On Leon Baptista Alberti

On Leon Baptista Alberti
His Literary and Aesthetic
Theories

Mark Jarzombek

The MIT Press
Cambridge, Massachusetts
London, England

This book was set in Baskerville by DEKR Corp. and printed and bound by Halliday Lithograph in the United States of America.

Library of Congress Cataloging-in-Publication Data

Jarzombek, Mark.
  On Leon Baptista Alberti : his literary and aesthetic theories / Mark Jarzombek.
      p.   cm.
    Bibliography: p.
    ISBN 0-262-10042-8
    1. Alberti, Leon Baptista, 1404–1472—Philosophy.   I. Title.
  NA1123.A5A35   1989
  195—dc20   89-33417
                                                                              CIP

Contents

Confrontation with the Arch-Aesthetic

Encounters and Misencounters in the Albertian Theater

Postscript: Alberti as Architect

Preface

It is a rash enterprise to write a book on Leon Baptista Alberti. It requires a multiplicity of competences—literary, philological, scientific, philosophical, legal, historical, and artistic—rarely found in any one person. All those who will find shortcomings and feel disposed to censure me I beg for understanding and, where indicated, for constructive help.

This book would have been impossible to complete had it not been for a Chester Dale Fellowship from the National Gallery of Art in Washington, D.C. (1985) and a postdoctoral grant from the J. Paul Getty Center for the History of Art and Humanities (1986). I would like to thank David Friedman, Stanford Anderson, Henry Millon, and especially Kurt Forster for their unflinching support. I would also like to thank Maria Frank and John Lawless for their corrections and contributions to the Italian and Latin translations.

Introduction

Leon Baptista Alberti's literary output constitutes a complex textual landscape of dialogues, dreams, poems, letters, descriptions, psalms, fables, and allegories. Some are written in *volgare*, others in Latin; some are complete, others incomplete; some are written with *amplificationi*, others are composed under the banner of *brevitas*. Some works were intended for a public audience, others for *familiari* only. Partly because of this complexity, the more complete and polished *De re aedificatoria, De pictura,* and *Della Famiglia* have received the lion's share of scholarly attention, although they constitute only a small segment of Alberti's total literary output. In recent decades the investigations have broadened as scholars of the caliber of Cecil Grayson, Eugenio Garin, David Marsh, Lucia Cesarini Martinelli, Gennaro Sasso, and Giovanni Ponte have begun to chart a more even-keeled approach.

The efforts of these scholars notwithstanding, the intertextual relationships among Alberti's works remain obscure, not only because of the hermeneutical difficulties Alberti's writings present but also because of the persistent preconception that the so-called minor writings and the aesthetic treatises belong to two different worlds. This misconception has proved difficult to dislodge, as it has its roots in the very beginning of Alberti scholarship, stamped as it was by nineteenth-century idealism, neoclassicism, and historicist progressivism. Alberti scholarship took on this cast at the turn of the century when there appeared in quick succession Hubert Janitschek's *L. B.*

Alberti's Kleinere Kunsttheoretische Schriften (1877), Paul Hoffmann's *Studien zu L. B. Alberti's Zehn Büchern: De re aedificatoria* (1883), Irene Behn's *L. B. Alberti als Kunstphilosoph* (1911), Max Theurer's translation of *De re aedificatoria, Zehn Bücher über die Baukunst* (1912), Willis Fleming's *Die Begründung der modernen Aesthetik und Kunstwissenschaft durch L. B. Alberti* (1916), and Julius Schlosser's "Ein Künstlerproblem der Renaissance, L. B. Alberti" (1929).

By the 1930s, Alberti scholarship was firmly entrenched in the field of art history, which pushed aside the literary or "ethical" works in an attempt to verify the thesis of a change of mental attitude from the Gothic to the classical revival, from Scholastic Aristotelianism to Ciceronian humanism, from medieval piety to Renaissance secularism, and from contemplative icon to empirical perspective. Writings of Alberti that did not fit into this pattern fell between the cracks. By the time of Rudolph Wittkower's *Architectural Principles in the Age of Humanism* (1971), Alberti's literary works had, for all practical purposes, been written off as irrelevant in discussions on Alberti's aesthetics. At best, they were scanned for a few promising quotes.

Even recent Alberti scholarship, generally aware of the nineteenth-century historicist perspective, has not freed itself from the traditional approach. Heiner Mühlmann, for example, in his book *L. B. Alberti: Aesthetische Theorie der Renaissance* (1982), though opposed to neo-Kantian idealism, continues to view the *kunsttheoretischen Schriften* in isolation.[1] Though he occasionally refers to *Della Famiglia*, *De Iciarchia*, and *De iure*, he dispenses with the rest of Alberti's output by relegating it to a different category: *studia humanitatis*.[2] Thus Mühlman too accepts the notion that Alberti's humanistic or ethical writings, literary rather than theoretical in nature, have little to contribute to Alberti's aesthetics.

Some attempts have been made to view Alberti from a broader platform. Two books come to mind: Giovanni Santinello's *L. B. Alberti: Una visione estetica del mondo e della vita* (1962) and Joan Gadol's *L. B. Alberti: The Universal Man of the Renaissance* (1969). Unfortunately, even here old biases remain. Assuming that Alberti's aesthetics alone imparts historical validity to the other works, Santinello attempts to demonstrate that Alberti's aesthetics is not localized in the treatises but is "traceable throughout the complex evolution of his thought."[3] Gadol also holds to the officially sanctioned approach. However, whereas Santinello begins with Alberti's "tedious," "long-winded," and "unoriginal" ethical writings and ends with Alberti's all-important theory of beauty,[4] Gadol begins with Alberti's theory of perspective and ends with Alberti's "unsystematic . . . and unoriginal" humanist writings.[5] The ethical and humanist writings are observed from the high mountain of Alberti's supposed ideal of harmony and proto-Enlightenment rationality.

Both authors tend to forget that the separation of aesthetics and ethics is a post-Kantian one and cannot automatically be applied to Alberti's writings especially since the terms "aesthetics" and "ethics" contain latent biases: the first is associated with such concepts as "reason," "theory," and "empiricism"; the second bears connotations such as "literary," "medieval," and "boring."[6] As I hope to show, Alberti's so-called aesthetic treatises, in accordance with what I hold to be his late medieval frame of mind, should not be viewed apart from his so-called ethical writings, as that would seriously distort the reconstruction of Alberti's philosophy. In fact, the working principle inherent in present Alberti scholarship—namely the strict differentiation of ethics and aesthetics—goes contrary to the innermost core of Alberti's speculations.

Eugenio Garin has brought a fresh impetus to Alberti scholarship. Investigating Alberti's writings with an open mind, he discovered a writer of astounding complexity. Though Garin, in the final analysis, also concedes priority to art historians, he must be credited with a breakthrough. In place of a distinction between "original" aesthetics and "derivative" ethics, he suggests a division into "rational" and "irrational," each with its own standards of originality. In his lecture "Il pensiero di L. B. Alberti nella cultura del Rinascimento" (1972), Garin holds that the stereotyped view of Alberti as the prototypical "universal man" portrayed in the "rational" works stands in conflict with the tantalizing, ambiguous language, the shifting tactics of expression, and the labyrinthine world of "ferments, solicitations, strengths, rebellions, survivals, heritages and memories" of the "irrational" works.[7] Garin points out that Alberti not only was a "disquieting writer . . . unforeseeable and bizarre" but that he opened up vistas on a world so disturbing that readers of his own time were unprepared to understand him.[8] Thus Garin turns the tables not only on those who neglect to take the literary works seriously but also on those who think of Alberti as a proto-Enlightenment idealist; he seems to see Alberti as a type of pre-modern irrationalist of Nietzschean dimension who has experienced the depths of "metaphysical anxiety."[9]

Although Garin attempts to redress the imbalances in Alberti scholarship—discovering in the process a "fantastic insanity" in Alberti's thought—he does not challenge the art historians' time-honored prerogatives. The treatises are still "rational . . . constructed classically in architectural equilibrium."[10] Garin does not explore whether Alberti's rationality stands in any type of dialectical relationship with the alleged irrational spirit that he discovered.

Garin's ideas eventually led to a consensus that Alberti wrote with a split personality, a "divided consciousness," as it has recently been phrased.[11] Lorenzo Begliomini, for example, claims that Alberti has "two faces," one "civic" (rational), epitomized by *De re aedificatoria*, the other "jocular" (irrational), as seen in *Momus*.[12] The terms "serious" and "not serious" have, of course, a certain legitimacy, as Alberti himself on occasion uses the terms "serious" and "ridiculous" to describe some of his writings.[13] *Momus*, a work that would fit into the category of ridiculous, is, however, by no means to be taken lightly. A penetrating social satire, it reveals more about Alberti's ideas on art and society than the serious *De re aedificatoria*. Dualities may indeed exist, but they have yet to be defined according to intrinsic criteria.

A further roadblock to a comprehensive understanding of Alberti's speculations is the artificial compartmentalization of his works along convenient lines of academic fields of specialization. Art historians study *De pictura* and the rules of perspective, literary historians his plays and dialogues; philologists dwell on Alberti's classical learning, while social historians concentrate on *Della Famiglia*. While no doubt much can be gained from disciplinary studies, the all-important context in this case remains unexamined. For example, *Della Famiglia* has long been regarded as revealing Alberti's thoughts on the family. Yet Alberti's views on the subject are incomplete without a consideration of *Theogenius*, a work that has been consigned to virtual oblivion, even though it was written immediately after *Della Famiglia* and deals with some of the same issues. Both *Della Famiglia* and *Theogenius* were published in A. Bonucci's *Opere volgari* of 1843–49, but only *Della Famiglia* was held to represent *the* Albertian view on family and society. Polarities, where they seem to emerge in Alberti's writings, should call not for division but for a rallying of disciplines and for a larger rather than narrower point of view, at least until their nature is understood.

There are no indications that Alberti emphasized one work over another. Rather, each work, regardless of its genre, assumed a specific, quasi-experimental role within the larger framework of his conceptual edifice. As I will seek to prove in this study, Alberti organized his entire oeuvre around a central scheme that cannot be reconstituted by studying any single work in isolation. To make progress in the search for the crucial and determinative elements of Alberti's thought, we have to include such writings as *Philodoxeus* (Lover of Glory, 1424), *De commodis litterarum atque incommodis* (On the Advantages and Disadvantages of Literary Studies, 1429), *Intercoenales* (Table Talk, ca. 1429), *Vita S. Potiti* (1433), *De iure* (1437), *Commentarium Philodoxeos Fabule* (1434), *Vita anonyma* (1438), *Theogenius* (The Origin of the Gods, ca. 1440), *Canis* (1441), *Profugiorum ab aerumna* (Refuge from Mental Anguish, 1442–43), *Momus* (1450), and *De Iciarchia* (On the Prince, 1468).

When read together Alberti's works yield information as to his ideas on the relationship between writer and society, on the assimilation of textual material, and ultimately on his own definition of humanism. Some writings deal with these topics more specifically than others, but all are in some way affected by it, in theory or in practice, directly or implicitly. Alberti's literary theory, however, cannot be separated from his aesthetic theory—it is directly related to and in fact determines his aesthetics.

Though Alberti's thoughts are in many respects *sui generis*, as will be shown, his thoughts are closer to mystic humanism than has hitherto been suspected, and this despite his oft cited proto-scientific bent and alleged lack of interest in theological matters. This pietistic wing, epitomized by Pico della Mirandola (1463–94) and Marcilio Ficino (1433–99), revived the medieval tradition that stressed the importance of the sanctified individual and the operation of grace.[14] In a hopelessly corrupt society secular remedies were seen as inadequate; the purification of society could only be accomplished by the immediate revelation of the divine plan in the lives of a few chosen individuals serving as *exempla*. By way of contrast, the secular wing, with which Alberti has normally been identified, believed that the power of the human intellect could bring about improvement largely through institutional reform and individual will. A close reading of his writings can only lead to the conclusion that Alberti's position within the spectrum of the humanist movement lies closer to the former than the latter.

Alberti may tend toward a pietistic interpretation of humanism, but his thoughts do not fit into even that category any too neatly. Pietistic humanism derived ultimately from the Platonic conception of the self-sufficient and purely rational being that, cleansed of the barnacles of passions and free from contingent, temporal limitations on its power, could open itself to God's grace.[15] If Alberti in certain instances seems to argue along these lines in his definition of humanism, it was ultimately to demonstrate the ironies inherent in such a view. Irony, of course, is totally anathemic to any kind of pietism. One could summarize that Alberti, though he rejects secular resolutions to social problems, does not become a spokesman for pietistic solutions either. The purpose of this book, therefore, is to move beyond the static image of Alberti as the paradigm of a particular point of view and see him as a thinker of merit and as a critic of the intellectual and cultural world around him.

Like other humanists, Alberti advanced his argument by means of a cumbersome apparatus of both classical and medieval provenance. This, combined with the frequent use of *exempla*, makes textual analysis delicate and complex, especially since repartee in terms of suitable *exempla* was often a veritable parlor game. In one instance, an Albertian interlocutor likens himself to a mythological figure throwing into the discourse "pieces of gold, gems and other precious things" so as to better make an escape from his student's critical eye.[16] That does not mean that *exempla* should be ignored, but that their theoretical underpinnings may lie elsewhere. In *Intercoenales*, with a glint of irony in his eyes, Alberti provides us with a list of some of the "almost infinite number" of writers he has studied: "Ennius, Caecilius, Licinius, Atilius, Trabea, Lucceius, Turpilius, Gallus, Naevius, Lucretius . . . Accius, Nigidius, Caecilium, Caecina, Cassius, Lucilius, Laberius, Afranius, Pacuvius, Sulpicius, Hortensius, Cotta, Fabius, Cato, Piso, Fannius, Vennonius, Clodius, Caelius, Macer . . . Pomponius Atticus, Varro," and, of course, Cicero.[17] Alberti's classicism, however, was a "secondary light," to use a term from his aesthetics, important but not necessarily primary. In his *Veiled Sayings* Alberti admits—and it can be easily verified—that "I won't deny that I invented some of these sayings in my leisure, and improvised others as I spoke."[18] Obviously, we must look beyond the classical gestures to the meaning. What one discovers is not only a complex world of survivals and revivals, but also a rather startling neo-medieval critique of humanism. The medievalisms in Alberti, far from "unfortunate," are employed purposefully and, self-consciously contrived, intended to throw contemporary values in doubt.

Though Alberti worked in the curia and was a priest, he was no naive *religioso*. Nevertheless, he derived much of his imagery from biblical and ecclesiastical sources. As we shall see, Alberti brings in theological themes not out of piety or convention but as ironic tropes to be shifted, reversed, altered, or lifted out of context. Doctrines such as that of the two planks, the two cities, *sub specie aeternitatis*, and *personae mixtae*, to mention only a few, taken out of context become powerful ready-made theoretical propositions and are indeed the very foundation on which Alberti's theory of humanism is constructed.

Dipping his hand into the ecclesiastical till again and again,

Alberti employs the material almost in a way that today we would call interdisciplinary in order to enrich, legitimize, and develop his own worldview. Of course, the classical and medieval both serve Alberti's strategy, but as the classical side of Alberti has been elaborated—and quite unilaterally so—I see it as my task to bring the medieval aspects of his thoughts also to light, particularly as they are an indispensable factor in his theory of aesthetics.

My main purpose however, is to follow Alberti's own development and to lay bare the internal consistencies of his thought. In order to arrange the complex material of Alberti's writings and make internal relationships clear, I have divided my discussion into three parts that overlap on occasion. The first part deals with the method Alberti employs to develop his cultural theories, a method based on a system of autobiographically tinged interlocutors that assume specific functions in a cosmological scenario; the second part deals with his theory of a fateful arch-aesthetic, and the third part investigates Alberti's views on the function of a belated humanism in the fundamentally flawed aesthetic world.

Alberti and the
Autobiographical Imagination

Introduction

A network of interrelated *personae dramatis,* all with autobiographical overtones, links the various writings of Leon Baptista Alberti. Philodoxus, Philoponius, Microtiro, Genipatro, and even Baptista, to name only a few, represent different voices in the Albertian polyphonic song of self; though each is intimately connected with Alberti, no single voice carries the melody exclusively. To see the characters in isolation would be to take them out of the context of an autobiographical methodology in which they serve the purpose of developing, testing, and elaborating theoretical concerns.

Unlike other humanists such as Poggio Bracciolini, Leonardo Bruni, and Lorenzo Valla, who put their dialogues into the mouths of public figures, Alberti employs the fictitious quasi-autobiographical characters—developed in a range of dialogues, descriptions, dreams and fables—as tropes that articulate a type of private philosophical language. But it is not a language that can be interpreted simply as a psychological self-portrait. Alberti's autobiographical methodology stands nearer the medieval idea of *exempla,* of patterns that repeat themselves again and again, and thus aims beyond a description of individual reality.

Burckhardtian views regarding the rise of the concept of individuality in the Renaissance have prejudiced the recognition of Alberti's *modus operandi.* Even Giovanni Santinello, otherwise sensitive to overarching themes, tends to interpret Alberti's works with an eye toward personal experiences, anxieties, loves, and other "contacts with life."[1] No doubt personal experiences are drawn on as raw material, but they are instantly typified, depersonalized, and transformed into generalizing postulates. One could by no stretch of the imagination distill a biography, in the standard sense of the word, from them. These tropes hide more than they reveal.

Initially, Alberti may have developed his quasi-autobiographical characters in order to extrapolate an image of himself as writer, but almost from the beginning he honed in on the tensions between author, text, and society. Soon he began to explore a wide range of characters who represent success and failure postulates, such as Philoponius, the radiant lawgiver, Libripeta, the weathered cynic, and Momus, the vagabond writer.[2] Beyond these characters, however, at the silent terminal point of his thought, is the search for a prototype humanist author.

Alberti's quasi-autobiographical method is part of an active, ongoing internal debate rather than a list of conclusions or a proclamation of received truths. Far from visualizing the ideal author as a static proposition or even as a sort of practical model, Alberti agonizes over the realization that his own definition of the writer involves a contradiction in terms. Writing is inherently unnatural both textually and ontologically; both texts and writers are artifices. Yet the ultimate aim is to enact the possibility of a life that is pure, simple, and spontaneously ethical—in other words, a life that is *not* the product of artifice. At what point Alberti arrives at this problem is not clear, but it takes shape very early on, certainly by the time he wrote *Intercoenales,* when he was in his early thirties.

This paradox is part of a historiographic proposition in which Alberti first constructs a positive theory of the relationship between writer and society and then disassembles his own carefully contrived theory. Whereas the temporal world, perceived from a conventional point of view, would appear mutable, and the spiritual one constant, Alberti shows, in ironic reversal, that the temporal world is ultimately immutable and the spiritual one ephemeral and endangered. As a result, Alberti defines the writer in a series of metamorphoses where writer and society, after their initial encounter, size each other up in a sort of bizarre dance involving masking and countermasking. Eventually the writer has to concede to the compulsive power of the temporal.

The implications for a theory of aesthetics, as we shall see, are profound. Art gives man the power to create a better world, but it cannot remove for him the consciousness of artifice. Unlike Plato, therefore, who held that only through the abolition of art can man prevent further alienation from the authentic, Alberti held that it is impossible to abolish man's predisposition to make art. For Plato the philosopher's task was to bring mankind into at least tenuous contact with a permanent, artless realm; for Alberti philosophy cannot possibly make such presumptions, as it is itself a manifestation of mankind's defective aesthetic psyche. No access to the authentic exists. The humanists, as Alberti defines them, can try, as did the philosophers, to orient mankind toward it, but since their message is also a product of the world-aesthetic, they too are corrupted by it. Mankind remains forever on the wrong side of an existential veil.

Essential to a proper understanding not only of this particular argument but of all of Alberti's theoretical speculations is a tripartite schema of characters: the saint, the cynic, and the "functionary." The three form the basis of a complex cosmology of Alberti's own making that brings to life his ideas on humanism and its paradoxical role in society. All three are linked to the "novice" who stands for the identity crisis implied in this cosmological scenario. The tripartite scheme is, as we shall see, the foundation on which Alberti constructs his aesthetic theory, which together with his theory of humanism was intended to confront the fierce realities of fifteenth-century intellectual and spiritual life.

As the tendency in Alberti scholarship has been to look at his writings piece by piece, none of this has ever been apparent. As a result Alberti lives more in legend than in fact. Here he is accused of lacking a coherent philosophy, there he is elevated to a forerunner of enlightened liberalism. Here Momus represents the *true* Alberti, there Giannozzo. Traditional views on Alberti must be held in check until we have followed the autobiographical itinerary indicated by Alberti himself.

Since this itinerary has implications far beyond the story line—and touches on the nature of the humanist task and the interrelationship between power, knowledge, and artifice—we cannot view Alberti's aesthetics separate from the "literary" works, as is done so frequently. In no case can the writings be divided into either-or propositions. The famous treatises, *De re aedificatoria* and *De pictura*, like the other writings, must be read against the background of Alberti's cosmology. The characters Momus, Enopus, and Gelastus, for example, conceived in a piece written at the same time as *De re aedificatoria*, are no whimsical vignettes; they are part of the theoretical matrix that must be understood before we can place *De re aedificatoria* and *De pictura* in the broader context of Alberti's thoughts. As I hope to show, Alberti's theoretical emphasis is neither on painting nor on architecture but on the nature of the literary task. To understand this task the reader must first acquaint himself with Alberti's quasi-autobiographical methodology.

Central to Alberti's thought edifice is the inseparable constellation of writer and text. The life of the writer and the life of the text are, for Alberti, interdependent. The appearance of one is synonymous with the appearance of the other—so too the disappearance. As Neofronus descends to Hades, his treatises are ripped apart by his relatives. When Momus is castrated and chained to the ocean floor, his *tabella*, having lost its force to convince, is thrown into Jove's unused library, where it falls into oblivion. The writer-text constellation can only be effective if it is both flexible and stable. The characters Baptista and Philoponius, as we shall see, represent such a success postulate. It is they who speak in the treatises where Alberti, once his attempt at authorial definition reaches maturity, implements a strategy of text-making.

But before we can follow Alberti's quasi-autobiographical journey and investigate the relationship between text and author, we must turn to his definition of humanism and the role it plays or should play in society. There is no better place to begin than his first two works, *Philodoxeus* (Lover of Glory, 1424) and *De commodis litterarum atque incommodis* (On the Advantages and Disadvantages of Literary Studies, 1429).

De Commodis Litterarum Atque Incommodis

Though *Philodoxeus* was written first, we will turn initially to *De commodis litterarum atque incommodis*, not only because it unambiguously states Alberti's definition of the novice writer but also—and significantly—because this text is not spoken through an interlocutor, as are so many of his other writings. We must not mistakenly assume though that it is spoken *in propria persona*. Carlo, Alberti's brother, to whom the text is addressed, serves merely as a foil. Since Carlo mixes the study of literature with mercantile pursuits, the speaker, taking on the role of a father figure, talks instead to a future novice who will not accept such compromises.

If they desire fame and praise, they should close themselves up at home and keep away everything outside that is elegant, pleasurable, and admired, so as to confine themselves to knowledge of literature with as much constancy as possible . . . . I would hope that my words can help students in this way: when they have grasped with their prudent reason all the things I have explained, then, with any assistance I can offer, they will be roused to see with greater clarity that literature does not look to wantonness nor promise empty or ephemeral things.[3]

In the opening paragraph "Alberti" contrasts his dedication to writing with Carlo's dilettantism.[4]

You [Carlo] have always found time for business alongside literature. I, however, have dedicated myself completely to literature, leaving aside everything else. I prefer in fact to neglect all other things rather than let a day pass without reading and writing . . . . People who desire praise rightly think it better to attempt something, even if not in every respect finished and perfect, than to wind up old and unknown in the field of literature.[5]

As a student in Bologna, the speaker explains, he had come to a true understanding of the difficulties and attractions of writing. He learned of the "dangers, torments, and misfortunes unending" and discovered that few would help him in his fight against the "defrauders, parasites, and emulators" who gave him not a moment of respite.[6] All this has not weakened his ardor. While others were "enjoying themselves at banquets," dancing under the "noxious influence of Venus," he willingly endured "long nocturnal lucubrations," "unending fatigues," and "constant preoccupations."[7]

Without doubt Alberti organized his experiences according to a theoretical framework that identifies first the writer and then Leon Baptista Alberti. Anguish and suffering, however real, are medals of honor demonstrating that the author has passed the obligatory initiation ritual that admits him to the house of literature.[8] Of central importance is the implied parallel between literary and religious callings. Much as a novice, the protagonist must endure suffering, reject riches and "futile fame," sidestep the "traps of ephemeral pleasure," and renounce family ties.[9] A pleasure of the spirit illuminates his path and makes him immune to "the infinite, inconstant, and unstable movements of life, and [to] the flux of desires and expectations."[10]

For me literature is the most joyful thing that could exist. While others were maintaining that one should place the cult of literature after all other disciplines, I, by contrast, was convinced that literature had to be put before everything else. Consequently, I began to apply myself to the knowledge of literature with much engagement, desiring with ferocious tenacity everything that was considered illustrious. There was nothing that with fatigue, anguish, and watchfulness I didn't try to reach and look for with an inquiry that was as careful as possible. I was really convinced that I had begun the most praiseworthy of all labors. In fact, I considered it suitable to a lofty mind to bear with patience the anguish and nightly studies and all the other pains and difficulties, out of a desire to acquire not only knowledge but also the fame that through literature I hoped I would be able to reach.[11]

"Fame," the speaker explains, refers not to temporal fame, but to immortal "glory" acquired once the writer has liberated himself from any residual attraction to the urban "marketplace" and learned to avoid the "snares associated with places of government."[12] When all connections with the temporal world have been severed, the writer is free to "marry literature," enter "the prison house of sheepskin manuscripts," and "bury himself for eternity among his books."[13] But just as a monk in the solitude of his cell can never give up the struggle to perfect himself, the Albertian writer, once in the "refuge of the library," cannot abandon his labors.[14] In fact, he now faces his most daunting challenge, the struggle with the codexes themselves: the "immense baggage of manuscripts."[15] Their sheer physical size leaves him exhausted and their number threatens to undermine his confidence. He fears he can offer little that is new: "With all my effort nothing comes to mind that has not already been developed in an excellent manner by the famous and illustrious ancient writers. As a result, it is hardly possible for even the most learned man of this age to say something better; nor can I produce the same sort of thing with equal skill."[16]

The novice undergoes these doubts and insecurities, so it is explained, not simply in order "to obtain praise and glory through writing . . . and become immortal" but also to learn about and to communicate everything essential for "a life that is good and blessed."[17] The message does not require the exercise of "rhetorical amplifications," for it has to remain "simple" and "humble," expressing only "truth, modesty, magnanimity, excellence, and knowledge."[18] Yet how is this message to be conveyed if the truly dedicated suffer "unending torments," if "everyone mocks them and despises them," and if other writers abuse the power of the word?[19] The "fallen" who give in to the "violent confusion of customs" no longer discern the difference between true and false efforts.[20] *De commodis litterarum atque incommodis* ends with an extensive exhortation from "an ancient author," who speaks as if in a vision, to the perplexed and exhausted young writer. It reads in part as follows:

Remember the past. Look to us for the old teaching and the intact wisdom. Then you can elevate yourself and sustain yourself against the inroads and the assaults of fortune. Put away your greed. Free your soul from the inflated hopes for *grandezza*. Flee these enslaving labors on behalf of wealth, of futile fame, and of the praise that corrupts even though you try to link it to writing. It will be foolish to run after these with a desire for something that will not follow from your activity. You would be more foolish to endeavor to obtain that which, if it does not come about, will bring you recriminations for unnecessary fatigues, and which, if reached, will bring you shame because of it. Strain yourself with a certain moderation. Exercise virtue with a particular diligence; you will not merely win the knowledge of doctrines, which is rightly seen as the companion of virtue, without also making yourself in time more fit for virtue through your hope, reasoning, and thinking . . . . He who wants to make his soul more splendid must certainly despise, hate, and abhor those vulgarities that one calls Pleasures, as well as those enemies of the virtues, namely Opulence and Riches.[21]

Although Alberti claims that this is "an unusual topic that has not yet been developed enough," many of the arguments were well known.[22] For example, the thesis that sensual and intellectual pleasures form antagonistic poles within the psyche was a topos reaching back to Boethius's *Philosophiae Consolationis*, which served as model throughout the Middle Ages for arguments that contrast the transitory nature of riches, honors, and power with the permanence of supreme good and perfect happiness.[23] Other topoi, such as the agonies associated with writing, the importance of maintaining faith in truth over riches, and even the difficulties associated with the immense bulk of books, can be found in a number of works, not the least of which was *Philobiblon* by Richard de Bury (1287–1345).[24]

De commodis litterarum atque incommodis, however, should not simply be brushed aside as a compilation of classical and medieval commonplaces. Here as elsewhere, Alberti deploys commonplaces strategically. In this case they serve to communicate not simply that writing requires self-abnegation but that it constitutes quasi-religious commitment. While the vocabulary may be classical, the syntax is medieval. The Albertian writer, as defined in this work, lives within the tried and tested realm of medieval piety. For example, in the thirteenth century it was often argued that *scientia litteratis* has small value unless the *homo litteratus* can prove his own high morality.[25] Even the thesis that the writer should dedicate himself to the "good and blessed life" derives from the late medieval criticism of empty intellectualism, which hankers only for adulation and ignores knowledge that leads to a good life with a clean conscience.[26] Alberti's devotional attitude to the undertaking of writing is meant to demonstrate lack of complicity with the temporal world. Writing, he would claim later, is "a holy and quasi-religious" act.[27]

While *De commodis litterarum atque incommodis* with its disdain for "the multitude" and its Ciceronian Stoicism goes through all the humanist routines, the thesis that writing is a quasi-religious activity is aberrant in the context of early fifteenth-century humanism.[28] Attacking an older generation of humanist writers (*maturis et perfecte eruditis viris*), Alberti envisions a new breed of writers who are not only moral agents of pivotal importance in society, but also men engaged neither in politics nor in *res gestae*. Alberti points out that these younger writers should "avoid the snares associated with places of government" and "flee all public administration."[29] "Let them [the older writers] treat the characters of princes, affairs of state (*gesta rerum*), and events of war,"[30] he warns.

We need only think of Leonardo Bruni. As papal secretary, head of the Florentine chancery, and author of the famous *Historiae Florentini populi* and *Rerum suo tempore gestarum commentarius* (begun in 1415), Bruni would be, from Alberti's point of view, disqualified.[31] Bruni's writings are—and were considered even then—examples of the new humanist concern with clear language and scholarly accuracy and as such served as model for writers such as Poggio Bracciolini (who, as Bruni's successor to the chancellorship of Florence, authored his own *Historia fiorentina*).[32] Though Bruni and Poggio were Alberti's superiors in the papal curia and though, as far as one can tell, his relationship with them was amicable, Alberti felt that *res gestae* was and remained no proper subject for a true humanist.

Alberti not only questioned humanism's vested interest in politics and its literary expression in the writing of *res gestae* but also voiced sharp criticism of rhetorical practices, holding that his own "humble words" are "distant to all rhetorical affectations."[33] Here he seems to be casting a reproving glance at Coluccio Salutati, often listed as one of Alberti's mentors, who championed *stilus rhetoricus*, intricate syntax, and exotic vocabulary during his tenure as chancellor of Florence.[34] Alberti rejects "the debasing use of rhetoric" even if its goals are valid. Petrarch's definition of great writers as setting "their hearers afire" and urging them "toward love of virtue and hatred of vice" by means of "sharp burning words" that "penetrate the heart, rouse the torpid and warm the cold" is nowhere endorsed in Alberti's work.[35] Writers, having to demonstrate sobriety and discipline, must reform themselves before they can attempt to reform others.

Clearly, Alberti interprets the distinction between *stilus humilis* and *stilus rhetoricus* in Augustinian terms as a distinction between Christian eloquence and pagan rhetoric: the first guides mankind's spiritual aims; the second, temporal ambition.[36] From Alberti's perspective the contemporary emphasis on rhetoric was no harmless development but a deplorable neopaganism. Rhetoricians and other "men of letters" embroiled in secular affairs serve as negative *exempla* of vanity, greed, self-display, and above all envy: "They try with great temerity to obfuscate and extinguish the glory, reputation, and fame of others."[37] As a consequence, the humanists, and not only the oft denounced Scholastics, guide the "ship of literature" to its destruction in the "tempest of society," prompting Alberti to ask,[38] "Who does not have before his eyes, as in a painting, the ruins and the destruction of the disciplines and of the good arts? Who has not lamented that such a loss, such a shipwreck, has happened in literature?"[39]

Alberti's advocating a return to the simplicity of an early Christian ideal in both style and life was meant to put the aberrations of contemporary humanism in perspective. He conceived of humanism not as a nascent movement but as one in a state of decline following a long history dating back to the founding of the Church. If humanism did not preserve itself as the dialectical alternative to temporal existence, then it had little to offer for the future. No naive believer, Alberti drew nonetheless on Christian thought patterns to launch a critique against contemporary humanism and perhaps against the Church itself. The humanist writer, in order to rid society of the "spirit of death," must conduct a martyrlike struggle on behalf of "good literature, the noble arts, and the divine disciplines."[40]

Though Alberti, in *De commodis litterarum atque incommodis*, outlines his literary ideology without interlocutors, theoretical concerns are already anthropomorphically animated in the autobiographical theater. The book, therefore, provides no empirically verifiable answers to specific questions about Alberti's life, as theory and autobiography appear in some circumstances as form and substance, in others as substance and form. A hermeneutical problem results: the discursive line yields a clear picture of the Albertian writer but a very unclear one of the author's *propria persona*. Does Alberti envision himself as a real protagonist or is he experimenting with an authorial pose? The historian is left in a quandary as to whether to read the work as reality, imagination, fantasy, or illusion.

Philodoxeus

The play *Philodoxeus,* written when Alberti was only twenty years old, set the stage for the exploration of the symbiotic relationship between writer and society that was to engage Alberti throughout his life.[41] The play contains in sketch form all the essential features of the private cosmology that Alberti was to develop and rearticulate in work after work. In 1434, ten years after the play was published, Alberti wrote a commentary on it and thus provided invaluable insights into the mechanics of his theoretical apparatus.

The allegorical plot centers around Philodoxus (Lover of Glory), son of Argos and Minerva. He is a poor but noble university student and evidently an aspiring writer, thus fitting into the novice pattern.[42] Alberti shows the protagonist already endowed with a saintly glow that will be an essential aspect of the historiographic pattern.

With the help of the sagacious and prudent Phroneus (Talent), married to Mnymia (Memory), Philodoxus attempts to woo the beautiful Doxia (Glory). He hopes that he can talk to her from the garden of the house of her neighbor, Ditonus (The Rich One). With some machinations Philodoxus is allowed into the house, sees Doxia through the window, and asks to meet her in the garden, but she invites him instead to the front door to make a public entrance, a gesture in keeping with the public nature of her allegorical function.[43] The quote describes the moment of conflict between the beckoning of riches and the call of Doxia: "I enter the house [of Ditonus, the Rich One]. I listen, I take a step, advance further, reflect, and turn back. Then I hear a voice, which, as it turns out, is that of Doxia. I beseech her for her help as I address her. She says that such behavior is not proper in such a private and secluded place and orders me to come to her house where she would wait for me."[44]

Philodoxus, "tormented with thoughts of doom and of anxious joy," does not jump at his opportunity, thinking himself unworthy, and so when Doxia's sister Phimia (Fame) asks him some questions to test his devotion, he leaves in order to meditate on his own worth. With Philodoxus gone, the sinister

Fortunius (son of Tychia, the Greek goddess of fortune), aided by Dynastes (Power), breaks the fence surrounding Doxia's garden and enters her house with the intention of abducting her.[45] In the tumult, however, he mistakenly seizes Phimia instead. Philodoxus, in his effort to save Phimia, calls on Chronos (Father Time), whose daughter Alithia (Truth) is a good friend of Doxia. Chronos, prodded by Tychia, eventually proclaims both men victorious; Philodoxus marries Doxia, and Fortunius marries Fame.[46]

In his *Commentarium* Alberti states that the play is meant to demonstrate that "the studious and industrious person, no less than the rich or fortunate one, can acquire glory."[47] We know better than to trust such a facile explanation. The play is a remarkably prophetical piece in which allegorical figures outline a complex historiographic program. To explain the play, some small digressions are necessary. Alberti's idea of Fortunius differs from the conventional topos. In the Middle Ages Fortune was imagined as a whimsical goddess whose interference in human affairs explained everything from accidents of fate to the impossiblity of an ordered society. Boccaccio's *De casibus virorum illustrium* is a typical example; fortune caused "the notable and alarming disgrace, miserable ruin, and death of kings, princes and other famous men."[48] Departing from this tradition, Alberti bestows on his Fortunius the sinister characteristics associated with infamy, generally defined as the practice of slandering the virtuous and supporting the vicious.[49] Fortunius, a conflation of Fortune and Infamy, is not arbitrary in his actions, as his "mother" Tychia would be, but willfully malicious; his attempts to wrong Philodoxus are calculated and deliberate.

Also central to the play is the differentiation between eternal and ephemeral fame,[50] each with its own time frame, a topos (dating back to Boethius and known to every medieval author) that contrasts the eternal configurations of the godhead with mankind's blind experience of earthly time.[51] Doxia represents the eternal, whereas her sister, corrupted and contaminated by Fortunius, represents the earthly. The three characters Glory, Fame, and Philodoxus, representing the spiritual, the political, and the literary, are, of course, also a reformulation of the medieval commonplace that saw society as divided into *oratores, bellatores,* and *laboratores,* that is, into clergy, warriors, and workers.[52] Interestingly enough, Alberti transposes the lowest order into the highest, for the "laborers" are writers engaged in a labor of the spirit.[53] Their representative stand-in, Philodoxus, must be visualized as having to prepare for a "sharp and difficult life."[54] Philodoxus, however, initially assumes that earthly fame would be the natural by-product of his efforts. His desire, like that of the "writer" described in *De commodis litterarum atque incommodis,* is to attain "fame *and* glory."[55] In the world of medieval reality, this could be conceived as a wishful reconciliation between king and pope united in the ideal realm of humanism. What is enacted, however, points beyond this configuration to a tragic flaw in man's psyche.

Alberti's stand on the age-old theme of the conflict between the temporal and the spiritual is considerably more adamant than Petrarch's. In *Paradiso* and *Divina Comedia* Petrarch contrasts the tranquility of former times with the restlessness of the materially minded present in order to explain that the writer must search out solitude to open himself to the spiritual. In later writings such as *Secretum* Petrarch opts for a more moderate position and allows the humanist a type of anxious coexistence with the temporal world. Claiming to base himself on Augustine, Petrarch holds that glory and fame are not incompatible; fame is sure to follow in the wake of glory.[56] Alberti, by contrast, stresses the incompatibility of the two; the double marriage effectively precludes Philodoxeus ever "marrying" fame.[57]

Alberti also interprets the topos of literary anxiety differently. Whereas Petrarch enters into the psychological complexity of human nature, which he portrays as constantly vacillating between the earthly and the divine, the protagonists of Alberti's literary mission, following the light of "truth, modesty, magnanimity, excellence, and knowledge," discover their freedom not in a more profound understanding of their own individuality, but in a total and ongoing confrontation with society. The resulting anxieties are not a form of existential self-doubt but demonstrate the difference in substance between writer and world.

In its allegorical imagery, *Philodoxeus* is closer in spirit to Boccaccio's *Amorosa Visione*. A dreamer has to choose between two gates, one opening onto a straight and narrow path, the other onto a luxurious garden. The first leads to immortal glory, provided that all ephemeral things and earthly joys are abandoned.[58] The second is an invitation to wealth, dignity, and earthly fame. Boccaccio's dreamer, since he represents earthly society, chooses the second gate, against the advice of Philosophy, who foretells his future anguish. Alberti's hero corrects the decision, so to speak; he explores the life—equally anguished but for another reason—found through the first gate. If Boccaccio's dreamer is an allegorical representative of the fallen writer, Alberti's Philodoxus is an allegorical stand-in for the hypothetically unfallen redeemer.

Ultimately, Alberti implies that a harmonious coexistence between writer, Glory, and Fame is not possible. The rift parallels—indeed parodies—the separation in the Christian world of Church and state.[59] With the violation of the "garden" the writer, no longer central to society, becomes an alienated and orphaned voice, and historical time, symbolized by Chronos, begins its ceaseless and futile churning. Chronos, though seeming to resolve the conflict, presides in actuality over a state of permanent discord. The writer is shown as incongruously aspiring to Gloria while the rest of society aspires to Fame.

This historiographic pattern, drawing on the theological problem of the irreconcilability of sacred harmony and earthly disharmony and the difference between God's atemporal nature and His presence in historical time, is not meant to rearticulate Christian dogma. In fact, *Philodoxeus* endangers some of the very fundamentals on which that dogma is based. For example, the destruction of the garden comes about neither because of the writer's disobedience to divine will nor because of his acquisition of knowledge but because of the emergence of ominous forces of destruction and a moribund urge, represented by Fortunius. Even more unorthodox is the postulate that the Albertian writer did not undergo a fall, making him by definition a misfit in society. This *tour de force* boldly transposes the medieval distinction between body and spirit into a distinction between society and the ideal humanist.

Leopis-Alberti

It is all too clear that, through the figure of Philodoxus, Alberti wanted to forward himself as *exemplum* of the "unfallen" humanist. In his short *Commentarium Philodoxeos Fabule,* written while he was preparing *De pictura,* Alberti defends himself against his critics. He explains that autobiographical references were deliberately woven into the fabric of the play, and into the prologue in particular, in the form of a subtext that requires that the reader recognize the self-referential notations: "So that my efforts would not be lost I added a prologue which I sprinkled with references to my studies, my age, and other important allusions to myself. My object was to claim, when I wished, the work as my own—and this I did."[60]

Here, as elsewhere, Alberti's autobiographical notations take the form of phrases such as "continual peregrinations," "a disconsolate youth," "studies of philosophy deep into the night," and "the evil plottings of detractors." Alberti drew on this repertoire of quasi-iconographic attributes not only to give his characters their proper autobiographic connotation but, in reverse, to steep his own life in archetypal meaning, just as he had in *De commodis litterarum atque incommodis.* Philodoxus's battle with Fortunius points simultaneously upward—to illuminate the higher cosmological battle between writer and society—and downward, to introduce Alberti in the role of protagonist. As is implied in the following passage, the authorial "I" of *Philodoxeus* refers to both the real author and the *genus* writer struggling "with sacred devotion" to be heard over the cacophony of evil. With great pathos Alberti declares that to "defend your Leon Baptista Alberti" is to defend the metaphysical and spiritual essence of society.

In sorrow at my misfortunes and at the bitterness of my enemies . . . I wrote this story as a kind of personal consolation . . . . Defend your Leon Baptista Alberti, who is the most devoted of all [writers] to his readers; defend me, I say, from the carping of the envious. Then, when time permits, strengthened by your hope and approval, I shall be able to peacefully publish other works of this type and, if Minerva wills it, greater works in time to come, so that you will be able to enjoy them and thereby come to love me better.[61]

The relationship between Philodoxus and Alberti is made even more complex by an additional distancing device. The play was allegedly written by a certain Lepidus (Pleasant and Witty)—of whom I shall have more to say later—whose manuscript Alberti claims to have discovered in an ancient Roman codex. "You want to know my real name?" Alberti-Lepidus taunts in the introduction to the play: "Here is the play, and its title is Philodoxus. Why do you stare at me? Why these gaping looks? That's what it's called! Oh, now I understand, you want to know my name. I will tell you. I am the mad dog, the idiot savant. You already know my name: Lepidus. Ha, ha, ha, and you are all charming as well!"[62] This sort of deceit had many fourteenth-century precedents, with some forgers actually specializing in the classicizing mode so as to tap into the lucrative market for ancient texts.[63] Alberti's purpose, however, is purely theoretical; he employed the ruse to make a stinging attack on a literary community which he saw as frozen in an attitude of blind deference to classical texts.

The work is marked by an eloquence that men learned in Latin literature praise to this day and judge even now to be the product of some ancient author. As a result, no one can read the work without the greatest admiration. Many commit it to memory, and not a few expend considerable effort in repeated copying . . . . When I realized that the work found such favor and was sought everywhere by scholars because it was thought to be ancient, by a fabrication I persuaded those who sought the origin of the work that it had been excerpted from a very ancient codex. Everyone quickly agreed, for the work was redolent with a certain ancient, comic diction . . . . nor was it difficult to believe that a young papal scribe would be the last person capable of such eloquence.[64]

The *Commentarium* was an attempt by Alberti to reassert his authorship, revealing himself not only as Philodoxus but as Lepidus as well. This introduces a hermeneutical issue surrounding the authorial self that Alberti does not want to have overlooked, as it is central to the ultimate message of the play. Since society instinctively stifles spontaneous spirituality, living texts are ignored by a dead society that holds only dead texts in esteem. Whereas Philodoxus enacts, on an allegorical level, the Albertian author's entry into the defunct society, Lepidus shows the play, as real object, thrust into the hands of the defunct literary establishment. The general and the particular, the allegorical and the real reinforce each other, with "Alberti" inhabiting both arenas.

In masking his identity so as to protect himself while attempting to gain a foothold in the polluted temporal world, however, the writer abandons his text and thereby actually loses his identity. But that is the plan, for the struggle to reassert himself is not so much a real one as another demonstration of the drawn out agony of a writer who, forced to go through the demeaning farce of disowning his text, will fail in his attempt to regain it. This spectacle both satisfies and ironizes the perversities that the temporal society inflicts on the writerly identity.

In this remarkable way Alberti commences the autobiographical game. He manipulates both commonplaces and autobiographical elements to create parallels between the plot of the play and the "history" of the play. The rejection of Philodoxus at the hands of Fortunius foreshadows the subsequent, and subsequently "proven," rejection of the play by the scholarly community. In reverse, by insinuating the text into the enemy camp of scholars, Alberti insinuates his now mythically tinged autobiographical self into the enemy camp of historical time once Lepidus is revealed to be Alberti and Alberti, Philodoxus.

Whether Alberti is an actor with cardboard weapons on an imaginary stage or a real warrior against a real enemy cannot be ascertained and is perhaps irrelevant. Nor can we determine to what degree we are dealing with a psychological profile, the profile of a historical reality, or something in between. However, in the distinction between Leon Baptista Alberti and Philodoxus, and between the text as authentic statement and the text as forgery, Alberti exposes the disjunction between the spirit of Albertian humanism and the flesh of society.

The problematical relationship between Alberti and his quasi-autobiographical personae and between writer and text maps out a sphere of aesthetic speculation that must be studied and understood prior to any investigation into Alberti's aesthetics proper. In the development of this personae, in moving back and forth between them and himself, Alberti in a sense abnegates his true self. The circumstances of his life become transformed; things are added and taken away, obscuring if not dominating the author, as Alberti attempts to define the exalted role of a model humanist. But rather than simply define an ideal self, Alberti explores the more difficult issue of the inherently alienating nature of textuality. He presents it here almost emblematically by first distancing himself from the text so he can later reappropriate it. But the process of reappropriation is by no means clear-cut nor its outcome guaranteed. The initial alienation of author from text, forced on the author by a dead society, is made to haunt the literary enterprise (as Alberti envisions it) to the end, with the struggle to regain the text becoming the central issue of his philosophy. The reunification of author with text can never happen spontaneously for in the process of distancing both text and author become objectified. Yet, as will be shown, Alberti continues to search for an authentic reappropriation of the text.

Intercoenales

The failure of the Albertian writer to attain both glory and fame is offset by the failure of the temporal world to fully subdue the spirit of the Albertian humanist. Ironically, this conflict is the driving mechanism of society, which constantly tries to throw off its conscience. Were it not for the writer's desperate attempt to establish a foothold in a world abandoned by God and to coordinate the temporal with the eternal, there would be no hope. *Intercoenales* (Table Talks) not only elaborates this theme but brings the autobiographical methodology into full bloom with characters such as Leopis, Lepidus, Libripeta, Neofronus, and Philoponius. Taken singly, each character is a humble song; together they are an operatic ensemble.

Written over a period of years between the late 1420s and the mid-1430s, *Intercoenales* is a collection of forty-three pieces of varying lengths comprising dialogues, dreams, fables, and allegories, all divided into eleven books. In its entirety, the work is hardly a minor undertaking; if the pieces were assembled into one continuous text, they would make a book of about two hundred and fifty pages. The original collection has come down to us in two sections, one dedicated to Alberti's friend, the mathematician and doctor Paolo Toscanelli, the other to Leonardo Bruni and Poggio Bracciolini.[1] Since the latter two were politically active and since both wrote histories of the Florentine republic, the dedication was not without ironic overtones.

Though some of the *Intercoenales* pieces show the influence of Horace, Lucian, and other Roman satirists, one should not view the work simply as an attempt to imitate classical authors or display classical learning. Over and above the common denominator Alberti always follows his own concerns, and indeed it is in the *Intercoenales* that the system of Albertian interlocutors comes for the first time into full view and helps to illuminate even earlier pieces. In the *Intercoenales* (though in piecemeal fashion) the truth begins to glitter through the rubble.[2] The interlocutors—I have chosen the most typical, though all of the others fit the pattern—connect the various stories and enable the reader to trace the broad theoretical issues. Each character defines a different segment of the larger ontological edifice, which is never revealed in its entirety but can be—and is meant to be—reconstructed by the initiate as if it were a jigsaw puzzle: Leopis, the aspiring writer; Libripeta, the bookish cynic; Philoponius, the student in a crisis of self-doubt; Neofronus, the victimized writer; Paleterus, the aged pragmatist; and Peniplusius, rich in literary talent, poor in money. Some are successful producers of texts, some are not; some speak with authority, some with cynicism; some live in the city, some in exile; some are inexperienced, others are mature. In later works many reappear, often transformed, to further expand the theoretical masterplan.

Apollo and Virtus

Before examining the "texts" of these *Intercoenales* writers, I shall focus on the "life" of the writer, from his initial appearance in society, as depicted in the first of the pieces, *Scriptor* (Writer), to his last appearance, as described in *Defunctus* (The

Deceased) and *Anuli* (Little Rings). This "life" symbolizes a struggle toward *beatitudo*. First, however, let us look briefly at the three *Intercoenales* dialogues *Oraculum, Vaticinium,* and *Virtus,* for they pick up where *Philodoxeus* and *De commodis litterarum atque incommodis* left off, namely in the postlapsarian world controlled by Fortunius and Chronos. They are the components of a cosmological system that will remain with Alberti to the end.

In *Oraculum*[3] Alberti employs a dream genre as defined by Macrobius in *Commentary on Scipio's Dream* (ca. A.D. 500), a book widely known in the Middle Ages and early Renaissance.[4] According to Macrobius, dreams can be divided into the following categories: *insomnium,* a nightmare; *visum,* a daydream; *visio,* a prevision of the future; *somnium,* a political allegory; and *oraculum,* a declaration by a venerable person. The first two Macrobius discounts, for they have no significance except for the dreamer. The last three—all of which appear in Alberti's writings—belong to the category of philosophical discourse. "We call a dream an *oraculum* in which a parent, or a pious or revered man, or a priest, or even a god clearly reveals what will or will not transpire, and what action to take or to avoid."[5] Such oracular figures appear throughout the Middle Ages in paintings, in literature, and in references to saints.[6] We only have to think of the oracles in Chaucer's *House of Fame* (I,ii).

In Alberti's *Oraculum* the role of venerable personage is played by Apollo, who speaks through a statue in a temple. As petitioners step before him in search of guidance, he attempts to orient them toward a productive life. The supplicants, however, want to bribe the god with gifts in the hope of achieving their goals by easy means. Since Apollo is made of stone, he obviously cannot receive the gifts. This proves his disinterest in worldly gain and keeps his message above suspicion. Having no human stake in society, he can return the gifts only with the admonition to put them to constructive use. Among the supplicants we find a Scholar, a Disputant, a Benefactor, a Lover, and, finally, a Poor Man. The first to appear before Apollo are a Money Grubber and a Magnate.

Money Grubber: Apollo, I beg you, grant my request. I bring this cart, laden with rustic tools as a gift to you.

Apollo: Keep these tools and use them by day; eventide you shall see yourself in them as in a golden mirror.

Money Grubber: Hm, I always tried to avoid hard labor.

Apollo: Well, that's the only way to avoid the shame of poverty.

Magnate: I beg you Apollo, grant my request. I bring you gems and gold coins. I fear envy.

Apollo: Distribute your money among deserving citizens.

Magnate: I don't know any.

Apollo: Then make sure that you are never alone with more than one person.

Magnate: That's impossible.

Apollo: Make an effort to keep many similar to you at your side.

Magnate: Too hard.

Apollo: Well, that's the only way to stop fearing envy.[7]

Obviously, the supplicants no longer live within the bounds of clear-cut categories where word and object coincide and to which Apollo wants to confine them. If each were to tend to his single and predictable task, society would function without friction, if automatically and blindly.

In the fifteenth century the term *virtus* often referred to a knowledge of the inherent logic of social interaction.[8] By combining *virtus* with *ratio* in the figure of Apollo, Alberti seems to be striving for a humanist amalgam of *virtus* and *doctrina,* the synthesis of which was one of the essential features of early humanist ethics. Salutati, for example, argued that philosophical speculation should strive to integrate the two concepts. Apollo's ancient wisdom, however, is not the bookish *doctrina* that Salutati had in mind. Alberti imagines Apollo more in the late medieval tradition that saw the god as a leader in the battle of the virtues against the vices.[9]

Oraculum, however, is not a mere homily or a static allegorical portrayal of reason. In fact, we have here one of the central themes of Alberti's exposition necessary to the proper understanding of later developments in his quasi-autobiographic journey. Because Apollo's advice falls consistently on deaf ears, attention is drawn to the fundamental miscommunication between mythic and historical time. The supplicants, caught up in temporal confusion, demand instant solutions to their problems, but Apollo, frozen in an archaic posture—indicative of the static nature of mythic time—refuses to comprehend the mad urgency and insists on the unilateral meaning of such terms as Scholar, Disputant, Benefactor, Magnate, and Lover. Apollo's immutability ironically places him at a disadvantage in his attempt to communicate in the ever-shifting panorama of historical time. This becomes apparent with the last suppliant, a Poor Man who has nothing to offer and thus provides no leverage. Literally lacking a name that would connect him to a primordial essence, he symbolizes the spiritual emptiness of the contemporary world. Apollo—from his point of view, quite logically—orders him to hang himself from the nearest tree.

Poorman: O Apollo, grant my request. Since I have nothing else to bring you, it is your power to enable me to bring even more than I could promise. If you will make me rich, I will give you silver tripods and golden candlesticks studded with emeralds. Well, what is your response? Apollo has grown silent; do the gods also spurn poor men? Please Apollo, grant me this one thing, I beg and beseech you. I cannot endure the poverty you gave me free of charge.

Apollo: Wretch! Hang your despair from a tree.[10]

The Poor Man, however, walks away undaunted, for the statue—literally out of touch—is unable to extend the arm of justice and enforce its pronouncement. The representatives of mythic time lack an effective foothold in the temporal world. Mankind has long since broken the contract that linked word to action, identity to being, and concept to definition. This scene embodies in a nutshell and even caricatures the futility of Alberti-Apollo's own humanist endeavor.

In a subsequent dialogue called *Vaticinium* (Prediction), which in many respects represents an inversion of *Oraculum,* we encounter Alberti's portrayal of the reality principle: man the deceiver and man the deceived. The dialogue centers on a Soothsayer who, though blind, can see directly into the hearts of men and spot their flaws.[11] Using his talent to drive a wedge between word and meaning, he is, of course, an Apollo-gone-wrong in historical time. Having set up shop in the city square, he extracts money in exchange for empty promises from all-too-gullible passersby. While Apollo had returned all gifts to the supplicants along with advice on how to employ them, the false Apollo, reigning unchallenged in the public forum, eagerly solicits "donations."

The Soothsayer, not just anticipating distrust but already integrating it into his deceptive scheme, laughs at the foolishness of the last of his supplicants who believes the Soothsayer to be a friend who actually says what he means. The Soothsayer takes the man's money and begins a long series of mathematical calculations until the supplicant leaves empty-handed and confused. The supplicant, of "peaceful, innocent and modest character"—a novice?—naively believed that money would not pollute the "faithfulness and constancy" of words.[12] While in *Oraculum* gifts were transactions given and received in kind, the introduction of money in *Vaticinium* is indicative of relativizing and a dangerous undermining of society's fundamental values.

Oraculum and *Vaticinium* must be seen in tandem. The statue of Apollo, an anachronism from the timeless "garden," contrasts with the cunning Soothsayer. The first represents a view from above; the second, from below. *Oraculum* gives an example of the voice of mythic time, but it is distant and ineffectual in real time; *Vaticinium,* perhaps a pun on the papal establishment, portrays the corrupt and insistent voice of blind temporality.

Virtus takes these themes one step further.[13] The goddess Virtus, portrayed here in a dialogue with Mercury, does not represent piety or even, as might be expected, appropriate moral action, which is the realm of Apollo, who concerns himself with society in general. Virtus is here to be understood as the champion of the talented and creative, standing in defense of the exceptional few. Though she is female, she is based on the classical concept of manly excellence and its medieval derivative, spiritual power.[14] Among her protégés in the dialogue are Plato, Polyclitus, Archimedes, Cicero, and Praxiteles.[15] She is, however, no more effective than Apollo in bringing her plans to fruition. Fortuna, having organized the mortals into an "army," drives her from the heavens. The brushes, pens, and chisels of Virtus's protégés prove of little use in her defense.

Virtus: Plato, the philosopher, began to offer some arguments directed against her [Fortuna], about the duties of the gods. But she was burning with rage. "Away with you, big mouth, she said, "for it is improper for slaves of the gods to speak for their masters in court!" Cicero also wanted to say something to sway her, but from the mass of armed men Mark Antony burst forth, mightily displaying his fighting form, and thrust a threatening fist into Cicero's face. Thereupon, all my other allies decided to make a hasty retreat. For Polyclitus with his brush, or Phidias with his chisel, or Archimedes with his sundial, or the rest of them having no weapons at all could hardly defend themselves against fierce armed men.[16]

With her allies in retreat, Virtus is left alone to face the barbarous army that "strips her and leaves her lying in the mud."[17] The other gods, unwilling to come to her aid, are only concerned with "seeing to it that the butterflies keep their beautiful wings . . . and that the melons ripen."[18] With the gods occupied with trifles and the *plebe* literally "soldiers of Fortune," Virtus finds that she has no place in the present scheme of things. At the end of the dialogue, she concludes: "I will forevermore be stripped of honor, despised, and exiled."[19]

Though *Virtus* is a piece essential to Alberti's cosmology, its general schema is a topos that strongly reminds us of Ovid's *Metamorphoses,* where "maiden Justice" fled the "bloody earth," inhabited as it was by "murder-hungry and violent men."[20] The topos was a common one. Richard de Bury, decrying the ignorance of many of his colleagues toward classical philosophy, tells of "admirable Minerva, [whose] soldiery is unmanned and languishing."[21] Richard felt that the restoration of high ideals could take place through the mechanism of improved scholarly research. Alberti, by contrast, suggests that the reintegration of society is not so much linked to the restoration of classical texts (as the ironies inherent in *Philodoxeus* imply) as to the reanimation of the lost arts that would lead to the revitalization of society's inner passion. This, his theory implies, can be accomplished by the writer who, as "son" of Apollo and Virtus, reactivates, by a sort of dialectic interaction, the waning potency of the exiled gods. "Whenever a man thinks and acts with

ragione e virtù, he will be like a mortal god," Alberti writes in
Della Famiglia, pointing to the only type of man who can restore
the knowledge of society's divine origins.[22] It is not the scholar
who will lead the world to a better state, but the inspired writer
who combines the *ragione* of social consciousness (*Oraculum*)
with the *virtus* of manly excellence and spiritual power. ·

Blindness and Insight

The choice the novice has to make between two time frames
that are, in Alberti's view, dangerously at odds—the theme of
Philodoxeus—comes now more clearly into view. An archaic
Apollo and an exiled Virtus, on the one hand, and a powerful
Soothsayer and a princely Fortunius on the other set the stage
for the arrival of a quasi-divine writer who will have to fight
Fortuna on behalf of his "mother" and the Soothsayer on
behalf of his "father."

Scriptor, the first dialogue of *Intercoenales,* consists of an exchange between two Albertian writer types, each representing
a different value in the experimental spectrum.[23] The hopeful
Leopis stands for the novice while Libripeta represents the
antagonist, the cynic—a typical opposition employed by Alberti
to develop his literary and aesthetic theories. Leopis, who has
just emerged from a month of isolation, announces that "I
have been busy with my books, striving to sow the seeds of my
reputation as a writer."[24] He encounters Libripeta (Book Fa-
natic) in the public forum, and a conversation ensues that,
though short, is significant, for it foreshadows Leopis's eventual
failure.[25] Leopis, still *scriptor* and not *auctor,* is blind to the
raging turmoil to which Libripeta wants to open his eyes. "Your
literary efforts," Libripeta predicts, "will be wasted (*operam per-
dis*),"[26] to which he adds: "You will be attacked by the crowd
of commoners (*vulgus*) who are especially quick to censure."[27]
He warns that the public will not take well to Leopis's high
tone: "Ha, ha ha, ridiculous fellow! Are you trying to accomplish this on Tuscan soil? In a land wholly shrouded in a fog
of utter ignorance? Where the land is desiccated by men's
burning ambition and greed."[28] But Leopis's writings will not

please the academic establishment either. Libripeta, "the dar-
ling of the learned," assures Leopis that he himself will readily
and forcefully attempt to "tear him down in public."[29] The
dialogue concludes with Libripeta's threat: "Watch out especially for *me*."[30]

This ominous confrontation between Leopis and Libripeta
at the very beginning of *Intercoenales* sets the tone for Alberti's
investigation into the literary experience. The motif will appear
again and again, in various degrees of elaboration. The exchange is not between Leon Baptista Alberti and another person but between the two extremes of Albertian self-
projection.[31] The name Leopis, though it may seem to imply
Alberti's identification with the character, is by no means to be
taken as a sign that he is identical with the author. Both Leopis
and Libripeta are artificial constructs, purely theoretical, ontological propositions that move under their own momentum
and serve as vehicles for the author's cultural critique. Leopis
is "blind" whereas Libripeta "sees." Libripeta, cynically, antici-
pates that unless Leopis's eyes are opened, he will sooner or
later succumb to enemies from among both the ignorant and
the learned, who form an unlikely but powerful alliance in
their combined effort to tear down all noble aspirations. Leopis, who represents the unity of author and text, a unity born
in naiveté, is a type of pre-Lepidus figure. One could say that
he hasn't "read" *Philodoxeus* yet, which means that he will not
graduate into writer status until he has experienced both alienation from society and from his own text, at which time, ironically, the glow of hope will have given way to wary resignation.

The contrast between mythic innocence and worldly disillusionment is followed up in the dialogue *Religio*, where Leopis
and Libripeta are once again the main characters, and where
Libripeta continues his campaign of "enlightenment."[32] Libripeta waits for Leopis to return from his prayers at the temple.
When he arrives, he is berated for being so naive as to believe
the priests, who as Libripeta points out, have the same motives
behind their actions as everyone else: greed, avarice, and lust
for money. Libripeta then launches into an attack on piety, and

argues that it is foolish and irrational to assume that the gods can be swayed by human desires.

Libripeta: As for all your humble prayers, pious one, they will be utterly disregarded. Besides, do you think that the gods are so similar to us mortals? Do you think that just like blind and careless men, they will suddenly form a plan of action and then just as suddenly change their firm intentions? Really, in the great scheme of things, as I am informed by the scholars on the subject, in the complex administration of the universe the gods govern by virtually immutable laws. Given that such is the case you madmen truly rave if you think that on the basis of your persuasive pleas the gods will change in thought or deeds . . . to do some new and bizarre thing.[33]

Libripeta clearly has the upper hand in the dialogue. He accuses Leopis of allowing himself to be seduced by the cunning of the priests, those "henchmen of the painted gods."[34] Contemptuous of Leopis's innocence, he even questions the significance of Leopis's literary aspirations, sneering that "you wear yourself out by your frequent literary vigils, but you still have much to learn about the evil and impiety of mankind."[35] Instead of crumbling under the embittered onslaught, Leopis nonchalantly proclaims in parting: "I remain unshaken, . . . the prayers and pledges of good men (*i buoni*) are not unwelcome to the celestial beings."[36] By definition, there can be no reconciliation between the cynic, who represents the enlightened earthly stance, and *un buono*, who represents the mythic world. Leopis's innocence marks him as not of this world. He is a novice in historical time, ignorant of its fallen condition. We can imagine him as a seed from the mythic garden that has drifted into the polluted world of historical time without a genetic coding that would enable him to function under the new conditions.

The themes associated with Libripeta derive partially from classical sources. In Lucian we read that the cynic has no patience with popular religion, in Heraclitus that he despises the contemptible multitude that in turn hates him, in Crates that he does not avoid human contact but that his virtue remains untouched; and in Diogenes we read that, rather than being blamed for his offensive public acts, he should be praised for his trustworthiness.[37]

The Apostolic creed had absorbed and transmuted many of these ideas. The various currents, however, too complex to elaborate here, all acquire an independence of their own in Alberti's thought. In *Somnium* (Dream), one of the darkest and most sinister pieces in *Intercoenales,* we see how these concepts influence Alberti's theory of the relationship between writer and society.[38] Just like the *oraculi, somnia* are not dreams in the standard sense; they serve, as we know from Macrobius, to illuminate covert political realities and were thus seen as part of the mystique of kings and rulers, a famous example being the *somnium* of King Henry I of England in 1130, in which the king was attacked by representatives of different elements of society.[39] By the beginning of the thirteenth century dreams had become a widely used literary genre employed by philosophers, theologians, saints, and lay writers.[40] If the dream was that of hell, it was certain to include themes of magic spells, rivers, meadows, and vapors, all of which indeed appear in Alberti's *Somnium,* which should also be seen in the context of fourteenth-century staged events in which the various spectacles of hell were acted out.[41] In this work, however, religious aspects are downplayed; it is instead an exposition of the sinister and repressed realities of the communal psyche.

In *Somnium,* actually a dialogue, the autobiographical *baton* passes from Leopis to Lepidus, whom we have already encountered as the fictive author of *Philodoxeus.* He brings us to the next stage in the protracted confrontation between the young writer and the voice of cynicism. In this scenario, Lepidus is still a novice and has not yet discovered his self-alienation, which will be the topic of another *Intercoenales* dialogue. Here Libripeta has to be interpreted as representing a premonition of Lepidus's future self.

In the story, Lepidus sees Libripeta emerge from a sewer hole. Unperturbed by his awkward position and the foul stench he exudes, Libripeta excitedly relates that he has just completed a remarkable voyage made possible by means of a magic spell that enabled him to penetrate beyond the order of the real world to experience the otherwise inaccessible turmoil beneath the surface.[42] In this subterranean world the insidious workings of society are shamelessly overt.

First, Libripeta came upon the River of Life, populated by horrible monsters—in actuality the unmasked visages of human beings. This was followed by the Valley of Forgotten Things, where he found such amazing objects as "great bags full of free speech, the sound of flutes and horns . . . charitable acts . . . and human authority"; he even found parts of his own brain![43] Only Stupidity was missing, the indispensable principle of human action.[44] Lepidus, aghast at what he considers to be Libripeta's "madness," interrupts the tale and asks, "*Quid tum?*" (What next?). As these are the same words that appear under the winged eye on the medallion made by Matteo de' Pasti—about which I will have more to say in a subsequent chapter—we may assume that this moment marks an important turning point.[45] Putting coal into the fire, Libripeta answers Lepidus's query by revealing that in the Valley of the Forgotten Things he saw all the literature on the "Good Arts."

Libripeta then continues his story, telling of a volcano that belched forth "objects of desire" in an ironically exaggerated response to the silly and vain demands of the men and women gathered at its base. Finally, after having crossed the putrid River of Life on the inflated carcass of a former lover, he came to his destination, the Meadow of Dreams, a place more horrible than any he had ever encountered. Instead of grass, the fields grew hair and were infested with lice. The lice, a metaphor for the voracious and evil urban populace (to which Libripeta had referred in his warning to Leopis), attacked the scholar, who was happy to find refuge in the sewers, through which he finally regained access to the deceptive calm of the world above.

Libripeta: Instead of turf and blades of grass, men's hair and beards, women's flowing locks, the fur of animals, and even lions' manes grew there [The Meadow of Dreams]. In fact you could see nothing in this field except hair of all sorts. Great God! How many dreamers I saw there! All of them digging up some sort of root which they ate, and they seemed wise and clever though clearly weren't. Suddenly a great mass of lice flew up from the field and nearly ate me alive. My only salvation lay in finding an escape. And so, raving as I was from my experiences in such a place, I took to my heels and found my escape where it was offered. The fates provided this sewer for me.[46]

Libripeta's journey taught him that the world is so deformed that it is literally "unable to speak."[47] The newfound wisdom, "learned from the sewer (*cloacarium prudentiam*)," leaves Libripeta with permanent scars.[48] It paralyzes his creative potential as a writer and stymies his ability to communicate beneficially. Though Libripeta can no longer write, he attempts, nevertheless, to warn that an untrustworthy order masks an ominous reality.

Being trapped in a "speechless" society for which he has no sympathy, his commitment is mainly to himself and to his "texts," which he safeguards ferociously for an undetermined future by keeping them "under lock and key."[49] The alienation Libripeta exposes is contrasted by Alberti with Libripeta's obsessive urge to hold onto and protect his writings. To open them up to society would lead to their certain destruction. Writer and text are ironically unified only as a sterile proposition. It is an anxious preservation that denies the living function of the text in a dead society.

Lepidus, though fascinated by Libripeta's story, has difficulty recognizing in it a lesson for himself and returns to his friends. At this point Lepidus, *inscitus sapiens,* possesses only a type of fool's knowledge.[50] He admits that he learned from Libripeta "a few quips" that make him seem worldly, but it is clear that he is still far from making a genuine intellectual breakthrough even though the seeds for that germinate already in him, as we know from the *quid tum.*[51] Libripeta is frustrated by Lepidus's inability to see the truth so obvious to him, and at the end of the dialogue accuses him of being "insipid . . . insane, and naive."[52] Lepidus, in turn, thinks that Libripeta is the insane one and advises the malodorous cynic to "take a bath."[53] Libripeta, however, prefers the honest stench of the sewer to the more pervasive but odorless "stench" of social corruption.

Though *Somnium* seems to sound the theme of *contemptus mundi,* Libripeta, the cynic, does not flee the city but remains, the better to speak of its evil. His very presence is a living reproof. Eventually Leopis and Lepidus will have to come to terms with Libripeta's negative wisdom, but that point has not yet been reached. The subconscious world is described as totally severed from the conscious world, which remains blithely ignorant of the enormity of its deviance. In almost Freudian terms, the subconscious is mute and refuses to communicate the trauma. While the *somnium* opens the dreamer's eyes, it simultaneously throws a pall over him; he is marked by the unmaskable and unmistakable stench of nihilism. In short, the dream is a form of catharsis that transforms the writer into an *auctor* with a type of x-ray insight into the workings of society, while simultaneously paralyzing his creative potential; he can no longer perform as author. In a society recognized as false the writer is alienated from his own identity and function. The joke Alberti plays on his audience in *Philodoxeus,* where he speaks through the mask of Lepidus, turns out in *Somnium* to be tragically serious. In *Philodoxeus* a mask was applied to permit the author to speak in a world that refuses to hear. In *Somnium* the argument is carried one step further; the only topic left to discuss is mankind's insanity. Blind sight opposes nihilistic insight.

Just as there is no communication between society and its repressed reality, there is no communication between society and its celestial counterpart. The gods, as we have already seen (*Oraculum*), living in a static unchanging sphere where norms are eternally valid, cannot comprehend the world given over to Chronos. As a result, they too suffer from blindness and speechlessness. This theme is developed in *Cynicus,* where Alberti elaborates once again Libripeta's negative wisdom.[54] Phoebus (the sun god Apollo) is sitting in judgment as the spirits of the dead come before him to be reincarnated as animals.[55] But as Phoebus is pronouncedly inept in his dealings with mortals, one of the shades with all the characteristics of Libripeta steps forth and confidently offers himself as interpreter. He declares himself well suited to the task, for "he knows mankind through and through" and indeed, as representatives of each social category approach, the Cynic (as he is labeled in the piece) lashes out in bitter words at their faithlessness, stupidity, arrogance, ambition, and criminality.[56] His judgments are used by Phoebus to transform the shades into animals, a stock device of medieval criticism.[57]

The shades can be divided into three categories: the religious, the temporal, and, for lack of a better word, the intellectual. The religious element of society is represented by the priests, who are accused of sluggishness, laziness, gluttony, and lasciviousness. They are turned into jackasses. The temporal world is represented by the magistrates and merchants. The former, because of heinous crimes, bloody murders, and sexual misdeeds, are turned into hawks, the latter, "that treacherous tribe," into dungbeetles. The Cynic focuses particularly on the third category, the producers of texts—philosophers, writers, poets, and rhetoricians—all of whom have abandoned the ideals of their profession. They are roundly condemned and are transformed into fireflies, mice, butterflies, and bees, respectively. One could read this critique as: a cold flaring fire, a gnawing away at books and reputations, a vain self-display, and an eager but mindless collecting.

This division of society parallels the arrangement in the garden of *Philodoxeus*, where Gloria, Phimia, and Philodexus had hoped to live in ideal harmony. Whereas *Philodoxeus* ends just as temporality has installed itself, *Cynicus* takes us further to show that in the mirror of truth each of the categories appears disrobed of its aura: Glory is polluted by her representatives, the priests; Fame by the magistrates, merchants, and other "soldiers of fortune"; and Philodoxus (the intellectual) by his latter-day equivalents, whether they be philosophers, who "no longer preserve divine dignity," writers, who "are no longer committed to wisdom," poets, who "suffer from hubris," or rhetoricians, who have "abandoned the principles of justice." Phoebus realizes that the Cynic's negative wisdom served him well and as a final fillip transforms him into a Socratic "golden-skinned gadfly."[58]

These four dialogues, *Scriptor, Somnium, Religio,* and *Cynicus,* map out two contrasting positions that create a dramatic tension calling for resolution. On the one hand we have Leopis and Lepidus, who represent primordial innocence. They enter the public domain, manuscript under arm, ignorant of the conspiratorial alliance between the *plebe* and the defunct literary establishment and above all ignorant of the divergence of word from meaning. On the other hand there is the malodorous Libripeta, the nihilist gadfly with a permanent writer's cramp. Viewing positive actions as futile and suspect, he discovers the paradox that the only way not to be claimed by the evil world is to honestly proclaim one's nonparticipation.

The Lost Garland and Newfound Wisdom

Libripeta's prophecy that Lepidus will eventually follow in his footsteps once he sees behind the mask of order is realized in the next frame, *Corolle* (Garlands), which shows the metamorphosis of the Albertian writer. Here the novice, contaminated by Libripetian doubt—the *quid tum* has taken hold—turns into cynic.[59] The goddess Laus (Praise), daughter of Virtus, enters the marketplace in search of a writer worthy of her garland and her hand in marriage. Envy accompanies her as an ironic counterpart. Praise rejects various suitors, including a rhetorician, a poet, and even Envy's favorite, a Libripetian critic, and bestows the garland upon Lepidus, who responds in typically Albertian terms: "I am one of those who delight in letters; furthermore, I always make an effort, while preserving my dignity, to be cheerful in private and among my friends."[60] Yet all is no longer well; Lepidus is undergoing a crisis of self-confidence. As Lepidus speaks, we can almost hear Libripeta laugh off-stage.

Fate has so determined it that from the time I first saw the light of day, not even the smallest thing has turned out the way I expected. It is a remarkable thing that all things happen contrary to my expectations and against my own plans. If I sow friends with service and kindness, I reap enemies. If I seek approval through liberal studies, envy is my repayment. If I strive to conduct myself peaceably and humbly by harming no one, I come upon detractors, accusers, secret enemies, and the most worthless traitors who disrupt all my plans and intentions. In sum, whatever I undertake, whatever I strive for, everything turns out different than I willed it.[61]

The nature of his transformation has not yet dawned on Lepidus himself, but is all too obvious to sharp-eyed Envy, who instantly tears the garland from his head. The "author" of *Philodoxeus*, who had once taunted his audience with "You know my name," is now stripped of the mask, to reveal not Alberti, as we might expect from *Philodoxeus*, but his Libripetian alter-image.

Lepidus: Why have you ripped off my crown so quickly? Why are you now destroying it [the garland] with your teeth in anger? Are you trying to kill me?

Envy: What is your real name?

Lepidus: My name? Lepidus.

Envy: You, Lepidus, the pleasant one? Nay, you are caustic, harsh, and mocking. Let us go, we will find no one in the whole forum worthy of the garland.[62]

Anxious and perplexed, his self-confidence shaken and his identity thrown into question, the previously amicable Lepidus suddenly finds himself revealed as a cynic. Praise returns to the heavens unwed; the attempt to reunite heaven with earth has failed.

Lepidus had assumed that his wholesome character, honesty, good intentions, and nobility of soul qualified him for the task. In reality, his mythic qualities have failed to take root. The gods, themselves unsure how to proceed (*Oraculum*), cannot forewarn him that the *naturale società a vera religione* is only a fiction.[63] Thus, instead of serving as link between the mythic garden and historical time, the Albertian writer finds no homeland in the temporal world; he, like Libripeta and Momus later on, can only wander through the city as through a foreign country. "Whatever road you choose, all is nothing."[64]

The metamorphosis played out in *Corolle*, where novice becomes cynic, is transposed in *Defunctus* into a different musical key. Here the metamorphosis is revealed as a type of death. An elderly novice, having failed while still alive to recognize that society is masked, undergoes the transformation to cynic only from the other side of the shroud.[65] The character Neofronus (Newfound Wisdom) brings this part of the quasi-autobiographical journey to its theoretical limits. On the surface

Neofronus had led a life worthy of much praise, as his funeral oration seems to indicate.

O you, Neofronus, the wisest among men, the most just and most happy, whose memory we are celebrating now with praise, certainly inadequate; how much better would it have been if we had esteemed you higher when you were alive! What honors, what esteem would not have been appropriate to have been circulated publicly in your life, you, who are now dead and mourned on such a grand scale by us? How we hold in highest consideration your memory, your excellent virtue, known among men and the object of universal admiration![66]

Typically, Neofronus had dedicated himself to literary endeavors with "constancy, industry, and diligence," producing numerous "elegantly written" books.[67]

After his death and awaiting his entrance into Hades, Neofronus, perched as a shade on the chimney of his house, avidly follows the events unfolding below. Since he had led a pleasant and undisturbed life, "full of compliments and praise," he is amazed to see occurrences that he would never have thought possible.[68] He witnesses the infidelity of his wife, who rejoices at his death so that she can be united with the gardener. To his shock he learns that his marriage lacked spiritual substance and was defective. Furthermore, he sees his good name defamed by his friends and his money wasted by his heirs.

Decrying the "tyranny of evil," the all-pervasive *insania*, "the vacuity of the human spirit," and the "contamination of madness" that infects everything, Neofronus exclaims disgustedly that the world is a place to which "even if he could, he would never return."[69] He realizes that his "newfound wisdom" has come too late (*tardum ingenium*) and that despite his excellent virtues, energetic literary efforts, and noble intentions, he has made no impact on society.[70] His ghost in Hades has more substance than his memory among the living.

Libripeta's prediction in *Somnium* that the writer's literary works will be lost is here acted out. Some of the codices containing Neofronus's "clear and elegant" writings are carried away, while others have the pages torn from them to be used as packing paper.[71] The death of the writer is paralleled by the death of the manuscript. Having left no living text, he discovers that he is unable to reach the level of those who are "eternal, incorruptible, and quasi-divine," for he and his texts have become victims of the "fallen, mortal, and fragile world."[72] Ironically, now that Neofronus can finally "see," his time on earth is up, and he must enter the eternal darkness of Hades.

In short, Alberti presents here the third stage of historical development. The first is the intact garden, the second, the destruction of that garden and the creation of two languages, that of mythic and that of historical time, and the third is an attempt to search for a common grammar—a search that fails (figure 1).[73] Alberti's prophets are ironic constructs; clad in the garb of mythic time, walking backward into society, they speak a foreign tongue behind enemy lines. Leopis (revealed as Libripeta) is eventually abandoned on earth by the higher powers that placed him there, and Lepidus (revealed as Neofronus) is lost to the echoless and sightless realm of Hades.

Lepidus   ----   *Death*   ---->   Neofronus: Belated Wisdom

Blindness   *Sight*

Leopis   ----   *Dream*   ---->   Libripeta: Sewer Wisdom

Figure 1

The Mendicant Exile

Leopis and Lepidus were demonstrated to be faulty postulates, as their inflexible, archaic natures refused to partake of earthly negative wisdom. Their suffering came too late to be transcended. In *Pupillus* (Orphan), Alberti sketches a different scenario—at once more tortured and more promising.[74] To regain the garland of Praise, and with it authorial power, the writer must be subjected to the negative aspects of the unnatural society and be functionable in it without losing his mythic core. He must withstand testing. This Herculean struggle, if successful, would result in saintly *beatitudo*.

The central character embodying this proposition is Philoponius (Lover of Hard Work). One of the most important
figures in the Albertian laboratory, he appears as protagonist
in two other *Intercoenales* pieces, *Erumna* (Mental Anguish) and
Anuli (Little Rings), both of which will be discussed later in this
chapter.

Philoponius, like Leopis and Philodoxus, is a "talented adolescent" full of literary ambition:[75] "He yearned to set himself
above the rich and powerful simply on the basis of his literary
accomplishments."[76] In the overall scheme of Albertian author
figures, Philoponius is more advanced than Lepidus, taking up
where the latter left off, outside the magic circle of compla-
cency and untested hopefulness. Again we encounter the iconographic insignia indicative of the theoretical line. "Yes, the
fortune of this young man was indeed bad"[77]; he "lost his
father," was "abandoned by his family," "robbed by his relatives, rejected by his friends," "expelled from his native land,"
"ill to the point of death," and "on the verge of starvation."[78]
Significantly, Philoponius is defined as a "mendicant beggar,"
foreshadowing a future incarnation, the vagabond Momo, who
was to transform vagabonding into the ultimate art.[79]

We know now that *Pupillus* is no autobiographical narrative,
even though the circumstances of Alberti's own life serve as
props.[80] Philoponius, as experimental postulate, is driven out
of the postlapsarian society once he is spotted as an outsider
from the mythic garden. He is banished from the city not for
political reasons but because he does not yet know how to play
the game. Inverting the Old Testament story of Adam's ex-
pulsion from paradise, Alberti depicts Philoponius as expelled
because he has *not* eaten from the tree of earthly knowledge.
This rather unorthodox version of the origin of exile stresses
the dialectical otherness of the Albertian writer who, as *exemplum*, is not a real mortal but an allegorical stand-in for society's
primordial wholeness. His suffering not only attests to the
painful initiation process that brings him face to face with
reality but also assigns to him the required iconographic insignia betokening his eventual transcendence.

Of course, testing is a topos in classical and medieval literature. Ovid's *Tristia* is a particularly appropriate example, for

Ovid—unlike Aeneas, who was accompanied by his companions—went into exile alone, leaving family, friends, and a devoted wife. Solitary confrontation of one's destiny was a frequent topos in medieval romances, which often end in the hero's *beatitudo*, provided he survives the machinations of his enemies. Fortitude proved by solitary existence is also a prerequisite in hagiographies, which is essentially what we have here in *Pupillus*. Unlike Ovid, who left Rome with the sobs of his family in his ears, Philoponius, who has no friends even among his closest relatives, is the *exemplum* of Christian meekness in a "rapacious world."[81] Philoponius, however, is not yet aware of his higher destiny. The gods, so he feels, endowed him with a talent he is unable to bring to fruition. Forced from the city where he assumed he would be effective, he feels marked for misery.[82]

Thus driven by so many misfortunes and overwhelmed in his raging mind by anger and indignation, the youth [Philoponius] lashed out in these words. "Why should I expect the gods to be kind to me in the future since I know that I am specifically marked from birth for perpetual misery? . . . I beg you, O divine audience, that hereafter no orphan shall rejoice for having obtained a better fate than I have endured. May they also find no sense of humanity among their fellow citizens; may they come upon no respect from their neighbors, and may they perceive no trust in their closest relatives . . . . May they receive all forms of hatred, envy, enemies, calamities, and miseries.[83]

There can be no doubt that Alberti is preparing Philoponius to discover the well-known Augustinian belief that life on earth is nothing more than an extended exile.

Suppose we were wanderers who could not live in blessedness except at home, miserable in our wandering and desiring to end it and to return to our native country. We would need vehicles for land and sea which could be used to help us reach our homeland, which is to be enjoyed. But if the amenities of the journey and the motion of the vehicles itself delighted us, and we were led to enjoy those things which we should use, we should not wish to end our journey quickly, and, entangled in a perverse sweetness, we should be alienated from our country, whose sweetness would make us blessed. Thus, in this mortal life, wandering from our native country where we can be blessed, we should use this world and not enjoy it.[84]

Philoponius's mendicant status stands not only for his Augustinian exile on earth but also for his Franciscan disdain for a pecuniary world in which he, as all mendicants, prefers to live as a stranger and a beggar.[85]

In the Renaissance, the state of exile was assumed as a regular pose by a cultural elite in imitation of Petrarch. Petrarch's exile, unlike Dante's, was not a bitter experience but was perceived by him as liberation. In *Remedies* (1366) he listed the advantages of exile: one can develop one's free will, demonstrate one's illustriousness, perfect one's sense of justice, and prove one's incorruptibility; above all one can claim a metaphorical fatherland not tied to a geographical place or subject to the vicissitudes of politics.[86]

Petrarch was not alone in contemplating the paradoxical situation—a topos dating back to the classics—that authentic virtues exist better outside the binding social framework.[87] His contemporary, the poet Bindo di Cione del Frate, described Lady Rome wandering about on lonely roads after being driven from the city by Pride, Envy, and Avarice.[88] The Florentine Matteo Frescobaldi compressed these motifs into a single ideogram: Avarice, Pride, and Luxury have exiled Prudence, Fortitude, Justice, Temperance, and their sisters.[89] In this inverse world the good people live *fuori i muri*, and the "wild folk" live like caged and dangerous animals within the walls of the city. It is in this context that we perceive Philoponius's exile. It links him with those benevolent forces that breathe the uncontaminated air *fuori i muri*. The negative result, namely, that the central position in society is forsaken, was for Alberti a historical given.

By Alberti's time the exile theme had already become a cliché. Poggio Bracciolini, with his usual wit, twisted it into satire on the occasion of Cosimo de' Medici's exile from Florence in 1433, offering the Florentine the disingenuous consolation that—having lost dignities, dominion, honors, wealth, and riches, which are all external things—prudence, magnanimity, constancy, probity, virtue, and faith are finally at his command. "Let Cosimo take refuge in the fortress of his reason and virtue. Studies are the true glory of the wise man in the theater of the world. Let Cosimo continue to cultivate learned

men and abandon the troubled world of politics."[90] Giovanni
Mario Filelfo even suggested that one should prepare oneself
with a repertoire of stock refrains to be used like polite formulas in encounters with exiles.[91]

Unlike his contemporaries Alberti still saw exile and suffering in a cosmological context. They are the source of the
writer's spiritual renewal and the iconographic attributes identifying the interlocutor as saint rather than cynic.

Intact Wisdom

The young novice, if he is to become saint rather than cynic,
must acquire "intact wisdom"(*prudentiam integram*)—the mas-
tery of the dialectic that synthesizes the physical with the metaphysical. In exile he will encounter his spiritual fathers, who
symbolize this union. These patronal figures, "remarkable, illustrious, and known for their virtue and knowledge of writing," sponsor his writerly identity. In Alberti's treatise on
oratory, *Trivia senatoria* (1460), the young Lorenzo de' Medici
Giovanetto (b. 1449) is advised to view his teachers Landino
and Gentile as his true "fathers": "Imitate these men, remarkable and illustrious, known for their virtues and knowledge of
letters, as your fathers, so that the fatherland can be more
glorious to have possessed in one single important family such
citizens as you, stamped by virtue and literary merit."[92]

The spiritual father instills in the mind of the novice the
principles of intact wisdom, with the hope that he can both
adapt to and transcend "mankind's disease-ridden life."[93] The
concept of intact wisdom is of profound importance in Alberti's
thought; it is the counterproposal to Libripeta's paralyzing
"wisdom learned from the sewer."[94] We find it described in the
closing pages of *De commodis literarum atque incommodis*, where
Alberti quotes from a supposedly ancient text. Much as in
Philodoxeus, Alberti argues here that if the ancients would speak
to us today they would insist on a metaphysical wisdom based
on spiritual wholeness. In his last work, *De Iciarchia*, Alberti
was to reaffirm this conviction. The spiritual father has to defy
even the biological father in order to guarantee that his protégé
can rise to the rank of "an earthly god of Virtue": "The papa

of the little one born in his house will say: 'He is my son.' I will reply, 'True. However, you have made him like all other animals born with two legs. I have made him like an earthly god of Virtue .... To whom would you say one who has been so ennobled is more indebted? To the papa (*babbo*), or to me, his true and best father (*vero e ottimo padre*)?'"[95]

It is one of these father figures, "a most honest, and quasi-angelic man," who in *Pupillus* saves Philoponius from death in the nick of time.[96] This process of growth is elaborated in another *Intercoenales* dialogue, *Erumna* (discussed in the next chapter), in which Philoponius is shown as graduating to a higher form of self-realization. For the moment, however, let us turn to *Naufragus,* where the theme of a father figure effecting a transcendence is beautifully epitomized in the allegory of a shipwreck.[97] Though the piece is told in the first person, we have by no means a personal experience, but a father figure addressing other *viri optimi.*

The voyage begins favorably enough with everyone in high spirits, but soon a storm breaks out and floods the ship. The only survivors are an evil-minded sailor, the "author," and an innocent young woman, standing for the novice; she is on her way to her marriage. Marriage here as elsewhere refers to a spiritual union. The three are trapped for several days in the damaged hold of the ship, which is filled with water up to the level of their necks. The foundering vessel is obviously a metaphor for society—a classical and medieval commonplace—and the three characters are allegories of human bestiality, hope, and innocence, respectively.[98]

As no salvation seems possible, the sailor attempts to murder the young woman to cannibalize her. His violent attempt to "feed on live limbs" threatens not only the life of the girl, who here takes the place of the ascendent Albertian writer, but the precarious stability of the vessel itself; the more the protagonist tries to restrain the sailor, the "more the sailor burns with rage." In an hour of desperate danger, as the ship is buffeted by high winds and the sailor goes raving mad, the paternal hero discovers that the goddess Hope has not abandoned them:

In this miserable situation, as you, gentlemen, might imagine with your understanding, what constant threats of death we overcame on one side only to await them on the other! With every swelling wave we saw our end grow nearer and nearer. Yet, O wonderful thing, never in so many dangers did hope abandon our minds, nor courage fail us, but rather we were always encouraged by the least little thing to hope for our salvation. And as I wondered at things and hardly believed that I would see the light of the sun again, I reflected that only one goddess remained to men in their wretchedness, Hope; she who "when all the gods ascended to the sky, fleeing the accursed earth, remained there as the sole companion to mankind [a theme Alberti elaborates in *Momus*]. She helps the shipwrecked man to see when no land is in sight, and to swim in mid-ocean . . . ." Therefore, it is no wonder that this goddess, who has never abandoned the wretched man beset by evils, even when all the other gods have deserted him, would not allow us to be overwhelmed by such evils.[99]

Sustained by their faith in Hope, the hero and the young woman manage to subdue the sailor and are eventually rescued by fishermen who bring them to shore. The young woman, now reunited with her bridegroom, is no longer the untested innocent; her impending marriage has become a metaphysical postulate.

A subplot of the story opens new vistas on the otherwise predictable resolution. Once rescued, the narrator learns that his brother, who had been traveling with him, has drowned and that his ring, taken from the body when it washed ashore, is, surprisingly, now in the possession of the young woman's bridegroom. The author, already the spiritual father of the girl, thus also becomes the spiritual brother of the groom. Once again conceptual links supercede biological ones. The death of the biological brother literally supplies the magic ring necessary to bond the bride and the groom under the sponsorship of the spiritual father. The novice status has been transcended.

The transformation of the girl into a bride allegorizes the transformation of the Albertian writer, when and if he survives the "shipwreck." Ideally the process must lead to a "marriage"—representing spiritual wholeness—as we have already seen in *De commodis literarum atque incommodis*, where the author marries literature, and in *Philodoxeus*, where the protagonist marries Glory.

Philoponius and the Twelve Rings

Let us now return to Philoponius, whom we have left in misery in *Pupillus*, to see how he achieves sainthood. In *Anuli* (Little Rings) a discussion as to Philoponius's destiny takes place among Philoponius's Guardian Spirit and Minerva, Hope, and the Council of Gods.[100] Philoponius's Spirit implores Minerva, Philoponius's "divine parent" (and the mother of Philodoxus, we may recall), to take note of her son, who, though tormented by Envy, Calumny, and Poverty, continues to worship assiduously at the spring on Mount Helicon sacred to Apollo and the Muses.[101]

Spirit: What an intolerable situation! Whenever he [Philoponius] goes to the sacred fountain on Helicon, he willingly and often performs the rite though it usually turns out badly for him. For example, once when he was there to perform the sacred rite, just as those do who claim to be totally dedicated to you, he looked at himself in the fountain and then lifted his eyes up to heaven. He then sampled the foliage hurled out by the source, when suddenly, as he started to raise a cry to posterity according to custom, Envy was there, and up ran Calumny. They came forth in a fierce and hostile attack and tormented him, disturbed and tore him away from the rite. Then the most savage of the gods, Poverty, persecuted him, wretched, oh, twice wretched Philoponius, with all variety of torment, with how many kinds of insult! I am a witness to this. In fact, I saw how the angry goddess was not able to turn this man away from his worship of you [Minerva], with all her insults and violence.[102]

Philoponius, in his own defense, explains that despite all his torments he has been able to fashion over thirty stones, with the intention of dedicating them to Minerva. The stones seem to refer to *Intercoenales*, which initially may have comprised around thirty pieces. Yet Philoponius, like Lepidus before him, complains to the goddess Hope that his literary efforts came to little.

Will you [Hope] deny that before thirty days were up I had produced more than thirty fine and excellent stones? You were there. Tell her [Minerva] what reward I was given for my efforts. One after another I produced them, ground and polished them and rendered them into various shapes. Even those stones that were more modest, these two [Hope and the Council of Gods] did not despise or openly scorn, but instead approved of them in lowered tones, saying that these stones did not have the appearance of ancient pearls [unlike *Philodoxeus*]—far from it—and then they went on their way. But need I mention the rest of mankind, or how often I was given the opportunity for regret by harsh times and evil men—not to insult any god, of course—for one and all cursed my efforts. For this reason, I feel justified in hating the two of you, by whose direction I came up against such obstacles."[103]

Minerva, to the Spirit's surprise, exalts in Philoponius's agony, reminding the Spirit of "the common saying" that suffering tests virtue: "Oh, you are ridiculous, Spirit! As for Philoponius, aren't you grieving at what will only contribute to his virtue? Does it utterly escape you what that common saying means, namely that just as yellow gold is tested by fire, so virtue must be examined by a time of hardship?"[104] Philoponius does not see the logic and turns away from Minerva and even from the Hope: "Away! You have long been planning my destruction and it disgusts me to listen to you! Farewell, towers of Rome! Farewell, to you also [Hope] and to whatever friends I had! And Minerva, farewell to you! Let me make my escape from here."[105] Just when all seems lost, Minerva calls Philoponius back and announces that the period of testing is over. Not having understood that Minerva was only testing him, Philoponius is now ready to be elevated to a higher form of consciousness. Unlike Neofronus, he had not turned into a cynic, leaving the "towers of Rome" more in sadness than in disillusionment.

Before I continue with the circumstances of Philoponius's elevation into sainthood as described in the second half of *Anuli*, I must make a detour to *Erumna* (Mental Anguish), where Philoponius's transformation is also discussed.[106] The two dialogues must be seen as parallel. At the beginning of *Erumna* we find Philoponius, predictably, sitting "in his library," suffering "mental agony," lamenting his "ill health," complaining about the "infinite evil actions of others," and decrying that "despite my versatile talent . . . I am destined for a life of complete misery."[107] To compound matters the "malodorous cynic" (Libripeta) turns up yet again, "like someone roused from a dream, his eyes stormy and his voice loud."[108] Haunted by his *somnium,* he ridicules Philoponius's melancholy and sadistically advises him to resign himself to his misery. Philoponius concedes that for a man of learning like himself, such a "rational" argument exerts a powerful attraction. This concurrence with Libripeta's diabolic rationalism indicates Philoponius's internal turmoil and incipient moral weakening.

An unnamed father figure now enters the scene. Aware that the Libripetian insights pose a danger to his student, he suggests a different line of reasoning to rescue Philoponius from his misery. He asks Philoponius to assume for a moment that he is engaged in a discussion with Fortune. What would Philoponius desire? Riches, perhaps? No, as a young scholar he must reject money because of the absolute evil attending it, not to mention the time-consuming process connected with its acquisition. Is it the patronage of princes that he wants? No, for a man of noble spirit cannot accept servitude (we shall return to this notion in a later chapter). Power, perhaps? No, for that would be in conflict with his literary calling. Thus, Philoponius, seeing "his own reflection" for the first time, finds his faith in the future restored. In gratitude, he praises his "father":

O most eloquent paragon of humanity, how your words have such weight and moment in my soul! Filled as you are with the salt of charm and suavity you have swayed my mind from anger to the moderation of equanimity and turned my thoughts toward total self-examination . . . . I must be quiet, yet I also must confess that I have received a great relief from tribulation. I thank you and congratulate you.[109]

Philoponius is now secure in his identity as the "most fortunate and blessed of men"; he can walk "in the temples, theaters, and fora," knowing that he will never be tempted to be other than himself[110]: "The more I ponder and reflect, the more I understand that there is no man more blessed than I . . . . And so, I have determined that the wise man wishes to be who he is . . . Great Gods! How much wandering in my mind I have done, pondering with nimble thought and learning, to arrive at this idea."[111] The "eternal war with Fortune" no longer poses any danger, for Philoponius is now confirmed as an "honest man, grounded in the best learning."[112] Unlike the cautious Philodoxus, the innocent Leopis, the confused Lepidus, the embittered Libripeta, and the belated Neofronus, he will become the true hero, the prototype, in whom temporal wisdom fuses with intact wisdom. As one element in a complex system of motifs, Philoponius is the only allegorical personification of stability.

Now that Philoponius has been "tested by the care of his elders and found to be free from any stain of vice or vulgar contamination"—that is, the contamination of Libripetian cynicism (*Erumna*)—the stage is set for his beatification, as recounted in the second half of *Anuli*.[113] Here Philoponius recounts that he was commissioned by Minerva to make twelve rings of gold, each with an engraved image (table 1). The rings symbolize the twelve rings of transcendence and define the spiritual essence of the author-hero.

The symbolism of the individual rings would hardly have struck fifteenth-century readers as farfetched; it has parallels in the mnemonic devices of biblical commentators and preachers, such as the seven mirrors representing the cardinal sins, or the nine magic springs representing the orders of angels.[114] One of the rings, depicting a fishing pole suspending a crown over a fish, alludes to the symbolism on the famous ring of St. Peter worn by popes to this day. This is, however, only the fourth of the rings, each of which is described and its *mysteria* explained. The order is such that the rings link the divine with the mortal, that which is guided by the spirit of God with that which is necessary for proper implementation of God's will on earth.

Minerva announces that Philoponius, having completed these rings, is prepared to stand on his own. The symbolic marriage of Minerva and Philoponius follows, presided over by Minerva's high priestess Hope. In a sense, Philoponius regains the garland Lepidus had lost. Not far from the marriage ceremony is a plane tree standing for charity and firmness of character.[115] Philoponius receives the first of his rings, significantly "the ring of the winged eye"—the symbol of the "all-embracing wisdom of God."[116] In lieu of the absent Virtus and the distant Apollo, Philoponius now takes his place as link

Table 1 The Twelve Rings of Philoponius

Symbol	Meaning
Winged eye in a crown	The reason and omnipotence of divine intelligence
Elephant ear in a net	The ability to hear everything and filter it through the net of reason
Diamond	One man needs many masks. Good friends combine as one.
Fishing pole suspending a crown over a fish	Learn to find good men among the rest.
Vestibule with open door and candelabrum	The spirit is like an open door seeking enlightenment.
Sailor on a ship gazing into the wind	Maintain wisdom in the flood of events.
Circle surrounded by hooks and flames	The circle of reason surrounded by hooks of passion and flames of anger
Janus with horn of plenty and staff of Bacchus	The public and private man with abundance and pleasure, tempered by justice and moderation, respectively
Theater stage with olive tree growing on it	One contributes the fruit of one's labors to the theater of public life.
Winged Pegasus flying over the ocean	The wings of talent that unite past and future
Bearded girl with plumb line hanging from her chin	The virgin spirit that guides pure judgment
Helmet covered with flies	Suffer the attacks of detractors with the steadfastness of a soldier.

between heaven and earth and in essence embodies the Albertian ideal of the perfect humanist.

Council [of Gods]: The ring is the symbol of joy and glory, and the eye is more powerful than anything, swifter, more worthy; what more need be said? It is such as to be the first, chief, king, like a god of human parts. Why else did the ancients consider God as something akin to an eye, seeing all things and distinguishing each separate one? By this we are reminded that we must render praise for all things to God, rejoice with the whole spirit in Him, fulfill a flourishing and manly ideal of excellence, knowing that he sees everything we do and everything we think. Then, on the other hand, we are reminded to be wide awake, all-embracing as far as the power of our intelligence allows, in order to find out all things that lead to the glory of excellence, delighting to pursue with labor and persistence what is good and divine.

Hope: Show your grace, gods! Oh happy omen! Give me that ring. Your hand, Philoponius! Hold out your ring finger. I promise you that you will enjoy a happy fate. Do you see high in the plane tree that pure white dove that softly coos and shows approval and sympathy for us with a flapping of the wings? Without a doubt . . . I see in this a promise that very soon those highest and mightiest fates which govern the affairs of even Jove the greatest and best, these fates shall be propitious toward you if ever they have neglected you till now. Oh, happy you! Minerva, show your support.

Minerva: Hurrah for him [Philoponius]!

Spirit: Congratulate him![117]

Philoponius, carrying his twelve rings, accompanied by Minerva, Hope, and the Council of Gods, joined by Zeal, Vigilance, and Industry, enters the law courts (*basilica*) where he will attempt to legislate over mankind. He has faith that the "learned will protect the learned" and that the message on his rings "will make the lives of princes, as well as of private citizens, happy and blessed."[118] This is the Albertian utopia: the Albertian humanist installed as honored lawgiver and quasi-divine prince. The program spelled out in the twelve rings is his platform.

Though Philoponius has attained *beatitudo,* uniting the "highest heaven and the deepest ocean," darkness still looms in his future. The plane tree to which the Council of Gods makes reference was commonly associated with martyrs (often St.

Sebastian) as it symbolized steadfastness and courage in the face of suffering.[119] The Spirit, in the closing of the dialogue, hints at a dark future awaiting Philoponius! "I can do nothing but shout [for joy] in a loud voice. I want the highest heaven and deepest ocean to hear me. But the times, the times! How few are found! Alas, I do not wish to contaminate the happy omens of this man with a sad prediction."[120]

The Writer-Saint

Philoponius is a proposition without equal in early Renaissance literature. He represents a challenge to contemporary humanist political opportunism. Having absorbed negative wisdom without becoming polluted by cynicism and having filtered out the "seeds of corruption, like a sieve" until all "is pure and simple," he is the ideal humanist author-lawgiver who has earned the laurels of *beatitudo* and the position of honor in the "basilica." The significance of Philoponius in respect to then-current humanist theories and practices needs to be discussed, especially since the character gives us fresh insight into Alberti's thoughts on the writer's role in society and his historiographic definition. I shall turn first to the thesis of literature as diversion and then to the Renaissance definition of the "great man" to show that the character Philoponius implies a rejection of both.

Throughout the Middle Ages, theologians in defining the role of literature emphasized those writings which profit the soul over those which merely please the senses.[1] *Joaca* and *fabula*, for example, were permitted by medieval theologians from Augustine on only if they carried a moral lesson. Even Dante argued that intellectual satisfaction must be set before sensual satisfaction.[2] By the fourteenth century, however, the orthodox position broke down as the recreational justification for literature gained in favor. The new approach was neatly summarized by Laurent de Premierfait in 1414 in his introduction to the translation of the *Decameron*.[3] Laurent explains that after the fall from grace, love turned into hate and joy into sadness. Man became "ignorant, worrying, brooding, grieving, and subject to the vagaries of fortune." Yet, Laurent goes on, writers, while unable to eradicate these ills, could provide comfort and solace "for the survivors."[4] Boccaccio, he concludes, is the model author, for his works keep our mind from dwelling on the vicissitudes of life. Poggio's *Facetiae,* with its courtly jesting, ribald humor, and sexual innuendos, would fall within this category. On the surface *Intercoenales* does not seem all that different. In the preface Alberti points to alleged humor and gaity, but in reality the work is sobering, conceived as a "bitter emetic" to cure the "grave cares of the spirit" and not as entertainment.[5]

As to Philoponius, there is nothing whimsical about him. Being the implementor of a quasi-divine mission, he must obey the rules of frugality. In a dedication of part of the *Intercoenales*—significantly enough to Poggio—Alberti explains that whereas other writers "feed on sweet and succulent grasses," he (Alberti-Philoponius) nourishes himself on the sparse and bitter fruit of the fig tree that grows in the ruins of a "fallen temple atop a lofty crag."[6] The temple, certainly not Rome or classical antiquity but mankind's (destroyed) spiritual homeland, is the fitting background for the fig tree, a standard scriptural symbol of conversion which represented, ever since Augustine, the manifestation of the divine pattern in the life of the saintly.[7]

In keeping with their mission, Alberti's quasi-saintly authors are endowed with a "talent and intellect that is in large part divine."[8] They must display a properly disciplined manner and deliver a serious and effective text in the struggle against modern day paganism. In the introduction to *Momus* Alberti explains that such singular beings should receive the honor due to them: "Without doubt, we understand that all things that are rare have a sense of divinity about them to the extent that they tend toward the divine, and as a result are held to be unique, exquisitely singular, and segregated from close association with the multitude."[9] Alberti goes on to explain, "We are instructed to call them divine and admire and honor them as gods."[10] Nothing could be further removed from such a claim of divinity than a mere diversionary palliative for *Weltschmerz.*

Nor can we view the character Philoponius as a forerunner of Pico della Mirandola's "dignified man."[11] Briefly stated, Pico, in his *De hominis dignitate* of 1486, holds that since man is both outside of the fixed hierarchy of things and at the center of the divine universe, he can elevate himself by means of his free will to perfect his god-given potential. Pico hopes that man will want to choose for himself the highest possible form of moral and intellectual life. For Philoponius, however, there is no choice; he is from the start a schematic figure. Though learning was an important part of his development, free will has nothing to do with it. As is well known, *De hominis dignitate* caused much controversy and was even found to be heretical. Given the overall tenor of Alberti's thought, one could surmise that Alberti would have sided with the critics.[12] Free choice individualism, even if couched in Pico's optimistic terms, was for Alberti the ultimate source of evil. His ideal humanist is defined as free from temporal contingencies but not from the ethical system. It is the all-important bond between stable eternity and fluid time.

As we shall see, Alberti's theme of the writer-saint implies a heresy of its own, but in its imagery it reflects the orthodox definition of Christ, as defined by the Councils of Ephesus (431) and Chalcedon (451), in which Christ is declared as having two natures, one divine and one human, both perfectly united in one person and one substance. The concept of duality, soon claimed by kings and popes alike, defined them as *personae mixtae* (combining spiritual and secular), *personae geminatae* (human by nature and divine by grace), or *Deus-homo, una persona, duae naturae*.[13] As a twelfth-century theorist explains it,

We thus have to recognize a *twin person,* one descending from nature, the other from grace . . . . One through which, by the condition of nature, he conformed with other men: another through which, by the eminence of [deification] and by the power of the sacrament [of consecration], he excelled over all others. Concerning one personality, he was, by nature, an individual man; concerning his other personality, he was by grace, a *Christus*, that is, a God-man.[14]

In my postscript I show that Alberti took this as the program for his design of the church of S. Sebastiano for Ludovico Gonzaga of Mantua. The open crypt represents the temporal nature of the patron, the chapel above, his spiritual essence.

But the concept of duality also carries with it a definition of power. A representation of Emperor Henry II, for example, shows the sacred dove above and the sword of justice below (see figure 2).[15] The king—but potentially any vicar of Christ—implements divine justice in the world. Is that not what is spelled out by Philoponius's iconographic emblems, the winged eye of ring number one right down to the helmet of ring twelve? Philoponius, as humanist saint-king, thus demonstrates the union of spiritual triumph and physical strength. Alberti is in a sense stealing the mana of invincibility to bestow it on his writers, who are effective not on account of their political abilities, rhetorical eloquence, or classical learning but due to their perfect "construction," which in an ideal world would be spontaneously welcomed. Philoponius, presiding not only in the earthly basilica but in the heavenly temple exemplifies the model humanist uniting law with devotion. The very words with which Alberti describes the temple in *De re aedificatoria* seem to evoke Philoponius's divine half: "The temple should be constructed so beautifully that the imagination is not able to conceive of a place more beautiful. Every part should be so prepared that the beholder is stupefied at the things so worthy of admiration and almost forced to cry out with astonishment: This place is worthy of God!"[16]

This brings us to the question of literary immortality. The unification of the two natures in the writer involves a new consciousness of the literary persona, an aesthetic which at first separates—all separations involve an aesthetic—the aspiring writer from his natural environment (*Pupillus*) but then attempts to close the distance between reality and ideal (*Erumna*) by means of the twelve rings. The writer, moving from novice to saint, can remove the aesthetic distance by means of a double marriage, for marriage symbolically annuls aesthetic distance, with Fame and Glory or with Praise and Minerva. Not only does he regain his literary identity, the separation from which (*Philodoxeos*) threatened to transform him into cynic (*Corolle*)

55

Alberti and the Autobiographical Imagination

Figure 2
Emperor Henry II as Judge, in the Monte Cassino Gospel (1022–23). Vatican, Otto-bon. lat. 74, fol. 193ᵛ (Vatican Library).

but he is a figure with all the attributes of power. This cosmological theory, outlined in the numerous stories of *Intercoenales,* is summarized in the closing words of *De commodis litterarum atque incommodis,* where literary pleasure is clearly a product of the *utilitas* that brings earthly praise, which in turn is a reflection of true glory: "You will find that writing is pleasurable, very useful to obtain praise and glory and very adaptable to produce the fruit that will transmit one to posterity and thereby guarantee immortality."[17] In this sense writers with their words wield a power that places them in direct conflict with other types of power. It is not politicians or soldiers who acquire glory but the writer. As Alberti would later reaffirm: "As the hand that warms and prepares wax so as to better receive the impression and seal of a gem, so studies cast the mind for all functions and rewards of glory and immortality."[18]

In this way Alberti answers the problematic raised in *Commentarium Philodoxeos Fabule,* where the ambiguous relationship between author and text was revealed as the result of stresses inherent in society. Because society is equated with the corrupt "body," writers uncontaminated by secular realities surprise their competitors (Fortunius, for example) by capturing glory *and* immortality for themselves.

Yet the equation is not without a remainder. Literary immortality, as Alberti defines it, involves a conscious manipulation of the persona in the present so that posterity will take, or rather mistake, its aesthetic nature as spontaneous reality, a ruse intended to throw a humanist shadow back over temporal power. In the process, however, the humanist writer violates the code of simplicity. Alberti confronts this issue in *Momus,* which will be discussed later.

Returning now to the more immediate question of literary ontology, it is clear that Alberti's concept of literary power challenges the Petrarchian notion of great men. Petrarch, in *De viris illustribus,* concentrates on Roman heroes in order to stress his thesis that the Dark Ages had destroyed the valuable patrimony of Italy.[19] These heroes demonstrate that fortune could be controlled by the strength of inner virtue; they were able "to perform deeds worthy of being remembered and imitated by posterity," a thesis continued by Lombardo della Seta when he completed *De viris illustribus* after Petrarch's death[20]: "Always keep in sight those men whom you ought to be eager to love because of the greatness of their deeds."[21]

On the surface this sounds very Albertian, but if we probe deeper it becomes obvious that Alberti's writers would never find a place in Petrarch's world. According to Petrarch, "doctors, poets, and philosophers" can never be great, as they are neither politicians nor warriors.[22] But that, Alberti seems to argue, is exactly why his writers *are* great. Philoponius "set himself above the rich and powerful *simply on the basis of his literary accomplishments*" (my emphasis).[23] He is great because as an apolitical aristocrat of the spirit he transcends all secular ambition. Alberti was the first to point out that his concept of the humanist hero flies patently in the face of the "antique customs" of great men. His writers should be honored "without hesitation" and receive "numerous recompenses" as tokens of approval.

What if, finally, contrary to all tradition and ancient customs of famous men, someone does find a way of becoming equally rich by means of his own learning; clearly, he would be someone possessed of better fortune, more profound knowledge, clearer authority, and greater attention to friends than other men. Likewise, his fluency of speech, ease of manner, talent, versatility, and shrewdness would be more acceptable and more adapted to the ears and minds of men. Indeed, such a man should be learned so that the state, not hesitating to entrust its existence to him, can become accustomed to sharing his frequent complaints and honors. But very few indeed are those who will attain this great height of renown.[24]

This brings us to Alberti's disenchantment with the prevalent humanist practice of serving political power (let us recall Dynastes's destructive alliance with Fortunius in *Philodoxeus*). According to this Albertian view Petrarch, Salutati, Poggio, Manetti, Bruni, Dati, and others had all betrayed the humanist cause by placing their talents wholeheartedly in the service of pope and prince alike. Petrarch was well known for his devoted services in the interests of the Colonna; Salutati, chancellor of Florence, was surely no objective recorder of the history of Florence. The famous pen of Poggio was put freely into the service of politics. Manetti, Nicholas V's secretary and private confidant, enthusiastically toed the papal line; Bruni and Dati were both propagandists for Florence, their writings supported by the state government.[25] Already then their services were viewed as establishmentarian. Pius II in his *Historia de Europa* makes it very clear that *studia humanitatis* is a prerequisite for the political career of a Florentine chancellor.

The prudence of the Florentines is to be commended in many things, but most of all in their selection of chancellors, for they do not seek out lawyers, as most states do, but those skilled in oratory and what is called the *studia humanitatis*. For they are aware that not Bartolus or Innocentius but Cicero and Quintilian teach the art of speaking and writing well. We have known three in that city, illustrious in Greek and Latin learning and in the reputation of their own works, who have held the post of chancellor in succession: Leonardo and Carlo of Arezzo and Poggio of the same city-state, who as apostolic secretary wrote letters for three popes. Preceding them was Coluccio, whose eloquence was such that Galeazzo, the ruler of Milan who waged a terrible war against Florence within the memory of our fathers, was often heard to say that a thousand Florentine knights did him less harm than Coluccio's pen.[26]

It has long been recognized that humanism moved outside of established scholarly channels, through state chancelleries or princely courts, and that it did not shy away from propaganda, official history writing, and panegyric praise.[27] But where humanists in general saw their actions as part of a new commitment to public life, Alberti saw only a selling out to temporal interests. Political power, academic approbation, and ecclesiastical garments all served to mask self-serving ambition (*Cynicus*). The perfect humanists of Albertian provenance received their patronage, so to speak, directly from God: "This intellect, this cognition, reason, and memory, all of it so infinite and immortal, where does it come from if not from him who is infinite and immortal?"[28]

Alberti held out the thesis of the independent author despite the fact that he owed his livelihood to the papal curia. None of Alberti's presently known writings, except *Vita S. Potiti*, which as we shall see later was also subverted to his purpose, were undertaken in the service of the curia. Thus he had no qualms when he accused his fellow intellectuals of betraying the higher goals of humanism. If we see (as we should) figures such as Philoponius as critiques of humanist theories and practices, we can no longer put Alberti blithely into the camp of those who proposed an ideal of man who determined his life by the assertion of free will.

The Five Ages of History

If Alberti rejected the very elements that we today conceive of as the main contributions of Renaissance humanism, it is not because he was naively medieval or sentimentally pious. His medievalism was deliberate, nuanced, and precise. It could perhaps be considered a neo-medieval critique of mainstream humanism. Though Alberti's thought may seem in some respects conservative, indeed reactionary, it is actually quite bold, as it contains an astounding heretical element. To explain this we must first review Alberti's historiographic vision, unique and *sui generis* among fifteenth-century thinkers. Though never explicitly stated in the works already studied, there are five historical stages that constitute the setting of the Albertian theater[29]:

1. The mythic garden and the hypothetically intact link between god, writer, and society. The garden is the spiritual homeland, so to speak, of the Albertian humanist.

2. The destruction of the garden, the beginning of historical time with its irreversible aesthetic, and the appearance and increasing momentum of the Moloch society.

3. The introduction of Libripeta, who reveals the *incommunicando* condition of the two worlds. He presents the first stage of a coming into consciousness, and a mapping out of the extent of social ruin and of the remoteness of the godhead.

4. The attempt made to address the problem by means of a savior postulate (Philoponius). The new Albertian author is a quixotic warrior who fights for the restoration of a reciprocal relationship between mankind and the deity to save man and reactivate divine potency. In this age Fortunius controls society, whereas Philodoxus, the embodiment of society's con-

sciousness, attempts to bond the world to the distant godhead (figure 3).

5. The final historical stage (to be discussed later), a critique of the theory of restoration. Alberti points neither to an eschatological future nor to a Christian-Petrarchian "rebirth." The world remains eternally "dark."

Alberti's historiography might be seen as a counter version to the fivefold vision of history discernible in Leonardo Bruni's *History of Florence,* which first describes the Roman Republic, then the rule of the emperors, the invasion of the barbarians, the new empire under Charlemagne, and finally the rise of the city-states of Italy around 1250.[30] Whereas Bruni employs the scheme to describe the secular history of Florence and the theme of liberty, its struggles and achievements, Alberti's historiographic vision is more in the nature of a creation myth and echoes concepts from Hesiod and Ovid. In *The Works and Days* Hesiod demonstrates a pattern that moves from peace to war, from joy to sadness, and from blessedness to anguish.[31] Clearly Alberti was an avid reader of Ovid, for many of his drastic descriptions of evil directly reflect sentences out of the *Metamorphoses* (indeed the theme of metamorphosis itself aptly describes the transformations the Albertian characters undergo).

The Distant Deity
.
.
The Writer-Saint
Truth, Modesty, Magnanimity, and Knowledge
.   .
.   .

Defunct Society   -   Defunct Gods
.   .
.   .
The Cynic

Figure 3
The fourth age of history.

The ultimate prototype for Alberti's idea of history, however, is the standard medieval understanding of history *sub specie aeternitatis,* which begins with the Garden of Eden and ends with judgment day, in all consisting of six periods. As first envisioned by Augustine and reiterated throughout the Middle Ages, the six ages were intended to illuminate the presence of a divine order that subsumed world history into the folds of a metahistorical progression.[32] *Sub specie aeternitatis* also argues that the only significant earthly events are those that portray the victory of faith, each incident subject of course to Apostolic approval. Though Alberti's historiographic concept has the outer form of history *sub specie aeternitatis,* it breaks the unquestionable ground rule, the precept of the centrality of the Church which dissolves only on judgement day, until which time the Church, with its organizational hierarchy, is the *only* possible means by which the faithful can attain salvation; the Church with its sacraments is the spiritual garrison against the armies of the devil. In Alberti's cosmology the humanist savior usurps the centrality of the Church. Taking up spiritualist arguments from the previous century—as well as anticipating reformist arguments yet to come—Alberti seems to suggest that the Church in its present state is a type of defective theocracy rather than a spiritual force.

To see the difference between Alberti's humanist historiography and the medieval canon more clearly, one need only recall the historiographic pattern developed by St. Bonaventure (1217–74) who, elaborating on St. Augustine, held that there were seven ages, the present being the sixth, in which the wine of revelation is adulterated by the water of philosophy.[33] The sixth age would end when the Holy Spirit would lead the Church into the full realization of the revelation of Christ. Though Alberti might have agreed that in the contemporary age philosophy was eroding society's spiritual core, he makes no concession to the role of the Church in mankind's salvation. It is nowhere indicated that Alberti's mystic humanist saints need the rituals of baptism, sacrament, or confession, much less an institutional backing. In Alberti's mystical humanism the writer-saints alone are responsible for God's commitment to human society and must be prepared for a mission that while futile must necessarily consume them. Had Alberti written somewhat earlier or somewhat later, when any statement that denied the mediating function of the Church would have been deemed heretical, he might have been called upon to defend himself.[34] Even in his age he had reason to proceed carefully—and the cagey and ciphered mode of exposition might have served that purpose—for Church discipline judged conduct lightly but controlled opinion with an iron hand. He might not have been burned at the stake, but he could have incurred a writer's ban like that imposed on Ficino for his ideas on magic, or he could have drawn upon himself a papal condemnation, as was the case with Pico della Mirandola, who published a controversial criticism of theological practices.[35] It is interesting to realize here that Alberti's beliefs, expressed in the middle of the fifteenth century, were not dissimilar to those of Marsilius of Padua, who was condemned as a heretic in 1327 for arguing that the Church had abandoned its original spiritual mission in favor of temporal power.[36]

Even a comparison with the Cathari heresy, farfetched as it may seem, is not totally to be dismissed. Catharism (derived from the Greek for "pure"), a widespread spiritualist movement during the Middle Ages, conceived of a life as developing around an independent group of *perfecti* who are protected and honored by the community simply on account of their self-abnegating dedication.[37] The Cathari heresy, which developed out of the early Manichaeanism that attracted even Augustine in his youth, was eradicated for the most part by the late thirteenth century but survived in Florence and elsewhere in the households of Italian nobility well into the fourteenth century. Though it was very much dead as an organization by the fifteenth century, its general scheme (if not its complex cosmology and its many theological abstractions) were by no means forgotten. The Cathari rejection of the Church as institution and Alberti's own implicit rejection of it in the definition of his writer who exists as an independent spiritual agent seem too close to be accidental and might imply some reformist sentiments in Alberti's thoughts that have so far gone undetected.

For obvious reasons Alberti never overtly emphasized any of

these theological implications, making it difficult to speculate on them. At least he was never accused of heresy, and the political climate during his lifetime was more lenient than that of the previous centuries. Since Alberti's author types only strike the chords of heresy softly, they could be misread as Christian warriors. In this guise they would certainly appear not only as acceptable and uncomplicated theological propositions but also as a reflection of the church militant.[38]

The Winged Eye—Quid Tum?

An analysis of Philoponius is only complete if we do not overlook the strong undertow of irony. In that respect alone he has little in common with the radiant ideal man envisioned by the Neoplatonists. Philoponius and Libripeta are inseparably linked. The first is a *perfectus,* handing down the laws in the basilica, with Apollo as father, Virtus as mother; Libripeta is his sibling opposite. Having lost all faith in humanity, Libripeta willingly suffers ridicule in exposing the terrifying absence of human virtues. Both attempt to change humanity. One insists on the potential for stability, the other on the fundamental absence of stability. In a sense one could say that each haunts the system of the other.

This brings us to the famous medallion of Leon Baptista Alberti made by Matteo de' Pasti (figure 4). The front of the medallion portrays the profile of a youthful Alberti, the back, the famous winged eye; below the eye is the inscription: *quid tum* (What next?). The date of the medallion is uncertain.[39] However, since the eye and the inscription also appear on a manuscript of *Della pittura* dated 1436, it is clear that Alberti devised this emblem in conjunction not only with *Della pittura* but also with *Intercoenales,* which was written during that time.[40]

Various interpretations of the medallion have been proposed over the years, but since most of them do not deal with *quid tum,* they could not adequately address the symbolism of the ideogram.[41] I suggest that the medallion represents the paradox of the fourth age of history. The question *quid tum?,* asked by Lepidus in *Somnium* upon hearing Libripeta's tale, represents the moment of shock that marks the transition from

Figure 4
Matteo de'Pasti, commemorative medal of Leon Baptista Alberti (National Gallery of
Art, Washington, D.C.). recto: Leone Battista Alberti (1404–72), architect and writer
on art and science; Matteo de' Pasti; National Gallery of Art, Washington; Samuel
H. Kress Collection (verso: within laurel wreath, a winged eye terminating in thun-
derbolts, and motto QVID TVM)

innocence to skepticism—from naiveté to an understanding
that the "Good Arts," the major ordering principle in society,
have been irredeemably lost in the sewer. Philoponius, with his
winged eye, transcends Libripeta's sewer wisdom. As a *perfectus*
defying all religious, political, and academic establishments he
is free from temporal concerns, and flies like Pegasus—whose
image appears on one of Philoponius's rings—with "wings of
talent" over the "turbulent waters," much as the winged eye of
the medallion seems to fly over *quid tum:* "We must be like
Pegasus in the course of life and in this labile age which drags
us along; in rushing to the port of a better life we must use
our wings so that we are not drowned in the waves. The wings
of men are the power of talent and the gifts of the spirit, by
which we advance steadily up to the heavens with an understanding of things. And through virtue and piety we are joined
to the gods."[42]

Against this background Alberti's medallion takes on a powerful meaning. Linking the voices of Philoponius and his bride
Minerva on the one hand and Lepidus-Libripeta and his lost

bride Praise on the other, it portrays the two alter egos of the writer: the saint-king and the cynic. The two cannot be seen separately; they are a symbiotic pair. One is icon, the other iconoclast; one is triumphant, the other militant. There is nothing in between except the defunct religious, political, and intellectual establishments. The implication is that the Albertian writer faces the paradoxical situation of being *both* icon and iconoclast. To resolve this paradox Alberti devised a third type of humanist, the functionary, who attempts to reconcile the two in the real world. But though the writer can wistfully envision such a reconciliation, it remains a fantasy, because for Alberti nothing can alter mankind's self-alienation.

The Humanist Drama

Alberti's preoccupation with the writer, with the relationship between writer and society, and ultimately with the historiographic function of writing is by no means confined to *De commodis litterarum atque incommodis* and *Intercoenales* but extends to his entire oeuvre. Most of the characters that appear in his subsequent works not only fit the pattern but expand the theoretical structure of Alberti's tripartite definition of humanism: the humanist saint, the cynic, and between them, for lack of a better term, the "civic functionary." All too frequently scholars have had eyes only for the middle category. The functionaries, to be introduced in a few moments, are especially important in Alberti's aesthetics, as they, much like painters and architects, set out to inhabit the real world in a way that the humanist writers by definition cannot. Each type must be seen in the context of the others, as their interrelationship delineates different strategies of contact between humanism and temporal world. Those who "make peace treaties" (writer-saints) differ from those "who administer justice" (functionaries) and those "who cure illnesses" (the cynics).[1] The first bring into existence the "flowers, true doctrine, and all elegant and praiseworthy things."[2] The second inhabit the flexible world of urban existence, and the third preside over the realm of mankind's "disease-ridden life."

Interestingly enough, Alberti's tripartite view of the humanist endeavor finds a parallel in the thought of Pope Nicholas V, who was known to Alberti already from his student days in Bologna. Pope Nicholas described his objectives as establishing peace throughout the temporal and sacred realms of the papacy, rebuilding the city of Rome, and building a library for the papacy that could guide him in governing the Church.[3] Though the relationship between Nicholas and Alberti is too complex to be entered into here, it is notable that the first of Nicholas's objectives parallels Alberti's writer-saints and the second his functionaries. As to the third category, library and government, Alberti, as we have seen, has two alternatives, a success version (humanist "fathers") and a failure version (Libripeta). Whether these parallels between Nicholas V's program and Alberti's theory were due to their common educational roots, whether Alberti and Nicholas communicated on these issues in Rome, or whether Alberti is in fact critiquing the Pope we will never know, for there are no records to help us in our investigation.[4]

Using our knowledge of the roles played by Philodoxus, Fortunius, Libripeta, Leopis, Lepidus, Neofronus, and Philoponius, we turn now in chronological order to St. Potitus, Baptista, Agnolo, Theogenius, Genipatro, Microtiro, Gelastus, Momus, and Enopus. Like modern archeologists we must refrain from hunting only gold bracelets and sift through the shards as well, even if this results in certain redundancies. Only by showing the overwhelming evidence of the pattern can the point be made which so strongly contradicts traditional interpretation of Alberti's thought. The argument will move, conveniently, from saint, to functionary, to cynic.

Saint Potitus

In the spectrum of Albertian characters, St. Potitus stands at the extreme end of the saintly humanism. He serves as model *par excellence* for the hagiography of the humanist. *Vita S. Potiti* (1433), composed at the same time as *Intercoenales*, has been largely ignored because it was held to have been written on command and because its content fell outside the perimeter of scholarly interest.[5] As I will show, however, this hagiography is particularly important in the definition of such transcendent writer types as Baptista, and reveals that Alberti, with his strategic skill, subverted all materials, undermining and ironizing their original context.

Vita S. Potiti, written by Alberti upon entering the curia as a sort of initiation exercise, was to be the first of a series of hagiographies ordered by the curia; for some reason, the series never progressed beyond the first installment. St. Potitus was by no means an obscure saint. A fresco of his decapitation painted by Spinella Aretino in 1391–92 in the Camposanto of Pisa was the centerpiece of a cult that survives to this day (see figure 5).[6] For the hagiography, however, there were few solid facts on which to draw. Predictably, Alberti used the opportunity to incorporate St. Potitus into his system. He not only produced "a more dignified version of the holy martyr's life," as he himself admits, but subverted the story surreptitiously to his own theoretical masterplan.[7] He transposed the illiterate young Sardinian into an articulate martyr, projecting onto him the now familiar autobiographic notations that point to the theoretical line.[8] St. Potitus is endowed with a gifted literary

Figure 5
Spinella Aretino, "The Martyrdom of St. Efesion and St. Potiti," in Camposanto of Pisa (1391). Reprinted from A. Lasinio, *Pittura a fresco del Campo Santo di Pisa* (Florence, 1832).

mind; his eloquence is such that "he was acclaimed and honored by even the most learned of men.[9]

The story begins with Potitus's elevation out of the physical into the metaphysical realm; he moves quickly from novice to sainthood by enduring the ridicule of the townspeople, by rejecting the wisdom of his biological father for the true wisdom of the Christian father, and by leaving home and country for exile in a secluded forest. Having no desire to pursue *vita civilis* or to acquire money and power, he enjoys his solitude far away from "the raw multitude" which "does not know how to make great things"[10]: "He thought it more beautiful to communicate with the beasts than with cruel and wicked men of which no city is without a great abundance."[11] However, as the story of St. Potitus proves and as the stories of other characters corroborate, the condition of exile too must be transcended. It is in essence only a form of testing. The humanist enterprise must not end in *contemptus mundi*.

The devil, eager to entrap Potitus, appears before him in the guise of a suave, handsome urbanite advocating the virtues of city life, the advantages of money, and the dishonor of intellectual solitude. When Potitus holds firm, the devil devises a more sophisticated strategy to entrap Potitus in temporal affairs. He infects the mind of the emperor's daughter with a profound illness so that the townspeople will call on Potitus to cure her with his miraculous healing abilities. And so it happens. Potitus gives up his life as a hermit, knowing that he must risk his life for the salvation of others. But he is stronger than the devil anticipated. Potitus not only heals the princess, but convinces her to become a Christian and even exorcizes the devil by striking her head, making the devil visible for all to see.

The emperor, afraid of Potitus's growing popularity, decides to kill him lest the entire populace embrace Christianity. Potitus, however, proves difficult to kill; the executioners try to burn him, feed him to the dogs, dismember him, and torture him, all to no avail; even when Potitus is thrown into the lions' den, the animals sit around and admire his "beautiful countenance." Only after a great struggle are the emperor's soldiers able to decapitate him, the event that is the topic of the Camposanto fresco.

The story of St. Potitus's martyrdom had to follow the well established principles of hagiography that traditionally employed themes of suffering, temptation, spirituality, and miraculous indestructibility.[12] Miracles in which the saint forces men of evil to behave foolishly and ineffectively were typical of *vitae sancti*. But this does not mean that the work should be ignored. On the contrary, it confirms the hagiographic elements so frequently encountered in Alberti's quasi-autobiographic exposition. In fact, the story dovetails neatly into the scheme of quasi-autobiographical postulates. Alberti seems to admit as much in the opening paragraph: "I wanted the early life of Potitus to be the first subject on which I could test my abilities. His youth was marked by a singular perseverance and by a multitude of miracles. Whoever makes the effort to study this youth will find much material for discussion and much application to his own life."[13]

Vita S. Potiti further elaborates Alberti's idea of history as developed in *Philodoxeus,* where the dialectic of eternal versus ephemeral values is played out. Since society speeds ever more rapidly away from stability, restoration requires a commensurately greater counter effort. Thus the combat Potitus had to wage, Alberti pointedly mentions, is far more intense than that of Christ himself. The devil (equivalent here to Fortunius), who had appeared to Christ in human form, has become now, because of his successes, a monster "exceeding human strength."[14] Thus the devil is not seen as an independent agent of evil, but as a mirror of the growth of evil in man's psyche.

Potitus knew the difference between these times and the ancient ones of Christ. In fact, the devil's tricks, namely the possession of ephemeral things, had in the beginning a human form as if to imply that the enjoyment and use of earthly goods was not adverse to mankind. Afterward the things [the devils] grew to a size more than human stature, because man—out of haughtiness and desire for grandeur— had become himself too haughty. And at the end they turned into beasts because of man's riches and excessive abundance of material things.[15]

Baptista

Baptista, appearing first in *Della Famiglia* (1433–34), then in *Vita anonyma* (1438), *Profugiorum ab aerumna* (1441), and finally in Alberti's last work, *De Iciarchia* (1468) assumes many of the hagiographic qualities of St. Potitus, in particular the saint's indestructibility. He too aspires to be one of the *uomini prestantissimi e rari* who resiliently and miraculously "emerge from life with undefeated and untroubled souls."[16] He inherits not only St. Potitus's early Christian meekness but his function; in the dangerous urban environment that is his home, he is triumphantly defenseless. The "bad-mouthers" are forced to admire him just as the lions felt compelled to admire Potitus: "He [Baptista] lived among envious and malevolent people with such modesty and equanimity that no matter how angry his rivals and detractors were with him, in the presence of the high and mighty they dared not say anything about him but praise and admiration."[17]

The best definition of Baptista is found in the *Vita anonyma* (as the text has been labeled by historians), written five or six years after *Vita St. Potiti*.[18] As usual, the character portrayed is not Alberti *in propria persona*. When Alberti wrote this *Vita*, he was a mere *abbreviatore* in the papal curia. Apart from the prestige of his post—which he shared with over a hundred others—Alberti had little power, money, or influence. At best he was known within a small circle of *literati*. Yet the *Vita* describes a man "famous," "known by not a few princes," and "loved by all."[19] Like a prophet, he was followed by admirers who "collected the utterances of his mouth as he walked."[20] He was so secure in his civic standing that "he did not need to wear the purple robes of his high office."[21] And, to top everything off, Alberti glowingly describes Baptista as "*meritamente elivato.*"[22]

"Baptista," like Philoponius, is the ultimate heretical *perfectus* endowed with an aura of mythic superiority. The *Vita* opens with these words: "In everything that was necessary for a noble and liberal education, he was—ever since the time of his childhood—master, sure of himself as a leading youth of his age."[23] Alberti even overplays Baptista's physical strength to demonstrate that Baptista is a being of an altogether different scale: "In soldierly exercises, he was famous in his youth. . . . He could throw a small coin of silver up high in a temple with so much force that one could hear the sound of it hitting the vault."[24] Like Apollo, he was able "to determine at just a glance everyone's defects,"[25] and, based on what he saw, he could make actual predictions: "Standing in front of the palace of d'Este, where in the time of Niccolo the Tyrant, most of the city's youth would be slain, he said: 'Oh friends, this pavement will perforce be slippery in the future because much blood will flow within this wall. . . .'"[26]

And so Baptista too, a saint-king, combining spiritual and physical strength in one being, employs his "versatile talent" (the same term was applied to Philoponius) to connect the heavenly with the earthly but—as always—not through politics but through "literature."[27] Since the humanist renounces all mercantile contacts, literature is the *only* fragile link that connects him to the secular. Intrinsically—and importantly—the writer is no "universal man." His contact with the world is by way of a very narrow path.

The path takes the form of a protracted struggle. He must show through bodily suffering that his study of literature is not equivalent to the acquisition of evil (as we remember, this was the topic of *De commodis litterarum atque incommodis*). Thus Baptista, "giving everything in himself to literature," suffers bodily weakness, emaciation, abdominal pain, temporary loss of sight, and singing in the ears—all iconographic attributes indicating that entering the realm of "earthly knowledge" is for him not equivalent to entering a realm of earthly sin.[28] Even Baptista's abdominal pain was a typical hagiographic complaint. For example, a contemporary of Alberti, the Florentine prelate Antonio Degli Agli (ca. 1400–77), wrote a *vita* in 1475 in which he takes up many familiar themes: youthful poverty, many worries, familial problems, temptations of the flesh, false accusations, and, of course, those abdominal pains, all of which did not deter him from his dedication to God, learning, painting, sculpture, and theater.[29] Whether Agli was influenced by Alberti is a moot point, for both authors took the hagiographic structure and filled it in with iconographical markers pointing to typical manifestations of the holy in the world.[30]

Alberti's *Vita,* however, is only one variation in the autobiographical subtext. Unlike Leopis, for example—who "lost the garland" and was unable to marry Praise and deliver his text—Baptista is portrayed as successful in elevating others to his level: "He was pleased with his writings, for his talent was not small. . . . He was praised by the good ones and the scholars . . . . Citizens who were still ignorant became so enraptured by his books that they became fond of literature."[31] Baptista's recreational habits serve only to demonstrate his purposefulness: Baptista, as was his custom, "would walk a few hours in the hills, or in the plain, for exercise, and then return to his study of literature and philosophy."[32]

Predictably, Baptista's efforts attract the jealousy of detractors, and on one occasion Baptista is forced to burn some of his writings to keep them out of the hands of numerous "slanderers."[33] Since Baptista possesses a steady, self-effacing patience, he transcends these trials and never permits himself any sign of spleen or irritability. Patience is important, for it allows talent to rise untainted to the surface: "He desired in all things a sense of moderation, all that is except for patience; in this regard he said: "One should possess either all of it or none of it."[34]

Baptista willingly and eagerly assumes his duty as a chosen one in the vanguard of those who preserve the myth of intactness. "Our real business," Alberti comments in the *Della Famiglia,* "is always to expose, by the very excellence of our conduct, those persons who are liars and frauds."[35] Baptista, representing the struggle of "the good, virtuous, and meek against the vicious, rapacious, and ambitious," forces evil men, assuming they are not won over by the innate beauty of his being, to resort to acts of jealousy, hatred, and violence thus exposing in piecemeal fashion the dark somniatic realities known to Libripeta.[36] Just as St. Potitus forces the devil into visibility, Baptista forces evil to demask itself. This cleansing function, which Apollo was unable to perform (*Oraculum*), is Baptista's cultural mission: "I [Baptista] will withstand you easily since with your lies you clarify for me who you are and who

I am. By grandstanding in this way, you reveal your arrogance rather than discomfit me by your insistent slander."[37]

Perambulating the city, Baptista, speaking through the voice of St. Potitus, points out in aphoristic manner the actions of evil men.

When he saw a wicked judge who strode in with one shoulder higher than the other, he said: "Here it seems the equal is unequal since the scales of justice do not balance."[38]

With the state safe from foreign threats, attention was directed at wicked citizens, and he said: "Doesn't it seem reasonable that after the rain stops, one repairs the roof?"[39]

"False ones, detractors, ambiguous ones, liars, the infamous, and all sacriligious and great robbers ought to be punished," he used to say, "because they destroy truth, reason, and very holy and rare things."[40]

Viewing the house of an ambitious man [he said]: "This inflated *palazzo* will blow its owner right out the door." And this indeed is what happened, for the mortgage on the house drove the proud owner into exile.[41]

There are the Letters to Paolo the Doctor where he foresaw future events of the fatherland years before they happened. And in this way he predicted the destiny of the Pope that actually happened twelve years later, and his friends and associates recall that he predicted insurrections of many cities and rebellions against princes.[42]

Baptista, we must not forget, is the product of an ontological aesthetic, a self-conscious configuration that renders him as a neo-primitive and one could almost say a *provocateur*. Alberti, of course, was aware of this paradox, having gone to great length to contrive it, as will become clearer in *Momus*.

Agnolo and Giannozzo

While Baptista embodies the saintly in an urban setting, Agnolo di Pandolfini and Giannozzo Alberti belong to a separate category, the humanist functionaries. Agnolo appears in *Profugiorum ab aerumna* (1441) and Giannozzo in *Della Famiglia* (1434, completed 1440). Unlike most of Alberti's characters, Agnolo di Pandolfini (1360–1446) was taken from real life; he was a venerated Florentine statesman and ambassador.[43] Yet, his real definition emerges only from within the context of the other Albertian characters. Unlike Libripeta, he remains free of cynicism and, at the age of ninety, is still a functioning member of society, burdened with law cases. He is, however, an intellectual mendicant, transcending love of country and even love of family and thus capable of bridging the gap between the Libripetian sewer and the humanist ideals. Although he never was in exile, he clearly perceives its intellectual advantages:

Agnolo: Some say: "Love your country, love your family, and benefit them as much as they want." But others say that the country of the human being is the whole world, and that the wise man, wherever he is, will make that place his own; he won't escape his country, but he will adopt another one, and he will be a lot better off there where he will not receive injury and where he can live without causing trouble to himself. Thus they praise that old saying of Teucer, a well-known and prominent man; he said that his country was where he could settle well.[44]

Agnolo, though not a writer in the hagiographic sense has produced numerous *documenti* dripping with good advice, for he—like all Albertian Humanists—understands the value of the text.[45] The *documenti* were collected by none other than "Baptista" and form the last of the three books into which the dialogue is divided.

For all excellent public affairs, for all well-thought-out plans of life, for all cultivation and ornamentation of the soul, it is essential to devote oneself to literature and to the learning and exercising of memories and warnings that scholars destine to posterity.... The documents collected and referred to ... will be by themselves so cultured that I don't doubt you will be glad to recognize them in my writings, regardless of my own eloquence and accuracy in speaking.[46]

Since Agnolo is also "like a father to Baptista . . . who eagerly follows him around," he makes sure that Baptista maintains faith in his own literary mission[47]: "This is an age so full of envy and perversity that that which should be praised and approved is vituperated by all. Nevertheless, Baptista continue with your work so as to be useful to your fellow citizens."[48]

Agnolo's presence in the city portrays the fragile continuity of society's spiritual essence. This is allegorized by the setting of the dialogue, which opens as the three interlocutors—Agnolo, Niccolo, from the family Veri de Medici, and Baptista—meet in a public temple. The temple, a *profugiorum* from mythic time, is described as a peaceful zone in a hostile world. On the inside, is a "quiet, springlike atmosphere, a pleasant grace, a majesty and a solidity, built for posterity"; on the outside is the "freezing" city, subjected to inconstant winds. The temple compares to Agnolo himself.

And certainly this temple has within itself grace and majesty: and, as I have often thought about it, I think I see in this temple a graceful delicacy combined with a full and strong solidity, so that, on one hand, each part of it looks as if it was placed there for pleasantness. On the other hand, I understand that everything here has been done and declared for posterity. Furthermore, here lives, so to speak, a springlike climate. Outside it is windy and chilly and freezing, but inside the winds are closed off and the air is tepid and quiet. Outside there are summer and autumnal blasts; inside there is a very temperate refreshment.[49]

The circumstance that few people visit the temple "despite its worth" implies that there are few who value the principles of "intact wisdom."[50]

Another functionary figure is also borrowed from Alberti's own life, his uncle Giannozzo Alberti, as described in *Della Famiglia*. Like Agnolo, he is actively engaged in urban politics, his discussions touching on issues that deal with the house, the shop, the villa, the farm, the manufacturing process and the managing of tenants. Alberti explicitly connects the two men in *Profugiorum ab aerumna:* "Agnolo and Giannozzo are the only two men he [Baptista] knows who are complete in all the values of life."[51] The two represent *prudentiam integram*. Intact wisdom, however, is allowed many variations, according to the talents of the individual who possesses it.[52] Giannozzo, being a businessman, is "craftier" and more astute than Agnolo; Agnolo, a magistrate, is credited with "a greater knowledge of literature."[53]

Agnolo and Giannozzo, magistrate and businessman, the two "fathers" of Baptista, symbolize the survival of the garden in the city. It is their duty to make contact with those who, like Baptista and Philoponius, cannot make contact with the world and can only communicate through their literary works and oracular statements. Both parties, however, face a difficult future, even if in *Della Famiglia* and *Profugiorum ab aerumna* Alberti portrays the "family" as functioning within the confines of the city. Baptista's paternal house, the mythical "ancestor of construction," as Alberti describes it in *Vita anonyma,* is "old, dark, badly lit and in ruins."[54] And indeed, in *Della Famiglia,* Lorenzo, Alberti's biological father, lies on his death bed, and Giannozzo is old, and in *Profugiorum ab aerumna* Agnolo is already ninety years old; obviously the *profugiorum* of civic humanism is an endangered realm.

Theogenius, Genipatro, and Microtiro

In *Theogenius* (The One whose Origin is with the Gods, 1441), a work written almost simultaneously with *Profugiorum ab aerumna* but in a way its sequel, Alberti describes a state of affairs wherein the humanist father figure retreats altogether. We are now moving closer to the third category of Albertian humanists. Though the two protagonists in the dialogue are not cynics, the tone of the book is dark. In contrast to the aged Agnolo, who demonstrates a modicum of authorial success—functioning uncontaminatedly within the city—the main characters in this dialogue, Theogenius and Genipatro (Father of Country), are in exile far from the city, which is now controlled by Tichipedo (The Child of Fortune) who is, of course, the Fortunius (Son of Tychia) of *Philodoxeus*. Theogenius and Genipatro, both refugees from the camp of the functionaries, find their task unfulfillable and embrace sainthood. Much as St. Potitus, they renounce life in the city and accept exile so as not to be numbered among the "bestial human beings" who "infest" everything they touch, desiring only to satisfy "the dark abyss of their stomachs."[55] In bucolic quietude they can now produce books which are "well composed, very correct, and full of teachings and wonderful kindness."[56] Their absence from the city, however, shows a deterioration of the scenario, for it is unlikely that they will return.

Alberti claims that the theme of "parental loss" was prompted by his own suffering on the occasion of the death of his parents.[57] "I want only to console myself in my adverse fortunes."[58] Since Alberti's father had died twenty years earlier and his mother several years before that, it is clear that he is referring to the death of Niccolo d'Este (1384–1441) of Ferrara, whose son Leonello was a recipient of a copy of the book. But the tenor of the book is clearly metaphoric; Alberti employs the theme of parental loss as a springboard to the topic of the humanist's orphaned condition. It is Agnolo who has died, so to speak, and now everything sways in the nauseating tyranny of *varietà e varietà*.[59]

In the dialogue Microtiro (Young Recruit), a novice and would-be civic functionary, has traveled out into the forest to find Theogenius, but with the city abandoned to Fortunius, he cannot yet make head or tail of the perplexing aesthetic that constitutes the very fiber of the city: "I face the malignity of perfidious and evil men who, conspiring, blaming, feigning, and with deeds, cares, industry, study, constancy, and diligence, and all art and fraud, continually annoy me by saying, doing, and pursuing things which cause poverty, hate, envy, hostility, and a bad life and great infamy."[60] Theogenius's attempt to convince Microtiro "not to give any value to fragile and ephemeral things exposed to change" is clouded by his own resignation[61]: "The soul, as Heraclitus claimed, purged of the crassness of earthly weight, escapes this prison as an arrow flies to the sky. I believe that you will find nobody who, after having left this life, would wish to go back to it."[62]

Whether Microtiro will grow to the challenge and return to the city to become a new saintly Philoponius or whether he will become a cynic is purposefully left open. This recapitulates the theme of the novice having to choose between sainthood or cynicism or, as gradually comes into view, an ironic combination of the two.

Gelastus and Enopus

Momus (1443–45), a mock creation myth, is typical of Alberti's homonymic style, in which various layers of meaning are interwoven.[63] The surface screens a subtler and more difficult message that deals with the inherent implausibility of the humanist program and the alienating nature of textuality.

This work introduces the category of the ultimate humanist cynic and will be dealt with more fully in a subsequent chapter. Investigating the fate of a writer who finds himself totally useless to society, it takes up the theme of a fatherless and textless society and brings it to a logical extreme. In *Philodoxeus* there had been no confrontation between the hero and the forces of cultural destruction. Philodoxus did not pursue Fortunius to the bitter end but accepted Gloria instead. In the *Intercoenales* stories *Corolle* and *Anuli* the struggle became more intense, and the possibility of a negative outcome was evoked; in the final analysis, however, Minerva guided her humanist suitor into the basilica. In *Theogenius* Fortunius was in ascendancy and the Albertian humanists were resigned to a life of isolation. In *Momus* many of these themes are brought to a conclusion with the character Momus attempting to hand over a *tabella* to Jove with a blueprint for a new and better world. Needless to say, the utopic moment will pass by unheeded.

Momus and a related character, Peniplusius, will be dealt with later. For the time being we will turn to the character pair of Enopus and Gelastus that functions in a self-contained subplot. Albertian voices in ironic antagonism to each other, the two bring the initial confrontation of Leopis and Libripeta full circle. One the innocent, the other the sophisticate, they speak to each other across the *terribilità* of existence. Gelastus (The Ridiculous One), a comic version of the novice Lepidus (*Corolle*), has recently died and is on his way to the river Styx. Like Lepidus of old, he still cannot understand that he speaks a "foreign" tongue. In his complaint, we recognize the familiar figure Alberti had first created some twenty-five years earlier.

Gelastus: Exiled from my country, I consumed the flower of youth in a continuous peregrination and in constant fatigue, pestered without respite by poverty and injuries from enemies. I have endured the evil deeds of friends, the pillage on the part of my relatives, the slander of rivals, and the cruelty of enemies. In escaping the hostile attacks of Fortuna, I fell into the abyss that was prepared for me. Though I was agitated by the convulsions of the times, burdened by preoccupations, oppressed by necessity, I endured everything with moderation, hoping always to receive better treatment from the gods and my destiny than I received. Happy was I if I could manage to draw some satisfaction from the exercise of the arts, to which I am always dedicated. Whether or not my writings drew me any profit, that I will let others judge.[64]

Gelastus represents a dead branch on the ontological tree, as he still has not penetrated the causes of society's *insania*, while tragically experiencing its effects: "There where I should have been given gratitude, I was given abundant envy, there where I expected aid for living, I found injury; there where good men promised to share their good fortune, the wicked gave more wickedness. You will say: 'This is the common experience of mankind, and one ought to remember that one is just a man.'"[65]

Just as Lepidus originally was haunted by Libripeta, we find Gelastus still pursued, more relentlessly than ever, by the cynic Enopus (The Color of Wine). Though intoxicated, Enopus has not lost his former sting. He is now an actor sophisticated in the art of role-playing and masking. When he sees Gelastus wander onto his stage, he cannot restrain his biting tongue and accuses him of having been too innocent and of having failed to protect his work. Gelastus, he points out, only "resembles the true one" and is not who he thinks he is (*Corolle*). Enopus even suspects that Gelastus's benevolence is only a farce.

Enopus: Gelastus repeats nothing but old clichés. What especially pleases me is the perfect artificial make-up of this Gelastus who resembled the true one in a remarkable manner.

Caronte [who is accompanying Gelastus to Hades] heard several things about Gelastus during his life, in particular that he was wise and learned. He also heard, however, that he was foolish and silly, and that everyone renounced him for being pusillanimous and neglecting to protect his dignity against grave offenses. People did not approve his principle to be continually useful to others and thus each day he was tormented and insulted. It was quite a different thing to deal with Enopus who was able to protect himself from injury and from the audacity of insolent people which he suffered with great tolerance.[66]

Gelastus's efforts to preserve the myth of the intact society have proved ridiculous and comic because, like Neofronus, he remained inexplicably naive. Enopus, though more capable, is not perfect either; and Gelastus, in turn, is quick to point this out to Caronte. Enopus lacks commitment to ennobling principles; "he accuses everybody, but represents nothing himself."

Appearing to be very different, both characters are similarly ineffectual. Neither seems to be able to escape from the other. The one is too uncritical, the other too critical; The one suffers because no one appreciates his benevolence, the other because no one appreciates his acrimonious wisdom. This debate, which represents the underside of Alberti's theory of humanism, featuring an ineffectual humanist cynic arguing with a ineffectual humanist saint, caricatures the ongoing struggle of society with itself. The fight between weak writer and drunk critic insanely accusing each other of falsity while the source of evil remains untouched emphasizes the ludicrousness of a crisis for which there is no cure. The gods, all the while observing this tragicomedy, break into sidesplitting laughter, which is certainly Alberti's own commentary on what he sees as the paradox inherent in intellectual commitment. It is this laughter that, as we shall see, precludes the theory of any utopian vision or any truly functionable plan for a better world.

The Autobiographical Trope

We have introduced almost all of the important Albertian characters and explored their respective roles. It should now be clear that the autobiographical elements are always and exclusively literary tropes. Alberti's exile from Florence (though terminated when he was twenty-four) is glorified into the writer's necessary exile from the city. The early loss of Alberti's father becomes the loss of society's center of gravity as allegorized by the figure of an inaccessible Genipatro. The youthful peregrination of the student changes into Leopis's journey in search of his literary identity.

With the help of these allegorical tropes, Alberti explored, almost in a workshop fashion, the variegated facets of the literary experience, projecting them onto a cosmological plane. The numerous variations of the writer-type are not isolated fictive elements, but are developed along diverse narrative tracks. One scenario begins with Leopis and ends with the

Neofronus, who belatedly laments the loss of his reputation and the loss of his writings. In another, Leopis becomes Libripeta, once he sees into society's subconscious. In still another, the novice becomes Philoponius, who emerges miraculously unscathed from the turbulence of society to be an effective practitioner in Alberti's tentative utopian vision. There is Baptista, whose *Werdegang* was modeled on St. Potitus. Novices, saints, functionaries, humanist fathers, and cynics all serve to map out the unrelenting history of mankind in a labyrinthian search for authenticity.

Libri Disvoluti

Seen individually, Alberti's writings always seem to swerve around something unexpressed. One piece ends with the author feigning suspense as to the outcome; another seems to have no resolution whatsoever. One is a fragment without ending, another a fragment without apparent beginning. Many pieces would be misunderstood without a broader context. In this manner Alberti continually points beyond each work and each character and challenges the reader to search for the external narrative. As a consequence, there can be no philosophy in the standard sense; the masterplan comes into focus only between the cracks, as it were.

Inconclusivity is both a reaction and a response to the virus of fragmentation against which there is no defense. Even Baptista's books are "fragmented and torn (*libris disvolutis*)."[67] The fragmented text thematizes the inherent uncertainty of intellectual life that separates image from argument and writer from text and refers to the authorial malaise that symbolizes society's malfunctioning. Since this applies to Alberti just as much as to his artificially created characters, Alberti's autobiographical journey cannot possibly be a mere rendition of his own life. Rather it stands in opposition to it, demonstrating the external pressures that disallow a naturally conceived autobiographical narrative.

Alberti seems prepared to accept the fact that as the theoretical armature takes on its ciphered characteristic the author disappears at the very moment he speaks; this is anticipated in and is indeed the very theme of *Philodoxeus,* where Leopis becomes the spokesman for Alberti, who refuses to speak in his authentic voice, given the inauthenticity of society itself. The oscillation of the characters and their constantly changing metamorphic patterns obstruct the view toward the author. At the very moment the Leopis-mask is pulled off in *Corolle,* we discover an unexpected transformation: Leopis has become Libripeta, and the moment of truth is lost. Alberti has allowed his self to be stripped of eminently concrete and legitimate attributes only to see it exposed to its own inauthenticity and to his own inability to reclaim the text. With the characters of Philoponius and Baptista, some precious time is gained, and the moment of realization is for the moment pushed away, only to surge forward all the more violently in later works such as *Theogenius,* where Genipatro and Theogenius compose their books in peace and solitude, but without any hope that humanist knowledge will ever translate into effective and benign action.

Because Alberti merges his theory of disjunction with the method employed to investigate it, his writings are hard to penetrate. In one sense, literary ontology gives way to a literary cosmology that is both a private language, needing to be decoded, and a public language serving as decoy. In reverse, Alberti uses a public language to articulate the private sphere, much as Agnolo employs fragments from "great and noble buildings" to construct his private study.[68] This conflict was never meant to be resolved, as it points to and is the product of the underlying aesthetic nature of human existence that just as it is denied access to its ontological center cannot reach beyond into the objective.

Confrontation with the
Arch-Aesthetic

Terminus a Quo

The divergence of word from meaning and being from image is the fundamental problematic in Alberti's writings. He returns to it again and again in one way or another. On the one hand, it represents the loss of authentic values. On the other hand, it represents an opportunity, a creative potential. The separation of being from image, the bane of existence and its very *raison d'être,* develops into a question of aesthetics since the experience of self-knowledge turns everyone into a master "in the methods of artificial (self-)construction."[1] This is exemplified in Alberti's willful interpretation of the figure of Narcissus in *De pictura.* Whereas medieval Neoplatonists thought of Narcissus as having lost himself in a transitory world of copies, Alberti holds that Narcissus was the first "painter": "I used to tell my friends that the inventor of painting, according to the poets, was Narcissus. . . . What is painting but the act of embracing, by means of art, the surface of the pool?"[2] Narcissus was not only the first painter but also the first human, having discovered the difference between being and image. Once the Narcissistic moment, equivalent to Adam's fall from grace, had occurred, man, severed from *società natura e vera religione* (as known by Apollo in *Oraculum*), was posited in chronological time (*Vaticinium*). Simulative obsession now dominates his psyche, and he is free to manipulate his image to the point where "in simulating we become what we want to appear."[3]

The area of dislocation, equivalent to an area of tension between subject and object, is the locus of an all-encompassing aesthetic in which all are "artists." Since the practice of simulation more than anything determines human behavior, from its most bestial to its most spiritual, the aesthetic moment cannot be reduced to a mere question of beauty. It is much more than that; it is the *terminus a quo* of human existence.

Aristotelians perceived man as preeminently rational, Stoics perceived him as social, and Neoplatonists as potentially divine. For Alberti, man is thinker *and* actor, a genetically coded masker. And, since aesthetics is not *eo ipso* linked to ethics, man creates an ambivalent world of displaced signifiers in which rationality becomes a mask for irrationality, virtue for evil, honesty for lies, and laws for lawlessness. Man, lost in a world of a thousand mirrors, can never reencounter his own authenticity. The humanist enterprise has the dubious mission of catering to this futile task.

In this respect Alberti's thought, though related to the classical theory of *mimesis*, differs from it in several important aspects. For Aristotle, imitation is natural to man from childhood on and constitutes one of his advantages over the lower animals (*Poetics*, 4). Not only is the mimetic capacity a potential source of delight, but it is equivalent to an innate urge to order the world, augment and complete nature, and in the process discover its rational organization. For Alberti, mankind's imitative capacity has no such optimistic connotation; it is devoid of that all-important ethical component fundamental to the ordering process. Art, far from being above everyday experience, is equivalent to it, for there is no human activity that is not in some way aesthetic. Indeed, it is mankind's aesthetic nature that drags him downward and that keeps him from becoming a rational, civic, and spiritual being. As we shall see, the Albertian humanist attempts an implausible critical rescue of the aesthetic domain. However, since aesthetics is an ontological given and ethics an unnatural, synthetic, and belated counterthrust, the struggle goes against the divine plan and must by definition fail.

The Human Prerogative

In a mock creation myth in a subplot of *Momus*, which I shall briefly summarize, Alberti gives us his version of the origin of man's art-making capacity.[4] An unnamed "painter," after fashioning men and women out of mud and shaping them in precast molds of copper, directs his creatures to his habitat, located "on top of a mountain," a place where they will find all "good things in abundance." They are exhorted to ascend directly and speedily. (In *De pictura* the comprehension of the rule of perspective is also "direct and simple," that is, for the "intelligent minds."[5]) The path to the land of "abundant good" is described by the painter as posing only initial difficulties (an argument also found in *De pictura*[6]). Men, willful in the face of choices, do not recognize the "simple and good" and break away in a foolish effort to imitate animals; this, as Alberti states sarcastically, is "a prerogative that had been permitted them by their creator."

Given the pattern of Alberti's thought, we may construe that the newly created beings stray from the path because they lack a text. As we shall see, Baptista with *De pictura* and Momus with his *tabella* attempt to correct the painter's "mistake," the former by handing to the painters a text that will guide their work, the latter by handing to Jove a text for the construction of a "new and better world." However, in the world created by the Promethean painter in *Momus,* which metaphorically describes the status quo of our world, there is no text, and mankind's art-making prerogative emerges as the source of eternal perplexity.

Having left the indicated path for the precipitous wilderness of brambles and thorns (society), the new men in uncontrolled simulative response to their environment progressively deteriorate from animals into monsters. (In *De pictura* Alberti relates how individuals who do not heed his instructions will tap around among unknown paths like blind men and get lost.[7]) When these violently transfigured men eventually try to return to the main path, they find themselves rejected. Constructing masks for themselves, they are able to mingle unrecognized with the few that had ascended directly.

No longer passive imitator, man has become an active speculator in the ontological realm. The differentiation between the good ones and the *fictiones* has disappeared. "Only with the greatest difficulty, by looking closely at the eye sockets, can one perhaps make out the difference."[8] Society, unable to distinguish between true and deceptive orders and between true and false discourses, feeds exclusively on the nervous energy generated by the perverse struggle it is waging against itself.

The Lost Ointment

The separation of word from meaning, of being from image, leads to an ambiguous relationship between man and himself (as reflected, for example, in Alberti's struggle to reconcile himself with Baptista and Baptista with Libripeta). The painful deviation from the principle of ontological immediacy, negating authentic existence condemns mankind to live and create in a shadowy world of wandering signification. This is the theme of the allegory *Patientia* (Endurance) from *Intercoenales*, which I will briefly summarize.[9] Exhausted from curing the diseases of mankind, the goddess Endurance, daughter of Necessity, has sought refuge on a deserted mountain side. Necessity, worried that her daughter's absence may cause even more harm among mortals, goes in search of her. When she finds her, Endurance explains that she went into hiding because she realized how ineffective her healing efforts really were; they consist only of "chants learned from old Chronos."

Necessity admits that such "inexpensive" cures cannot heal the truly ill and gives her daughter an ointment "prepared from the essence of hard work and diligence, expensive stuff indeed" (ethics). For a brief moment there seems some hope that mankind will have its primordial intactness returned. Predictably, Endurance "accidentally" drops the vial (the painter delivered no text, and Jove rejects Momus's manuscript) and the ointment is lost forever. Endurance returns to her previous practice of giving to the ill "berries of flattery . . . the herbal plaster hope, [and] little speeches of consolation." The potion that could cure is replaced by a palliative, truth by deceit, and Necessity, representing the congruence of word and action, by Endurance, a "student of Chronos."

The Art of Simulation

The simulative urge, part of the ontological definition of mankind, running concomitant with the dialectic of spirit and body and presided over by Chronos, develops its own trajectory through time. The "art" of simulation, "a gift by the goddess Deception at the beginning of time," plays itself out as history.[10] "In the beginning," Alberti writes in *De re aedificatoria*, there were a few basic building types, all "derived from nature." Eventually, however, society developed into such complexity that "the various kinds of buildings have become almost infinite."[11] Not only did the types of buildings increase, but buildings became subdivided into component parts that are themselves "like smaller houses."[12] The momentum away from "nature" cannot be arrested, but the resulting fragmentation could be controlled by a continuous and conscious ordering process. The absence of an aesthetic "theory," however, has carried architects along on the drifting currents of time. They have lost the "footsteps of nature" and now produce buildings "out of whim."[13] In *De statua* we hear Alberti complain that "not surprisingly artists" (much like rhetoricians) "in creating similitudes, eventually arrived at the stage where . . . they were able to make any similarities they wished."[14]

This movement toward ever greater arbitrariness is also the thesis of Alberti's often ignored panegyric *Canis* (1441), a tongue-in-cheek eulogy on his dog. In spite of the humor implicit in the situation, Alberti begins on a rather serious note with a discussion of the function of eulogies in contemporary literature. He holds that over time there has been an increase in the writer's ability to create rhetorical images, as compared to ancient times "when excellent men first began proclaiming in their writings the immortality and virtue of their contemporaries."[15] Just as in *De statua* Alberti here claims that "things went so far that some, not satisfied simply with praise and honor, raised with their writings the reputation of those who have behaved most virtuously to the point where they were called gods."[16] Alberti then points out that now we can even create things which have never existed in reality. "Besides all this, others invented fabulous things that could not be absolutely believed, only to isolate and exalt manly excellence."[17]

Alberti's panegyric is a ribald metaphor for the compulsive progression inherent in the simulative process. Not without self-ironizing humor Alberti, living up to the historiographic expectations of the present, endows the dog with all the characteristics typical of a Philoponius or a Baptista. He is prudent, virtuous, brave, and blessed with a singular talent and moral wisdom. Not only does he come from an ancient and illustrious lineage (his father was Megastomo: Big Mouth), but his image is linked with all of the famous canine heroes of the past. We even find him credited with a knowledge of the liberal arts!

In *De re aedificatoria* Alberti, in a more serious vein, delicately inserting a piece of social criticism into the text, contrasts his own age—hoping that someone will "rise to reform it"—with an earlier one where the "writings of the fathers were still extant."[18] He then describes how princes of old were content with modest statues depicting their victories, but after learning to associate their victories with divine power, they began to create grander monuments to perpetuate their own names rather than honor the name of god, "all rising to such a pitch that whole towns were built simply to honor the fame of an individual."[19] A few paragraphs later we hear of sculptors who, prompted by the excesses of their princely patrons, repeat the historical pattern. They create sculptures so large that they required many pieces of stone. In painting the same seems to hold true, for today, when "incredible prices are asked for painted panels," the art of painting is far beyond the stage where "man was mindful of his nature and origins."[20]

Paddy Chayefsky's 1960s play *Gideon* seems to take the words out of Alberti's mouth. The theme of the play is the progressive rebellion of Gideon against God. At the play's opening God inspires Gideon, who is absolutely obedient to him, to win battles over Israel's enemies "for God's sake." As the play progresses, Gideon begins to win battles "for God and Gideon," then "for Gideon and God," and finally "for Gideon" alone. As the play closes, Gideon declares full independence from God.[21]

Civitas Perversa

Whereas medieval Aristotelians argued that art and nature form a symbiotic pair, Alberti argues that mankind's art-making capacity is a by-product of his native instinct to deceive and is equivalent to a separation from the wholesomeness of nature.[22] Aesthetics and ethics derive from divergent impulses: the former is given as a troublesome prerogative free of charge; the latter—"expensive stuff indeed"—is distilled from hard work and discipline, the ingredients of the "lost ointment." Since the simulative capacity is without the imprint of an ethical coding, society, left to itself, degenerates into a quasi-Augustinian *civitas perversa*.[23] Alberti, at his most medieval, sees the city as marked by persistent worldly clamor; in his cosmology the true God is remote, and Fortuna has replaced Virtus and the Soothsayer, Apollo.[24] Given over to the "fraudulent, false, perfidious, reckless, audacious, and rapacious," the city, a "spectacle of frenzy," sways in the growing tyranny of "human variety, differences of opinion, changes of heart, perversity of customs, moral ambiguity, and obscurity of values."[25] It is a "vision of horror, stupefaction and monstrosity!"[26] Greed reigns in the proverbial marketplace, the realm of Fraud and Chronos—the two gods that Alberti associates with the alienated realm of the arch-aesthetic. Man, far from being a potential candidate for spiritual transcendence, is despised by the rest of creation. "There is no animal as hated as man himself."[27] His disruptive activities prevail wherever one looks:

Theogenius: The other animals are happy with the food their nature requires. . . . Only man is constantly investigating new things and hurting himself in the process. Not satisfied with the space he has on earth, he wanted to cross the sea, venturing I believe out of this world. He wanted to rummage about beneath the waters and the earth, inside the mountains, and he even tried to get above the clouds.[28]

Instead of serving as the model for mankind's activity, nature is the target for his criminality. It cannot defend itself. Sounding a theme from Ovid's *Metamorphoses*, Alberti has Theogenius describe man's relentless defilement of nature.

Nature had the metals; she hid the gold and other minerals underneath the mountains and desert places. We, miserable men, dig them up and bring them to light and use them. Nature scattered shining gems in a way and in a form that to her, as an excellent teacher, seemed the most appropriate. We collected them even from the farthest and most remote regions and chop them up and give them new shape and a new look. Nature separated one tree from the other; we adulterate them by bending them and joining them together. She gave us rivers for our thirst and ordered their course to be free and speedy. But rivers and springs, like all things of nature, though perfect, bothered us and so, in spite of all this, we go looking for wells. And still not satisfied, with a lot of efforts, and so many expenses, and so much solicitude, we—the only ones among the animated creatures who are annoyed by natural water and other excellent liquids—found how to make wine, and that not for our thirst, but in order to pour it as if the only way to pour it was by the cask. . . . We like nothing except that which nature denies us, and we are delighted only when we make efforts to displease nature in many ways. . . . In fact, we so dislike things that are natural and free that we turn ourselves into servants.[29]

Man, the fabricator of *fictiones,* unable to tame and order his creative urgency and driven by a "homicidal urge," wages a battle against all forms of stability. In *Templum* foundation stones, jealous of capitals, rise up in revolution; in a short subplot in *Momus* sailors mutiny and murder the captain after a cruel game; in *Profugiorum ab aerumna* Ulysses's house is transformed into a tavern; and in *De commodis litterarum atque incommodis* the blind mob turns a deaf ear to "solid and clear virtue."

Priests, the "henchmen" of the painted gods and devoted to Mammon, are "befouled with every blot of shame.[30] [They are] lazy, indolent, arrogant, greedy . . . and distinguished as authors and artificers of crimes and evil deeds."[31] There is also the "treacherous tribe of merchants" and, above all, there are the defective rulers.[32]

In character and life they were intoxicated with conceit, and were cruel and merciless. In presiding over their magistracies at home and in interpreting the law, they plundered wards of the state, widows, and all the weaker citizens. In performing their duty they did not safeguard liberty but rather conducted everything arbitrarily in relation to their intolerable lust. They detested all citizens who seemed desirous of freedom. They raped adolescent boys and freeborn girls. Those who opposed them in these crimes, either by intervening or openly resisting, were punished by being forced into exile or into prison.[33]

At the root of all this evil is the separation of mankind's art-making prospensity from his ethical potential. "Industry, constancy, diligence, and art" are put to evil purposes instead of good ones; even virtue serves "as a cloak for sin and a veil for crime—a stain from which no human thought, no discourse, no judgments, no custom, and no opinion is free."[34] Mankind's aesthetic abilities do not elevate him into the realm of higher potential, but rather alienate him from his ability to distinguish good from bad. "Asked whom he [Baptista] thought to be the worst of men, he answered, the wicked ones who want to behave like good ones."[35]

False Intellectuals

The ambiguity of artifice may separate man from himself, but it is, ironically, the bond that connects him to society. The unlearned and the learned share this knowledge, the unlearned in the form of blind instinct, the learned in the form of conscious strategy. Thus the ultimate artificers in the historiographically determined realm of the arch-aesthetic are the intellectuals. Far from advocating, let alone practicing, an ethical life, they exploit the disjunction between word and truth. *Philosophi, poeti, litterati, eruditi, docti in lettere, obtrectatori,* and *eloquenti,* all "instructed and educated in *gymnasii* and libraries," have usurped the intellectual center of society under the veil of a mystifying discourse.[36] As always, we should not be too zealous in asking which particular philosopher or writer Alberti may have had in mind. Each group represents a different manifestation of the separation of ethics from aesthetics.

Philosophers

The Albertian humanist saints and the philosophers are, or should be, "the trustees of the human mind and moderators of our souls."[37] The Albertian humanist interprets this as a plan of action, the humanists-gone-wrong as a smokescreen for bombastic discourse: "Ah, I can almost see them now, disputing with such majesty in their words and gestures, with such severity in their sentences suitable for syllogism, with such weightiness of opinion that they darken our souls. It would appear a sacrilege to think them wrong. . . ."[38]

Full of overblown pride, these philosophers reject the path of true virtue "to pretend and dissimulate things on the outside of their faces."[39] Isolating themselves so that no one can accidentally look behind the mask, they undermine the relation-

ship of trust they should have with society: "Whenever he used
to see those vain and ambitious ones, who styled themselves
philosophers, walking through the city and displaying themselves, he [Baptista] used to say: 'Look! Here are our wild fig
trees that love their sublime and sterile solitude—because it is
public!'"[40] Instead of shedding light on "the good and just life,"
they speak about "forms, accidents, substances, rest, and motion,"[41] when they are not otherwise trying to "invent, defend,
and adorn sentences that are more beautiful than true," rein-
forcing an aesthetic that separates words from actions.

So it is that many [philosophers] when they loaf about can reason
well about difficult and hard things that they themselves would not
be able to bear well at all. . . . Thus, if these very learned and outstanding men, inventors, defenders, and adorners of sentences that
are more marvelous than they are true, could not—according to less
learned men like us . . . value the ephemeral as worthless and could
not reduce their fear of adversity, then we—inferior in mind, condition, and profession, and weaker in position—what can we do?[42]

In a *Prohemium* to one of the eleven books of *Intercoenales*
addressed to Poggio, Alberti allegorically describes the philosophers as vultures "swooping down from the very ether under
the stars in search of some lifeless cadaver."[43] Despicable also
are the sophists who cannot be trusted even if they speak the
right words.

Philosophers: Mercury, we are your favorites. . . . Phoebus, show us
favor, for we preserved the dignity and divine influence of the gods
among men in all our writings. In our way of life we kept ourselves
aloof from any intercourse with corporeal and mortal concerns, since
we always kept heavenly and divine things in view, and as a result
the task is on you to see that we are not again thrust back into any
hateful heap of flesh.

Cynic: O wanton tribe! Dishonest! Insolent! Are you not utterly
ashamed to proclaim the law even to the gods? Do you judge this
your right because you were so imbued with such great and glorious
arrogance while you lived among men that you dared to prescribe
ill-considered laws of universal nature not only to private citizens,
peoples, and kings but even to the whole earth, and to the stars
above? I advise you of one thing Phoebus: If you give ear to these
sophists, they will argue face to face with you that you are not a god!

They [the philosophers] claim that they deserve grand things from the gods, claiming that they shed much light on the good and just life (*ad bene beateque vivendum*), and that they made men fear the gods. In short they demand that you give them the form of a lion, others the form of elephants, eagles, whales, and of other grand and noble bodies of this sort.[44]

In summary, one could say that philosophers are unsuitable models for imitation; they "stifle that which with so much power determines our soul."[45]

The Holy Disciplines

Alberti's criticism of the philosophers cannot be reduced to the level of the general humanist protest against dry Scholasticism, as it is only one segment of a broader critique that includes all writers, be they poets, rhetoricians, *litterati*, or *eruditi*. Since this aspect of Alberti's thoughts has been rarely analyzed, it is necessary to turn to each one separately. To start with, the poets. Though defended by Boccaccio, Petrarch, and Salutati, poets too perpetuate intellectual fallenness.[46] The Cynic states: "Watch out, Phoebus! Don't think that those men here have such talent that they can imitate the ancients who created such humorous stories about you gods. They have only plucked one or another line from the ancient authors, and yet they want to be held in such esteem that they claim Musaeus and Orpheus their inferior."[47]

Under more violent attack are the *eruditi* and *docti in lettere*, among whom Alberti certainly numbers his humanist colleagues. In *De commodis litterarum atque incommodis* Alberti argues that the *eruditi* "know only how to offer their delicate ears, almost as if it were sufficient for them to refine their ears by erudition, rather than to refine their souls and hearts."[48] Because knowledge for them is purely an aesthetic issue, they remain morally immature and thus unfit to direct society. "The learned are nothing more than stuttering babies," blind to the true potential inherent in their craft.[49] Having long since abandoned the kind of knowledge necessary to improve the lives of others,[50] the "humanist academic" (*docto in lettere*) prefers the lure of money.

Among the [various] classes, there are the literary men. The common folk see them as ridiculous, deride and despise them, especially when they are not rich. Then again, as for those who manage to become rich (a rare event) let those men know that honors are not due to literary pursuits, but to wealth, not to virtue, but to fortune. Indeed, let them note how many would be worthy if only their eyes were not blinded by the splendor of gold or of the toga. Without your gold or with the toga laid aside, you will be ignored. So it is. Whoever is richest is deemed worthy of honor and respect. Therefore, no one is esteemed a sage on account of his wisdom, expertness, illustriousness, and knowledge of excellent questions. [He is esteemed a sage] only if he can proffer something thought worthy of praise and admiration in the midst of the mob with the aid of gold and riches.[51]

Since writers not only seek monetary gain with their efforts but also burn with envy, wallow in frivolity, and cannot function outside their libraries, Phoebus turns them into mice. Theoretically, "writers commit the deeds [of the gods] to literature, describe the cycles of time and the changes of fortune," but the humanist Cynic sees them as gnawing mice.

Cynic: Ours is not the same care and concern as theirs in the study of literature. These are the sort who, when you read their works, can say nothing that is free from untruth. They have created invincible leaders, stirring addresses, mountains climbed and seas crossed, and finally conquered people who have never seen an enemy!

Furthermore, holed up in their libraries they thought they appeared learned far and wide by gnawing away at the reputation of truly accomplished men. And they burned with such great envy that they did not want anyone but themselves to be considered learned. In the midst of such frivolity they brag that they have bequeathed to posterity the immortality of their names.

Phoebus: I do not think it laudable that these men set about to appear like flesh and blood as they were so insubstantial. Therefore, they shall become mice.[52]

Rhetoricians, the next in line in Alberti's critique, feed the fires of alienation by readily exploiting the circumstance that "there is nothing more flexible and malleable than the word; it yields and inclines in any direction you choose to move it."[53] As a consequence, their efforts "destroy truth, reason, and all the very holy and rare things."[54] They are far worse than the relatively harmless poets. The Cynic declares: "You are more worthless than the poets because you have staked your primary claim to glory on the fact that you are trained to win favor by applauding and flattering, and by dragging into hatred and contempt whomever you wish by slandering them with your curses."[55] In *De commodis litterarum atque incommodis* Alberti gives an example of the abuses practiced by rhetoricians: "It would not be appropriate for us to imitate the famous Greek rhetorician Isocrates, who is said to have praised with his orations that worthless tyrant Busiribe, but to have attacked Socrates, the most noble and venerable of philosophers."[56]

Contemporary rhetoricians who "impudently employ portents and fictions and other bold abuses" are treated with particularly heavy sarcasm in *Vaticinium*.[57] Most of the clients of the Soothsayer are wise to his deceptive discourse and seem to escape relatively unharmed, yet both the Soothsayer and his supplicants are trapped in a world of mutual suspicion. Only one client naively believes that the soothsayer "speaks as a friend."[58] "Let us have a good laugh at that character," the soothsayer snickers to himself after having enticed the man to give up four gold coins for nothing but empty promises, "he is genuinely insane."[59] One cannot describe the alienation of discourse more aptly.

Ironically, rhetoricians, specialists in the art of manipulation, drag along the dead weight of accumulated formulas. In the introduction to one of his *Intercoenales* dialogues Alberti compares their art to a flute that has been rendered useless by the overlay of unnecessary decoration: "The flute was made of ivory, and on it were decorations in precious stones, and a representation, beautifully etched by the inspired hand of a craftsman, of the whole history of antiquity. Indeed, the king of gods himself could have played it with no slight to his dignity. This pipe had one flaw: it produced absolutely no sound."[60] Alberti emphatically distances his own work from these abuses. In *De commodis litterarum atque incommodis* he carefully points out: "My discussion will leave aside many of the rhetorical forms, devised to strike one's imagination, and [it will] ignore various other ways of arguing, because I don't want to bring about the contempt of students by showing them myself how writing can be so lacking of values."[61]

Let us now turn to the critics, who, instead of engaging in productive discourse, are accused of settling for pedantry and self-congratulatory bookishness. Though Alberti conceded the excellence of old texts, he felt that critics used them to browbeat contemporary writers: "It is not our task to look with great watchfulness at the most famous and elegant examples of ancient eloquence which, no matter how hard we strain, we can never reach."[62] Because of their destructiveness, critics are numbered among the most spiteful of human beings.

From their eagerness to dispute and their lust for conquest it developed that, even at great danger to themselves, each worked to bring disaster on all the others. . . . I will not recount the bitter struggle to do injury and seek revenge that arose from this situation, nor will I recount the grave discord [present in the field of literature], from which utter destruction easily follows; the whole sad matter lies before your eyes.[63]

Libripeta, of course, is the critic *par excellence;* he keeps his vast library "under lock and key" and no longer writes.[64] In *Oraculum* he is chastised by Apollo for nonproductivity. "Give men a reason to praise you," Apollo advises. Libripeta, however, knows that Apollo, locked in the stony confines of his statue, is ignorant of the arch-aesthetic the knowledge of which is his own expertise. He answers with stubborn finality: "Hard study is all too tedious and anyway it is easier to appear learned than to actually be so."[65] "So become a detractor," Apollo advises. The goddess Envy recognizes the Libripetian detractor as her offspring: "Do you think I do not know my own offspring . . . ? To criticize everything, to condemn the acts and words of all, to be irritated by the common sewer of good and depraved, learned and ignorant, to damn to ignominy the true and the false without discrimination."[66]

In the description of the River of Life in *Fatum et Fortuna,* critics, while not singled out by name, obviously belong to those "suspicious, jealous, and calculating" swimmers who frustrate the progress of others while they themselves cannot swim at all. Their hands are forever soiled by the muddy reeds to which they hang.

"Who are those that I see struggling in the waves amidst the reeds with their heads barely above water? Tell me, I pray you, about all that I see."

And the shades answered: "They are among the worst of mortals: 'suspicious,' 'jealous,' and 'calculating,' as you call them; with their perverse nature and depraved habits they do not swim, but amuse themselves by impeding the strokes of others. They are similar to those that you see contriving, by fraud, to steal with one of their hands, now a floating skin, now a board, while the other hand clings tenaciously onto the rushes that grow in the mud under the water. These rushes are the most irksome of things in the river; and this kind of activity is such that those who engaged in it muddy their hands which remain muddy forever."[67]

Most critics employ an "anything goes" mode. What is needed instead are reliable critics giving nuanced judgments.

Each man will criticize the writings of others according to his own whim and not according to the subject itself, and he should. Furthermore, no more learned men will be on hand to supply a reliable verdict; instead, there will be mere opinions that contradict the views of others. Some critics find pleasure only in things that are ornate and bombastic. Others view what is painstakingly executed as cold and harsh. Others eagerly read only to taste and sniff the flowery elegance of well-rounded sentences.[68]

Normally quite discrete, Alberti felt strongly enough about the abuse of literary power to write a public letter, *Protesta,* sent anonymously to the judges of *Certame Coronario,* the famous literary competition held in Florence in 1441, in response to their refusal to name a winner.[69] He accuses the judges of having, out of political considerations, sabotaged the selection of the most deserving work—presumably his own: "There are probably people who would judge you as not upright since you did not forbid in time what you knew to be harmful."[70] "In your divine wisdom," Alberti continues, speciously, "you knew this to be harmful . . . for which one of the participants did not put aside all his private cares and domestic matters to perfect his poems," only to find his efforts wasted?[71] Taking up the position of the "common people," Alberti points out that not only were the participants injured, but the judges, those "learned men" with "delicate ears" full of "nothingness," lost an important opportunity to stem the suspicions and discontent rampant among the citizens of Florence. In a sarcastic tone, Alberti addresses the judges:

If Orpheus, Musaeus, Homer, Virgil, Ovid, Statius, and your Apollo too were living in this age and had found that a certain other poet competitor had been crowned with victory, on what basis would they blame the person who crowned him? If they said: "This crown—and a laurel crown at that—is unbecoming," at this point, if you, most eloquent men, were mute and without tongue, we commoners would answer in your place with these words: "And for what reason is the crown your own insignia, when the harlots have it too? If the laurel is what makes you poets, would sausages make a poetess? This man was crowned because in that contest he was indeed excellent and above the good ones; and you were inferior to the lowest and very bad poets by remaining silent. Given that he who writes is called a writer, and he who sings a singer, and he who plows a ploughman, doesn't he who writes poems, tell us, deserve to be called a poet [especially] when those [namely the judges] who just stay silent and reprove the others demand to be considered poets, nay, the princes of poets?"[72]

The rapacious hunt for fame endangers the integrity of literature and turns it into a free-for-all. In a short allegory, *Fama* from *Intercoenales*, Libripeta describes how writers dismember the sacrificial bull (of literature) in the vestibule of the temple of Fame, which significantly enough "is not far from the temple of Fortune": "We decided to slaughter the bull right there in the vestibule of the temple and to distribute him cut up in pieces so that each of us could individually carry the pieces into the sanctuary. Some of us got a whole limb, but each took up his respectable piece, but I myself took up the belly that had been left behind on the ground."[73] The quote refers to the appropriation of literary material to carve out an ill-gotten fame. The story continues with the priests attempting to drive the writers away. In the struggle, however, the belly Libripeta is carrying breaks over his head, its contents spilling over him. This associates him with the bad odor of nihilism.

The *litterati* are also chastised in the preface of book 7 of the *Intercoenali*, where Alberti sets forth a fable in which contemporary writers are shown desperately and ludicrously chasing after the moon (Ciceronian eloquence) which night after night eludes the traps set for it.[74] The story is a warning to those who believe that in imitating excellence one can become excellent oneself: "If indeed things are now as I see them, then there is no one with however brief exposure to literature [the "moon of erudition"], no one who has glimpsed some species of eloquence even from afar, who at the same time is not quick to conceive a hope that he will soon turn out to be the greatest of orators."[75] In actuality, "eloquence, is a variegated thing" and not as simple as the image of the moon would suggest[76]: "In judging the written work of others, almost to a man, we are all so fastidious that we want to be in perfect harmony with the eloquence of Cicero, as if everyone in that earlier time thought the best authors to be also duplications of Cicero. Fools!"[77]

It was perhaps the discovery of Cicero's *De oratore* at Lodi in 1421, which excited the fantasy of fifteenth-century humanists, that elicited this statement.[78] At any rate, the seeming ease of a skilled orator such as Cicero is a carefully guarded artifice that cannot be mechanically copied just by having the right books.

When they realize that mastering the act requires more work than they imagined in their indolence, they merely rush out armed with a supply of books, as if through books alone, and not through rigorous study, they could achieve an understanding of oratory. Since each person imagines that he himself has sufficiently mastered the study of oratory surpassing all others, the result among us is that we are worn out, not by striving for recognition, but by criticizing and attacking the good reputation of others.[79]

We come now to the final group of writers, the *eloquenti*, who, "eager only to taste and sniff ornamental elegance," are described in a *Prohemium* of book 4 in *Intercoenales* to Poggio as gluttons relishing the "full juice of vulgar eloquence." *Eloquenti* are compared to heavy-set oxen wallowing in the muddy riverbanks. In their indolence they follow the path of least resistance. A she-goat feeding on a scraggly fig tree (wisdom) in the ancient ruins of a fallen temple is Alberti himself.

"Hey there, lusty one," said the oxen, "what recklessness led you to spurn the grassy bank and make for that steep and thoroughly inaccessible path? Don't you know that it is better to fill yourself on sweet succulent grass than to crave rough stubble and the bitter fruit of the wild fig tree? Not least of all, you should take care that you don't learn to regret such precarious travel on the cliff's edge."

They say that the she-goat had an answer for the oxen: "Come now, you lumpish, soft-footed wretch, don't you know that, as the mouth assists the stomach, the feet dutifully assist the mouth? Besides, I have the appetite of a goat, not an ox. What I eat is all the less agreeable to you because you are not permitted to touch it. Moreover, your sedge is less pleasing to me because it is available everywhere even to the most indolent creatures." Alberti then concludes: "My dear Poggio, I feel that this very thing is clearly happening to me while I am engaged in writing my *Intercoenali*. There are quite a few readers who wish to graze and be nourished in more luxuriant and spacious fields of eloquence than I offer.... However, once my audience has heard the story of the she-goat they will have no cause, I hope, to criticize me."[80]

The demise of the literary world, as Alberti sees it, is not simply an internal problem; it has come about because society demands a defective spiritual center. The "tempestuous and violent changes in mores (*morum tempestates procellas*)" have left literature "in a shipwrecked state (*naufragium in litteris*)."[81] The multitude is free to dictate its will to the *litterati* and infiltrate their ranks without seeking spiritual improvement: "Thus we see all the holy disciplines of writing loaded and disfigured by the dregs of humanity.... The bumpy, scrofulous, twisted, ramshackle, stupid, dull, and incapable ones, unable to do anything else, all these devote themselves to literature."[82] As a result writers instead of fighting the arch-aesthetic, support it, thus polluting the "spirit" of humanism. Literature no longer attracts the "noble and illustrious ones," for they are turned away by the very image of an art so debased.[83] A painter comes forth and asks: "Who does not have before his eyes, as in a painting, the ruins and the slaughter of the disciplines and of the arts? Who cannot experience sadness at the loss and great shipwreck which happened in literature?"[84] Philosophers, rhetoricians, critics, and men of letters are all afloat on a defective barge—

A small ramshackle barge without oars,
Made up of broken-bottomed wicker baskets,
It is not possible for the Muses to do something anymore,
Since the bow leaks so copiously.[85]

Nature as Patron

Società natura e vera religione is the immovable and permanently unattainable vanishing point toward which existence needs to be ordered. It stands between the crumbling authority of intellectual discourse and the dubiousness of mass judgment. The "beginning in nature," therefore, has to be interpreted on a semiotic level both by Alberti when he writes and by his artist-postulates when they make works of art; the writer has to orient his soul according to the principles of a society supposedly at one with nature. Only by means of this illusion can an attempt be made to take control of mankind's simulative urge.

When Alberti states in *De pictura* that the theory of painting is taken "from the basic principles of nature," he does not mean that he is going to nature as an empirical "observer" but simply that he is not under the sway of temporally contaminated conditions.[86] The writer enacts the Narcissistic process of "returning to nature," in order to harness it to ethics. Leopis, for example, spent nearly a month in isolation[87]; Baptista "withdrew for over ninety days" to write *Della Famiglia*,[88] and Philoponius spent thirty days at the fountain on Mount Helicon.[89] Even Agnolo points out that "when I write, I see and hear nothing but myself,"[90] thus guaranteeing the purity of the authorial psyche. The Albertian writers bracket themselves out of temporal time to demonstrate that they are orienting themselves "to nature." The student painter follows suit, for the mathematical rules of perspective that the painter employs to organize his painting are said to be a type of mental imitation of nature.[91] "A spherical surface is like (*imitatur*) the outside of a ball."[92] Though both the painter and the writer later make changes, the beginning of each enterprise has to be anchored in an assumed original oneness of being and image. This was the case, for example, when the first architects designed shelters "in imitation of animals."[93] "The ancients . . . made their works chiefly in imitation of nature. They made apertures always in uneven numbers, as nature herself has done."[94]

Nature is the metaphoric locus of integration. In the lyrical opening paragraphs of *Theogenius* we encounter Theogenius (The One whose Origin is in the Gods) composing his treatises in the blissful solitude of a forest far away from the city.[95] In the vicinity bubbles a fresh spring that yearns to greet Theogenius with his own reflection so that he will have near to hand the means to activate his imagination. Within the context of Alberti's thought, we must read Theogenius as representing the joyous, untroubled, and humanist union of being and image.

Theogenius: Here columns erected by nature are the steep trees that you can see. There, above us, are the delightful beeches and firs whose shadows cover us from the sun. All around wherever you turn your eye, you will see thousands of reflected colors of various flowers shining among the green grass and the shadows, surpassing the brilliance and the light of the sky. . . . And here close by is this silver and pure spring, witness and arbiter in part of my studies, which always smiles at me and flows around me, caressing and hiding at times among the foliage of these very fresh and charming grasses, and at times with its exuberant waves it raises itself and babbling sweetly as it bends toward me, greets me; at other times it shows its tranquil and joyful waters to my eyes, anxiously waiting for me to look at my images (*specchi*) reflected in it and in so doing contemplate myself.[96]

Alberti's use of the nature topos stands in marked contrast to the debonair Renaissance attitude that saw nature as that ambiguous realm of physical delights. The forest in both Petrarch's *Canzoniere* and Boccaccio's *Amorosa Visione* serves as a metaphor for both innocence and seduction, whereas Theogenius's forest is a metaphor for the intact realm.[97] It brings to mind such medieval writings as the *Descriptions of Clairvaux* by an anonymous Cistercian, where sturdy oaks, graceful lime trees and pools of pure water inspire the devout toward meditative quietude.[98] But Alberti's humanism is not a monastic escape. Its arena is the unnatural city. When Baptista and Microtiro, for example, enter its "turbulence" as humanist missionaries, they are endangered; they speak a foreign language and do not aspire to the urban ways. As Agnolo points out, true philosophers though dedicated to the "good and praised life" can live only on the periphery.

Agnolo: And if we have to speak about their lives and customs and establish the reason and manners of the good and praised life (*modo del vivere bene e lodati*), let us discuss those many other people, and even the philosophers, who are happy with one worn-out piece of clothing and with a study much as a putrid and despicable vase, and living only on cauliflower and rejecting all fragile and ephemeral things to such a point that they don't even want to take for themselves a bowl. I won't tell you about this because I don't want to be wordy, but you, O man of letters, remember this well and think how these people acted.[99]

If nature had not become their symbolic patron *in absentia,* they could easily have "rotted away in literary vigils."[100] Even Baptista needs nature to remind him of his higher commitment: "Seeing the fields flower in springtime . . . he would be seized with melancholy and rebuke himself thus: 'Baptista, you must give man the fruit of your studies.'"[101] Since his writings were created in response to a demand by nature and not contaminated by temporal ambitions, Baptista freely "gave every artist copies of his great and worthy treatises"—a sign of his spiritual otherness.[102]

The Belated Aesthetics

Whereas true writers can circumvent the patronal system by declaring their allegiance to the invoked purity of nature, artists and painters are dependent on the patronal system for their very existence. Despite this and other differences which will be discussed later, both writer and artist share the historiographically determined condition that points them back to nature. As opposed to those who have "lost the way," Alberti's fictive "humanist" architects as defined in *De re aedificatoria* follow "the justness of noble works" and actively bring the memory of an intact society to public recall.[103] "Beauty, here, is in the service of cultural survival and helps counteract self-destructive impulses in society: "I would go so far as to say that a work cannot be better protected against violence and injury of man than if its forms have dignity and beauty."[104]

Dignity and beauty, therefore, must be understood within the context of Alberti's historiography of simulation. The first architects may have "imitated" nature, but today's architects live in the given arch-aesthetic zone of self-objectivization. Thus, the beauty they strive for in their work ironically involves the same masking principle employed in negative simulation; ugly parts should be concealed and handsome elements should be enhanced: "Beauty . . . is obtained by means of ornament, by painting and concealing things that are deformed, and by trimming and polishing that which is handsome, so that the unsightly parts might be rendered in colors less offensive, and the more lovely parts with more delight. If this be granted, we may define ornament to be a kind of heightened brightness and improvement."[105]

The main difference between the arch-aesthetic and the new aesthetic is that the latter is performed openly and is, in principle, almost a communal effort. Above all, it is a process dominated by an ethical point of view that keeps it from being subject to abuse. The inauthentic is no longer a threat but an advantage for those seeking permanence and true beauty. Thus Alberti advises his brother Carlo to review the treatise that he had dedicated to him, *De commodis litterarum atque incommodis,* and "make changes according to your judgment, and by removing these errors render the work grander and more dignified," and, so it is implied, more permanent.[106] The new aesthetic, which "corrects, as far as possible, defects in the model while still maintaining a likeness (*similitudine*)" hinges exclusively on the proper, public and positive use of simulation.[107] The process of "taking away, increasing, and altering" as described in *De re aedificatoria* constitutes a counter-aesthetic in step with a complex society.[108]

The painter, cleansed of moral imperfections according to the exhortations outlined in book 3 of *De pictura,* is free to collect the beautiful things that "are dispersed here and there."[109] In this way he simulates Baptista who, "anxious to know everything, simulated ignorance to learn the knowledge of others. . . ."[110] Ultimately, the functionaries of Alberti's aesthetic "theory," painters, writers, and architects, arrive at *simi-litudine* by choosing only the beautiful and assembling it into a new configuration: "[Zeuxis] believed that . . . beauty . . . could not be discovered in nature in one body alone; thus he chose from all the youth of the city five outstandingly beautiful girls, so that he might represent in his painting whatever feature of feminine beauty was most praiseworthy in each of them."[111] Alberti's counter-aesthetic theory thus suggests that an attempt must be made to entice man back to a consciousness of Apollonian order. The artist, entering quasi-deceptively into the faulty scenario, learns its rules in order to take presimulative control of mankind's compulsive, a priori urge to simulate.

This is the implied premise in Alberti's address in *De pictura* to "his" painters, who are in direct competition with the arch-aesthetic world of shifting images, of *varietà e varietà,* of a thousand masks, where "everyone can express an opinion" and everyone is an "artist," even if a false one.[112] Knowing "how impossible it is to imitate something which does not continually present the same aspect," Alberti instructs the painter to follow the rules of perspective and insert a "veil" between himself and the image to be painted, to stabilize the constantly shifting aspect of the image. Thereby "the object seen will continually keep the same appearances."[113] This does not mean that Alberti disapproves of painterly variety; on the contrary, "The mind takes great pleasure in variety and abundance."[114] To say anything else would imply that the painter is out of touch with the reality of the historigraphical dilemma that attempts to link mankind's expert understanding of variety with an illusory immutable reality.

The procedure is equivalent to the attempt to unite fame with glory and the physical with the spiritual. The man in the street is attracted to the painting by its "variety," as that is what he understands. "When spectators dwell on observing details, then the painter's richness will acquire favor."[115] Once the spectator is in the proximity of the image, simulative habit takes over. The spectator cannot help but "mourn with the mourners, laugh with those who laugh and grieve with the grief-stricken."[116] The perspectival order, by which all "random confusion" and "tumultuous appearances" have been deleted, then guides the spectator from the vacillating to the stable. *Società natura e vera religione*, instead of disappearing at the vanishing point, will issue forth from the picture plane into the real world. The spectator becomes an extension of the *istoria* which, since it has been ordered in the soul of the humanist painter, orders the spectator's soul as well (or so it is hoped).

In Alberti's theory there is no place for an autonomous work of art, and, therefore, there can be no concept of beauty that can be reduced simply to a set of criteria; much less can there be art as a pure expression of inner feeling, as later centuries might view it. A work of art is an alternative to, but also a product of, aesthetic forces that already exist and have been at work in society since the beginning of time. In this way Alberti's counter aesthetic challenges not only the original historio-graphic, aesthetic moment in which the incongruity of reality and image was created but also the arch-aesthetic that is so serviceable in the proverbial marketplace. In the process of becoming complex, the world became impoverished, as evil could be more easily simulated than truth. There was, as Mo-mus discovered, no way of looking behind the mask. Alberti's aesthetic theory does not propose to look behind the mask (it is, after all, a mask in its own right). It does not aim at ultimate truth or, for that matter, at a return to archaic simplicity or austere Benedictine rules, as one might suspect, but points beyond the variety of existence to the vanishing point of human existence, the *società natura e vera religione*. Instead of stripping the artist of historical dimension, it makes him functional within the given disjunction—indeed, able to celebrate it—as he attempts to engage the potential latent in the irreparable break with reality. It literally throws him back into the face of "history" as a counter proposition. The artist must attempt, one could say, a critical rescue of the simulative capacity of mankind.

The Prince and his Ottimo Artefice

Numbering among the members of a select group of *perfecti* in a position to order the simulative principle both within them-selves and in others and thereby to link the aesthetic with the ethical is, of course, the Prince, as defined in *De Iciarchia*. As humanist functionary, he is "first guide and moderator for others," a philosopher in the true and original sense.[117] Since *De Iciarchia* is spoken in the hagiographic voice of Baptista, we should perceive him as being sponsored by the humanist and educated in the humanist ideology of textual *autorità*. The Prince, like all the *pochi e rari*, must integrate *ragione* and *virtus*, social consciousness and manly excellence.[118] Thus he must not only have "prudence, ability, cognition of things, and authority" to guide others toward "a good and desired end," but he must also be "illustrious on account of his wisdom, experience, and talent."[119] This distinguishes him from the "common multitude" that, in an ideal scenario, sees him as an emulative ideal. As Baptista, the appropriate mentor, says: "One becomes virtuous by imitating and getting accustomed to becoming similar to those who are just, free, magnificent, magnanimous, prudent, constant, and who in all aspects of their life are governed uprightly by discretion and reason."[120] In this ideal situation, the members of the multitude, living under the benign rule of the prince, see themselves as part of a "blissful family" where everyone "becomes important and brings to excellence the capacity residing in him, rather than relying on fortune; one can wish for nothing more than that together with the whole family all will be blissful, honored, and most happy."[121]

As the goal of Alberti's civic functionaries is to serve as arbitrators in the realm of disjunction, they must move from ontological ideal to epistemological action by descending to the level of the "many" who cannot bridge the gap. This excellent cleverness (labeled variously *ottima astuzia* or *ottimo artefice*), "which is rare in this world," was something Apollo, in *Oraculum*, was, rather comically, unable to accomplish.[122] Alcibiades, however, as described in *Della Famiglia*, excelled in the art of adaption.

In Sparta, the land of thrift and exercise . . . he appeared frugal, rugged, and unlettered: in Ionia he was delicate and charming; in Thrace he learned to drink hard and enjoy himself with these people as well. He knew how to adapt himself to situations so well that in Persia, a land full of pomp and delighting in show, he surpassed

Tissaphrenes the king in his haughtiness of manner and magnificence of display. To adapt quickly to situations and to make friends, it is necessary to study the gestures, words, customs, and conversations of others. One must learn what pleases, what saddens each one, what moves him to anger, to laughter, to talk, and to silence.[123]

The Prince especially must be skilled in infiltrating the mentality of his subjects so that he can assert himself beneficially. Baptista is the model, for he "simulated ignorance to discover the talent and ability of others."[124] But Baptista has no political ambitions; he prefers the pose of distant saint. Yet Alberti can extrapolate from the definition of Baptista the ideal ruler-functionary who must adapt, quickly and easily, to the different types of people in his domain.

Baptista: Various and different are the souls and minds of mankind. Some are quick to anger, some turn easily to mercy, some are acute, suspicious, credulous, contemptuous, experienced, bitter . . . [etc. etc.]. It would be profitable that our prudent prince continually explore, probe, and understand hour after hour the mores, life, and facts of each of them so that he can use with each excellent, most suitable and motivated ways of commanding and so that he can adapt the variety of his orders according to the variety of souls.[125]

The ideal Prince has to realize his "aesthetic" self-consciously. But whereas others would lose themselves to the mask, the Prince, the brainchild of Philodoxus, Baptista, and St. Potitus, must be shown as pure in his intent to unite fame *and* glory in his *persona mixta*. Baptista states: "This emulation, with which you search for fame and glory above all others, comes from the correct bearing of talent and the generosity of spirit, acquired not with slander but only with the virtue which sits in you."[126]

The theory of simulation which lies at the heart of Alberti's theoretical edifice has, of course, a long history in Western intellectual thought. For our purpose, it will be adequate to point out that Alberti's thoughts follow along the lines of Averroes, whose theories dominated the school of Bologna, Alberti's alma mater. Averroes saw the inherent divisions in society as a potential source of strife, isolating the intellectual and theological elites from each other and from the masses.[127] Averroes argued that the ultimate task of leaders should be to establish parallel but not identical understandings of what was good for society on all levels of its hierarchy. Leaders have the responsibility not only to rule those below them but to guide them toward goals beneficial for all. The highest form of intelligence is that which can infiltrate others. In his treatise *Philosophy and Religion* Averroes describes a certain Abu Hamid who "tried to awaken the nature of men, for he never attached himself to his books. He was an Asharite with the Asharites, a Sufi with the Sufis, and a philosopher with the philosophers; so much so that he was, as has been said [sic]: 'I am a Yeminite, when I meet a Yeminite: if I meet a Ma'adi, I am one of Banu Adnan.'"[128]

Averroes makes it clear that these singular individuals do not use their simulative capacities to deceive but to draw men upward. Similarly, for Alberti, the talented individual dissembles the resistance of the unlearned for their own and society's benefit. In a remarkable affirmation of the theory of simulative pedagogy Alberti-Agnolo explains in *Profugiorum ab aerumna* that the teacher of dance does not begin by laying down the abstract rules of a theory which the student must learn but by following the student's own unlearned movements. Only when he has completely empathized with the student's movements can be begin to exert his control. Eventually, a reversal takes place, and the student imitates the teacher. The student thus not only acquires the art of dancing but also comprehends the art of simulative transfer.[129]

Since astute cloaking of intent is something "that must not be visible," as Giannozzo warns in *Della Famiglia,* the Albertian humanist may be forced on occasion to compromise his virtue.[130] But this, according to Averroes's well-known interpretation of Aristotle and Plato, should not be feared, as long as astuteness is concomitant with salutary intent; in fact, rulers may even lie in order to encourage the virtuous conduct of the citizens.[131] In his *Elementa picturae,* a technical treatise on geometry, Alberti warns his colleague Theodorus, to whom he is sending a manual for his classes, that "in order to avoid skepticism [on the part of the students] I think from the first you should direct the work of your students *before* they realize what ends you are determined to accomplish" (my emphasis).[132]

"When all is said and done, the students will judge and evaluate us as they wish."[133] The instructor, anticipating this, however, will obviously conduct himself in such a manner that "the students shall be exceedingly grateful."[134] Alberti's Prince embodies this line of reasoning; it is not enough for him to possess the valued tools of perspective, the insignia of his identity; he must make good use of them. Baptista states: "It is one thing [for the prince] to hold the right angle, the straight edge, and the pen, and it is another to put them to good use."[135]

If the prince does not absorb the instructions, that is, if he does not use the tools of perspective or the text or the advice of the humanist-saint by his side, then he will inevitably fall into the practice of false pre-simulation. This is the scenario in *Momus*, where Jove refuses the role of humanist functionary. *De Iciarchia*, written after *Momus*, is like an answer to Jove. More about that later.

The Intact City

In an ideal situation there would be no disjunction between humanist and society. The two would be in tune, the world would be at peace, and the relationship between being and image, on the one hand, and word and meaning, on the other, would be ordered. Above all, the arch-aesthetic would not have risen independent of ethics. This *società natura e vera religione* is, though eternally inaccessible, a perspectival vanishing point that must order the discordant world. The closest we come to a description of this humanist fantasy is book 8 of *De re aedificatoria*, which describes a leisurely itinerary from the country to the center of town. It portrays the intact city in harmony with the humanist and the memory of the *natura società e vera religione*.

In the first two of the ten chapters into which book 8 is divided, we find the author in the countryside, traveling along a highway, viewing "houses, villas, a fine hill, now a river, and now a spring, now an open spot and a rock, now a plain, wood, or valley."[136] As he nears the city he comes upon sepulchers of great families and monuments to heroes. In chapter 3, still on the outskirts, he passes graveyards with obelisks, pyramids, and small chapels. In chapter 4 he pauses to read some of the inspiring inscriptions. In chapter 5 he describes large watch-towers that symbolize the city's watchfulness and sturdiness.

At the beginning of chapter 6 he announces: "It is now time to make our entrance into the city."[137] Going through the city gates and over bridges and following the streets, he observes the bustling squares, the protected porticos, the triumphal arches, and the various types of markets. In chapters 7 and 8 he comes to the public theaters and other places of diversion such as amphitheaters, public walks, and porticos where philosophers converse. In chapter 9 he comes to the end of his journey, the spiritual, political, and intellectual center of the city, "to be used only by the principal citizens."[138] He describes the senate house, the temple, "free from all contagion of secular things,"[139] lakes for swimming, groves dedicated to the gods, arsenals, and finally a library that also houses a collection of mathematical instruments. The last chapter describes the bathing establishments, which are not part of the central city because they require too much space. By closing his discussion with *terme* Alberti makes a conceptual link to the spring that the traveler had seen at the outset of his journey, alluding as much to spiritual as to physical cleanliness.[140]

A city controlled by a tyrant would be prisonlike so that the inhabitants could be controlled (V,1); a city ruled by a king would be dominated by his palace (V,3). But in this city the library takes the central position, preserving textual consciousness and standing for civic intactness. It contributes to the same collective memory evoked at the beginning of the itinerary by the sepulchers and monuments.

We must not automatically lump this description in *De re aedificatoria* together with other writings of the time that were also part of the general fifteenth-century groundswell of urban consciousness. The descriptions of Florence by Leonardo Bruni, a papal secretary, and Goro Dati, a silk merchant, are for all practical purposes descriptions of the secular city, its institutions, political armature, and great buildings.[141] The journey described by Alberti is inherently theological. The essential clue is Alberti's discussion of the mathematical instruments in the library, the instruments needed to observe the

planets. This, of course, is in line with the Augustinian under-
current running through Alberti's thought. Augustine defined
Christ as one person, two natures: "He is far above all heavens,
but his feet he has on earth."[142] The optical instruments at the
end of the itinerary and the activity of walking at the beginning
are unmistakable allusions to this Augustinian metaphor, which
can be perceived as defining the ideal humanist city. Again
ecclesiastical concepts are shifted into the humanist camp; the
image of church as the body of Christ is elegantly translated
into the city as body of the humanist.

Genipatro (*Theogenius*) and Agnolo di Pandolfini (*Profugiorum ab aerumna*) would be ideal inhabitants of the humanist
city, the first the ideal writer-saint and "father of the country,"
the latter the ideal civic functionary. Members of great lineages,
they developed themselves physically and spiritually, entered
the public domain, and, late in life, were elevated to promi-
nence. Culminating their careers, they delivered the texts that
secured permanent fame: Agnolo, the *documenti* "gathered" by
Baptista and assembled in book 3 of *Profugiorum ab aerumna;*
Genipatro, "numerous well composed books . . . , very correct,
full of teachings and wonderful kindness, and welcomed by
good people and scholars alike. They will make him, as we
hope, immortal."[143] Immortal indeed, as he combines—recalling a discussion earlier in this book—Apollo's prophetic
wisdom[144] with heavenly talent, because his father, so we are
told, "is his sincere intellect" and his "mother his upright reason."[145] Thus his writings are enjoyed by scholars and citizens
alike; they represent *autorità*[146]: "I frequently go to temples,
theaters, and the houses of the first citizens, where they among
themselves often read and discuss me and my studies."[147] Genipatro is veritably identical with the city. He embodies permanence in a world of flux. Everything is "in him": "Every single
thing is in me and cannot be robbed. Mine and with me are
the knowledge of letters, certain parts of the Good Arts, and
the care and love of virtue, all excellent things for a good and
blissful life."[148]

In this ideal setting, Genipatro's function as a "trustee and
moderator of the human soul" would be highly valued; a seat
would most certainly be reserved for him in the *palaestre* as

defined in *De re aedificatoria*[149]: "The ancients, and especially the Greeks, erected in the very middle of their cities those edifices which they called Palestre, where those who applied themselves to philosophy attended public disputations. They were large spacious places, full of windows, with a free prospect on all sides and raised seats and porticoes running around a flowery green meadow."[150]

The flowery meadow in the very heart of the city symbolizes mythic time successfully embedded in historical time. The image also appears in a letter to Leonardo Bruni, Alberti's superior in the curia, in which Alberti describes a series of ten paintings. The first portrays Mother Humanism, followed by her daughter Kindness, who begot Benevolence, who begot Peace, who begot Contentment. The last painting, that of Contentment, focuses once again on the peaceful, meadowy courtyard of the library: "The painting shows a woman with a serious and mature aspect. Using a small bundle of beautifully arranged flowers as a pillow, she rests in a flowery field among a multitude of books. With uplifted eyes she praises the sun and holds her hands out in adoration."[151] If the humanist scholar can stretch out contentedly in the inner sanctum of the palestre at the center of the city, then the city is at peace. His own soul pre-simulates a well-ordered state.

This leads us to Alberti's drawing of himself standing in a flowery meadow with a book in his left hand (figure 6). The stance is a well-known commonplace—it can be seen in hundreds of medieval frescoes and drawings—that Alberti wants to claim for his hagiographic self-definition of the humanist. The new authorial icon is not that of a Christian saint handing down the text of God but, once again, of a humanist saint embodying the reconcilability of irreconcilable realms. Alberti, of course, is not above presenting himself in the elevated role of ultimate model.

In the city of contented humanists the public gladly renders to the princes and humanist instructors "the thanks they are due." Glory and Fame can now exist alongside each other in harmony, as if their dialectical opposition had never been set in motion.

Figure 6
Self-portrait of Leon Baptista Alberti (Biblioteca Nazionale, Rome).

Glory springs up in public squares; reputation is nourished by the voice and judgment of many persons of honor, and in the midst of people. Fame flees from all solitary and private spots to dwell gladly in the arena [together with Glory], where crowds are gathered and celebrity is found; there the name is bright and luminous of one who with hard sweat and assiduous toil for noble ends has projected himself up out of silence, darkness, ignorance, and vice.[152]

This city exists without friction between those who govern and those who are governed, between those who define the urban identity in their texts and those, including the writers, who put it into practice. It is the implied counter-proposal to a creation-gone-wrong.

It is in the [ideal] city that one learns to be a citizen. There people acquire valuable knowledge, see many models to teach them the avoidance of evil. As they look around, they notice how handsome is honor, how lovely is fame, how divine a thing is glory. There they taste the sweets of praise, of being named and esteemed and admired. By these most honorable joys, the young are awakened to the pursuits of excellence and come to devote themselves to attempt difficult things worthy of immortality.[153]

A Iove Principium Musae

At the end of book 2 of *De re aedificatoria* Alberti pauses to outline, in the form of a "holy and religious" prayer, the main features of the city.[154] Moving from the physical to the spiritual—in accordance with the principles outlined in book 8—Alberti mentions first the public domain of the city: "We pray that we may have a happy and prosperous ending, with strength and happiness to the city and its inhabitants, their fortunes increased, their efforts successful." There follows an allusion to the contented humanist who inhabits the central precinct: "[We pray] that we may have a contented mind." Then comes a reference to the city's historical consciousness: "[We pray] that we may acquire glory." Alberti then speaks of the purpose of the central precinct, where the principles of continuity are preserved: "[We pray] that the good and benevolent things are continuous and follow one on the other." Or, as it sounds in Alberti's Latin:

Caeterum praestare quidem arbitror, si omni opinionum incerta su-
perstitione despecta rem ipsam sancte et religiose aggrediemur. "A
Iove principium Musae: Iovis omnia plena." Ergo purificato animo
et sancte pieque adorato sacrificio inchoari tantam rem perplacebit,
his maxime habitis precibus ad superos, quibus poscatur, ut opem
auxiliumque praebeant operi et faveant caeptis, quoad fauste feliciter
prospereque eveniat res, sitque longa cum sua suorumque hospit-
umque salute et salubritate, cum rerum firmitate animi aequabilitate
fortunarum incremento et industriae fructu et gloriae propagatione
bonorumque omnium perhennitate atque posteritate. De his
hactenus.

The Great Defect

Past prickly thorns, through sharp underbrush
Across rough waves, through cruel war,
Wherever I pass, one thought overwhelms me
And will make me white-haired and old before my time.

My thoughts are so many that
If yes and no in my head take hold of me,
When one closes and the other recloses
I will certainly shrivel up from pain.

But you, sincere Father, who knows
the works and the hearts of us the accursed,
Why don't you concern yourself with our great defect?

Your justice which is so waited for,
As Dante says so well, from which I take strength:
The sword from above does not fall quickly enough.[155]

Alberti's reference to Dante in his sonnet involves a misreading
of *Paradiso*. Dante's "La spada di qua su non taglia in fretta,"
which Alberti rewrites as "la spada di lassù non taglia in fretta,"
is only one part of a sentence that goes on to say "nè tardo,
ma ch'al parere di colui che disiando o temendo l'aspetta,"
which means that the sword from above strikes neither in haste
nor tardily "expect as it seems to him who awaits it with desire
or with fear" (canto 22, line 16). Dante believes that mortals
should console themselves in the knowledge that the clock of

God's justice functions at its own imperturbable speed; Alberti, however, sees a "great defect," a miscommunication between the divine and earthy time frames. Earthly time lacks consistency; at one moment it speeds up—turning the author "white-haired and old" before his time—and at another slows down—"the sword doesn't fall fast enough."

Because of the great defect, the realms of the psyche, much like Freud's concepts of the id, the ego, and the superego, cannot communicate with one another. Neither the sewer below nor the divine realms above serve as poles for the orientation of the earthly, which is trapped in the horizontal world of Chronos. Alberti's tripartite system of saint, functionary, and cynic can be viewed as an effort to bring the problem into the open and thereby make it accessible to healing efforts. Each attempts to break the barriers that insulate chronological time, one from above, one from below, and one from within. This is the purpose of the counter-aesthetic that functions on all three levels: on the first to postulate a pure and uncontaminated realm, on the second to compromise with it, and on the third to accept total but open disorder.

Microtiro

In the Albertian view of history Adam's eating the forbidden apple developed into the ongoing feast in which mankind now revels. Theogenius, surviving only on that which he can grow with his own hands, expounds on the symbolic of devouring: "Man has taken an oath to go all the way to the bitter end to commit cruelty and atrocity. His stomach desires to be the public graveyard of everything; herbs, plants, fruits, birds, quadrupeds, worms, and fish. There is nothing on earth or beneath the earth that he does not devour. He is a fierce enemy of what he sees, and of what he does not see. He wants them all to serve him."[156]

The Albertian humanists, not partaking of the feast, are driven back into the garden of Eden, as it were. This is enacted in *Theogenius*, where we witness the collapse of the Albertian humanist enterprise in the face of the powerful arch-aesthetic. History has to return to the status quo of temporality and humanism to its status as peripheral. *Theogenius* is actually a before and after shot compressed into one piece. If Genipatro represents the "after" (namely Baptista in exile), Microtiro, a "young recruit" of the humanist cadre, represents the "before." He is not yet a Baptista and on the verge of becoming a Libripeta. At this fragile juncture Microtiro has to learn of the arch-aesthetic before he can be channeled into one or the other of the types of counter-aesthetic. He has to realize that he will find himself surrounded by "betrayers, adulators, petitioners, obstructors, lascivious, frivolous, immodest, vicious, and harmful men."[157] They had pushed Genipatro into exile where he finds "wholesome work" in the garden at the expense of being no longer capable of improving society, which is ruled now by the arrogant Tichipedo (Child of Fortune). (The similarities to *Philodoxeus* are numerous.) Tichipedo, who had taken the path to riches and fame, meets with all the predictable consequences; his sons are murdered, his brother commits suicide in prison, his house is plundered, his wife dies during an aborted childbirth, and he himself is eventually sold into slavery. Tichipedo has all too well adapted to the arch-aesthetic and as a negative *exemplum* serves as a demonstration of its consequences. Genipatro in order to escape the arch-aesthetic was forced to renounce all interest in urban affairs, even though he is the "father of the country." By implication he leaves behind an orphaned family. Fully aware of the irresolvable dialectic of fame and glory, he knows that the proud procession of a humanist into the town can never be enacted. He laments that "rarely does it happen that the good ones are able to lead in their republic against the wicked ones. The more they know the more they live in danger of expecting a terrible fortune."[158]

Alberti never resolves the suspense he introduces. We are left to wonder whether Microtiro will attain Philoponian transcendence or opt for a limited personal peace, as even St. Potitus originally had intended. Should he return, a negative ending is in store for him, for Alberti pointedly refers to Alcidiabes, who initially in *Della Famiglia* seemed the very model of princely control but who in *Theogenius* has become the tragic victim of envy and his own spiritual otherness: "Alcidiabes, who was rich, fortunate, and beloved and who had an almost divine mind, was in every way prince of his citizens. However, after having ennobled his fatherland with his virtue and victories, he died in exile and in poverty, having lost all his possessions, because the masses always dislike those who are not similar to them in life and customs."[159]

The message Alberti wishes to convey in his dedication of *Theogenius* to Leonello d'Este is never clearly stated. Is he being advised to abandon politics and exile himself, as an Albertian humanist would? Or does it suggest that he avail himself of the services of a humanist adviser, such as Alberti, to effect a reconciliation of humanist and society, bringing him back from exile, as it were? Though these options are never spelled out, Alberti's *Theogenius* is clearly unlike contemporary dialogues by Leonardo Bruni and Poggio Bracciolini, who portray the humanist movement in glorious action; here it is shown embattled, on the defensive, and of dubious effectiveness. The ideals that govern its existence, namely frugality, modesty, and perseverance, are useless within the urban confines. With a certain longing, Alberti looks to distant India where "those who are good and very learned rule the republic and take care of its laws."[160] The Albertian humanist is not accorded such a central position in the city, which has been usurped by "barbarians" who live not outside it but within it like "caged and dangerous animals."[161]

The Final Shriek

Without memory of the origins (Theogenius) and its father (Genipatro), the city speeds toward destruction. The "I" of social conscience is inevitably, and paradoxically, dragged along with it. Time (historical time) is untrustworthy, and Virtue (mythic time) is "tired," leaving the Albertian humanist abandoned in the middle.

If I suffer, no one should be surprised,
Because one wants what one likes.
I don't know when the soul, lost among so
Many perils, will have any peace.

Miserable that I am! On what should
My vain hope, weak and false, hang?
I cannot dislike the ones who do this to me.
Love, what does one do? Why don't you advise me?

Time would be good to advance your course,
But since tired virtue is already failing,
I can no longer trust either of them.

But if restraint extends to compassion,
I believe that help will come in time.
If not, you will soon hear the final shriek.[162]

Encounters and Misencounters
in the Albertian Theater

The Author-Text

Having explored Alberti's literary ontology and its concomitant domain of aesthetics as the primary alienating phenomena of the human psyche, we will now investigate in more depth how Alberti viewed the various roles that humanism plays in its protracted confrontation with the arch-aesthetic world.

If Alberti was not the first Renaissance thinker to notice the tension between knowledge and power as one of the essential problems of his age, he was the first to create an elaborate speculative system in response to it. By the mid-fourteenth century humanists had secured for themselves highly privileged access to power. Petrarch sitting at the table of the Colonna, Giannozzo Manetti writing the biography of Nicholas V, and Giovanni Pontano in the service of Alfonso I of Naples are only several of the famous instances of humanists' influence in politics. There were of course patrons who enjoyed the purely intellectual benefits in their contacts with the humanists. Piero de' Pazzi's famous "conversion" from princely pleasures to princely learning, Isabella d'Este's court at Ferrara, and Montefeltro's support of humanists are well-known examples. But the alliance of knowledge and power was by no means a happy marriage and was subject to suspicions, abuses, and excesses. One need only think of the numerous invective battles, of the popes and princes who competed for the employment of certain humanists, of the biases Poggio and Salutati displayed in their writings, of the bitter polemics against the Church waged by Valla, and of the purging of humanists, including Alberti, from the curia in 1464 by Paul II.

Alberti today may, in some circles, still be defined as a Renaissance Man, but Alberti himself would hardly have defined his age as a renaissance. What he saw were the ominous signs of cultural deterioration in general and of a faulty definition of the humanist task in particular. Instead of eagerly submitting to the powers that be, humanism should stand back so that the specific roles of knowledge and power can come into full view. But Alberti does not opt for simple solutions. Humanism is itself a paradox, for, as Alberti envisioned it, the humanist writer, having to reveal the underlying evil in society and to postulate a cure, faces the situation of having to "know man through and through" and yet remain uncontaminated. It is through this paradox and the anxieties it produces in the writer's psyche that the turbulent nature of the communal psyche is revealed, even if at the same time the possibility of hope is diminished.

Because of this paradox, humanism of the Albertian cast, though it aims at a better world, is suspicious of aloof Neoplatonic idealism. Whereas Neoplatonists would see the world as a degenerate form of the ideal, Alberti sees the world and the ideal as leading separate existences. The humanist program as he envisions it can attempt to create contact between the two realms, but it cannot necessarily change the real world for the better. In fact, instead of postulating a distant but potentially attainable concordance of words and things and of man and identity, it exposes and grieves over all instances of "misfitting," itself included. Its own separation from society (equivalent to historical time itself) in a sort of ripple effect initiates a series of other separations, beginning with that of the writer from society (something artists are challenged to repair, as we shall see) and ending with that of author from text, which, in its finality, is the *terminus ad quem* of social existence, standing for and replicating the original separation of word from meaning, image from being, and necessity from endurance. Though Alberti's humanist saints suffer and articulate the troubles of the temporal world through their expression of hope, the Albertian cynics point to the omnipresence of aesthetic alienation and to the fact that the temporal world is not perishable at all but rather prevailing. It is the spiritual world, not the temporal, that is ephemeral and endangered.

Alberti has learned from his own autobiographical method that the struggle to arrive at an authentic self—possessing reason, piety, and a sense of social responsibility—is complicated by the difficulty of fusing aesthetics (an ontological problem) with ethics (an epistemological one) in a seemingly spontaneous and natural way. In facing this difficulty humanism cannot avoid employing the very thing it attempts to counteract, namely aesthetic alienation, as this is the only human means of effecting change. The humanist aesthetic, employed in full consciousness of its double-edged nature and its primordial drift, makes the writer potentially more potent than those officially in charge, but also painfully complicit in the archaesthetic he is combating.

Alberti would always remain in the ivory tower, for to enter the fray would deny him critical distance and indeed the validity of his theoretical speculations. There were those, however, who, thinking along more simplistic lines, seem to have wanted to bring ideas very similar to his into the real world. Girolamo Savanarola (1454–98), for example, hardly ever mentioned in discussions on Alberti and in some ways miles apart, is in other respects oddly close. What Alberti saw in the abstract—and through the veil of irony—Savanarola took literally as a program of political reform. Does not Alberti's writer-saint suddenly come to life in the figure of Savanarola? Indeed the problem posed by Alberti, namely how the writer can wage a war for the spirit of mankind without himself becoming contaminated, describes the very problem faced by Savanarola. This is not to say that Alberti's works, ciphered as they are, were meant to call forth a real fighter-saint, but only that Alberti placed his finger on the pulse of his times.

Though the issue of knowledge and power constantly seems to weigh on Alberti's mind, he does not search for easy answers to the problem but asks the polemical question: Can knowledge and power coexist and contribute to a better world? His answer is an ironic yes and no. Such a union can only contribute to a better world if both parties are recognized as combatants with differing *raisons d'être*. Only then can any clarity be achieved between "who you are and who I am," to use the words of Baptista. All-too-peaceful coexistence hints at falsification, whether it be the misappropriation of power by false intellectuals or the drawing of intellectuals into temporal matters. The underlying tensions between the literary self—the only possible locus of uncorrupted knowledge—and the ever shifting world of power can never be allowed to fall from view. Moral consciousness and political consciousness must coexist in a dialectic so as to maintain the myth of compatibility. The Albertian humanist, therefore, can never attempt a unilateral, Savanarola-style takeover, for he must by definition be in retreat.

To make visible the struggle between the world and the Albertian humanist, between *Realpolitik* and the exiled voice of conscience, and between the arch-aesthetic and ethics, Alberti appropriated, as we have seen, the historical model of the struggle between emperor and Church, rephrasing it as the struggle between temporal government on the one hand and the humanist government in exile on the other. The aims of the two enterprises are legitimately at variance. They should not and ultimately cannot coincide. Each has its specific function in the aesthetic realm, the first to perpetuate it, the second to transform it from barbarism to culture.

As we have seen, Alberti outlines not one, but several different interrelated humanist encounters with the arch-aesthetic. There are four ways in which contact between the two realms can be achieved instead of three because the middle proposition (the functionaries) is composed of two variants. The following chapters will cover the various scenarios, which can be briefly summarized. First, there is the attempt to bypass the arch-aesthetic by envisioning an implausible totalizing domination of society by the writer-text constellation. Second are the civic functionaries who, well aware of the dangers inherent in the arch-aesthetic, attempt to restrain it by means of its own weapons. Unlike Machiavelli's, Alberti's princes are bothered by their consciences because on the one hand they are unable to fulfill their saintly destiny and on the other hand they feel threatened by the potential incursion of a paralyzing cynicism in their psyche. Third are the artists, ignorant of the arch-aesthetic altogether—instruments of a counter-aesthetic strategy enacted by the humanist mentor. Finally, there is the vagabond unmasker, the ultimate cynic who, destroying all illusions, prefers vagabonding to the artifice of the first, the openly advocated astuteness of the second, and the naiveté of the third.

The functionaries, proposed by Alberti as a fusion of cynics and saints and represented by the prince, Agnolo, and other "fathers," embody the reconciliation of these contradictions and the realization of a moral life, thereby charting a potential course for human action. Alberti's definition of the functionary, which begins to appear only in the middle dialogues *Della*

Famiglia, Profugiorum ab aerumna, and *Theogenius,* is part of a broadening investigation into the civic humanist compromise with *Realpolitik.* It is clear, however, that Alberti's functionaries are intended to demonstrate the unmanageability of the arch-aesthetic. In the final analysis, they turn into failure postulates. The search for real-life prototypes like Agnolo and Benedetto stalls, as we find out in *De Ichiarcia,* Alberti's last dialogue, where Baptista spins out a fantasy of a utopian functionary prince in front of a crackling fireplace on a winter's night.

The failure of civic humanism leaves the field open for painters and architects to enter the fray and attempt to infuse humanist ideals into the unwilling world. Their lack of power and vested interest makes them immensely suitable vehicles for the implementation of a humanist ideology suspicious of all collusion with *Realpolitik.* The absence of a power base makes them innocuous enough in that world so as not to provoke its rapacious forces. Practicing simulation openly and as it were naively, they are not perceived as a threat in the arch-aesthetic realm and thus unknowingly import the contraband ethics. They are a Trojan horse left behind by the Albertian humanist—the ultimate counter-deception in a deceptive world.

Ironically, the artists are themselves deceived, for the text they must follow hides the author's textual stratagem. While in *Philodoxeus* it is still implied that the real author will throw off the mask and take his bows, as indeed he does, in the treatises on painting and architecture the impenetrable mask hints at no irony. Here Alberti, exploring the totalizing mask, has structured himself out of the text. Knowing that Alberti did nothing without profound deliberation, could we not speculate that the extinction of the author in *De re aedificatoria* and *De pictura* was intended to abolish the lingering presence of the authorial aesthetic—Alberti's *own,* that is—in the allegedly nonaesthetic text and enforce a congruence of word and meaning? If we hesitate to suspect Alberti of devising this elaborate mask, we need only remind ourselves of the creation myth in *Momus,* where it is stated that only with the greatest difficulty and by looking carefully into the eye sockets can one detect the mask. Thus it is fitting that we end with *Momus,* where Alberti, in the fourth and final attempt to formulate a position against the arch-aesthetic, articulates the reversal that has long been rumbling underground. In *Momus* the shifting strategies of masking, counter-masking, and unmasking that take place between Alberti and his authorial poses, between writer, text, and audience, and between the power structure of society and humanist conscience are brought to their logical, ironic conclusion.

The Mortal Gods

In *Corolle* and *Fatum et Fortuna*, Alberti evokes the fantasy of the successful union of writer, text, and society. This union is not forwarded as a utopian ideal since it exists outside of historical time. As long as it remains in the realm of humanist fantasy its validity seems plausible, but placed within the context of *Realpolitik* it becomes, of course, a travesty, which is the ambiguity played out in *Corolle,* where a "rhetorician" outlines the rules that supposedly guide his life. His complicated diction and his flowery style are intended to show that he has not forgotten what a humanist writer is, but he does not follow what he espouses. Alberti uses this fallen writer not only to exemplify the arch-aesthetic alienation from the ethical foundation but also to exemplify the implausibility of utopian hopes for mankind. The rhetorician, as in a trance, parrots the high ideals of humanism in a tortuous, labyrinthine, unending sentence. Contained therein, however, is a list that moves from that which is "given" to that which the writer must acquire, from divine talent to earthly learnedness. The list, in fact, is almost an outline, albeit in an ironic setting, of the *Vita* that describes the life of Baptista.

Authors must be endowed with singular and outstanding talent.

They must model themselves on venerable, serious, and learned men.

They will win special thanks from good men, a type of divine regard.

They must hope from the immortal gods for immortality.

They must not only have good character and learning but virtue and fortitude.

They must provide strenuous lucubrations for their state and fellow citizens.

They must work with highest devotion, vigilance, and effort.

They must not neglect the standards of ancient learning.

These famous men will cling together in mind and thought.

Nature must be their guide.

They bolster the fragile and failing hopes of men.

They must know that it is from the depravity and the corrupt reasoning of the inexperienced that improper reasonings emerge.

They must strive for what the Greeks call *pronoia* (providence).

Through virtue (manly excellence) they build the path to the heavens.

Their art of exposition must not be loose and free-flowing but should be based on an ordered method of speaking.[1]

The rhetorician's failure to understand what he is saying exposes the mistake inherent in the creation of the world; it has no built-in affinity for textuality. That was the great flaw described so colorfully in *Momus*, where, as we have seen, the "painter" fails to hand a text over to his proto-humans ("The Prerogative"). As opposed to the dire reality ironized in Corolle, Alberti describes in *Fatum et Fortuna* of *Intercoenales* a counter-creation myth that shows the "simple and uncorrupted" writer-saint at work. In this *somnium* Alberti describes a "demigod" standing on a mountain looking down on the circular River of Life that girdles it. Existence in this river is precarious and endangered: some souls are struggling on inflated bladders, others on overloaded ships; some are even swimming unaided. A shade, speaking to the dreamer about the difficulty of negotiating survival in this river, draws attention to a group standing apart from the multitude; they are described as *diis persimiles*. Carried by their wings, which represent "truth, simplicity, and talent" (Alythia and Phroneus we have already encountered in *Philodoxeus*), they put their "divine endowments to good use" in the "admirable enterprise of constructing rafts" (texts?) to help others negotiate the toilsome River of Life. Alberti understandably claims that "in a marvelous way," he "sees himself among them."

Shades: But now, offer supreme honor to those you see there set apart from the multitude.

Looking in all directions, I said: "In truth, I see no one who is separated from the multitude."

And the shades: "How can you miss those who with wings on their feet, fly with such agility and rapidity over the waves?"

Then I said: "I see but one; but why should I do homage to him? What have these done?"

Answered the shades: "Does it seem to you that those have little merit who—simple and uncorrupted—are considered by men to be divine? Their wings represent truth and simplicity, and their winged sandals signify contempt for transitory things. Justly, therefore, are they considered divine, not only because of their divine endowments but also because they were the first to construct the boards that you see floating on the river. Those boards, upon which they carved the name of each of the liberal arts [lit., the good arts] are a great help to those who are swimming.

"Those others are also similar to the gods, but they do not entirely emerge from the waters because their winged sandals are imperfect; these are demigods, and they are most deserving of honor and veneration as they are immediately below the gods. It is their merit to have enlarged the boards by adding pieces of flotsam to them. Further they engage in the admirable enterprise of collecting the boards from the reefs and the beaches, in order to construct new ones and to proffer these works to those who still swim in midstream.

"Render, O mortal, honor to these. Render them the thanks that they are due for having offered excellent help with these boards to those negotiating the toilsome River of life."

This is what I saw and heard in my sleep; and I seemed, in a marvelous way, to have somehow managed to be numbered among the winged gods.[2]

As the passage makes clear, there are two different types of rafts, those made *ex nihilo* and those that are repaired. The theme draws on a commonplace medieval theological distinction between first and second planks.[3] The first plank is the ritual of baptism that neutralizes original sin. The "second plank after shipwreck," as it was commonly labeled, is the ongoing sacrament of penance, which helps against the constant threat of actual sin. Just as the first launches the soul into temporal time, the second helps in restoration when underway. In defining his demigod humanists who are engaged in either writing new texts on the "good arts" (i.e., counter-proposals to the "bad arts" of the arch-aesthetic) or restoring old ones, Alberti transposes these most basic of Christian principles into working propositions of his salvation myth.

That Alberti—ever so modestly—sees himself in such an exalted position should come as no surprise. Is not *De pictura* a "new raft?"[4] Alberti lets it be known that "This is a topic never treated before."[5] *De re aedificatoria,* on the other hand, is like a repaired raft, reassembled as it is from Vitruvius's shipwreck.[6] These texts then are part of the alternative creation myth, in which mortals are given the option to make use of a textual raft in the dangerous River of Life, a raft ordered according to divine principles and devoid of vested interests. A paradox emerges. The world as it historically developed is an aesthetic one; the counter-proposition, however, which aims to diffuse mankind's aesthetic nature so that it once again can recognize the "pure and simple," also involves an aesthetic both ontologically and textually and is far from spontaneous. In this strange postulate involving an allegedly nonaesthetic art of text making, the demigod writers, represented as "most deserving of honor and veneration," should be nothing less than the guardians of society. And in *De re aedificatoria,* we hear that "The guardians (*intellegeret genus*), appointed over men, should be some other kind of beings of superior wisdom and greater excellence than common men."[7]

Intelligentia, which comes "directly and simply" and was commonly associated with angels and deities, differs from *ratio,* a more limited human knowledge. It is not accidental that the young Philoponius was saved from death by some quasi-divine guardians, *intelligentes honestissimi,* as he was to join their ranks (*Pupillus*) after having been purged of his initial resentment (*Erumna*).[8] Only then could he emerge metamorphosed as a lawgiver speaking only what is pure and simple, as dictated by his second ring. Baptista, not so much the lawgiver as the ideal uncontaminated guardian-mentor, also speaks in *De pictura* in a manner "that is simple and beautiful," perfectly simulating an intact bond of trust between students and humanist instructor.

The humanist writers are deserving of honors because, as Alberti asserts in *De commodis litterarum atque incommodis,* they place others on a path toward "an honorable and happy life very much similar to that of the gods (*deorum persimilem*)" and thus may claim to stand *outside* the arch-aesthetic compulsion.[9]

Alberti leaves little doubt that his humanist godlike instructors have a sacred trust: "The virtues of painting are that its instructors, seeing their exertion so praised, feel themselves to be almost simulating God (*simillimos intellegant*)."[10] Embodying the spirit of social conscience and preserving all excellent things into posterity, the phantasmagoric Albertian demigods, "uniquely and exquisitely singular" and designed in opposition to the hard-nosed *Realpolitik* of fifteenth-century Italy, preside over the ethical-aesthetic realm without falling prey to its premise of distortion: "My fond wish is that whatever is most proper and most beautiful, and that whatever helps run the republic and preserves all remarkable things to posterity should be termed, one might go so far as to say, sacred."[11]

While Plato held that the arts lead man ever further from the ideal and cloud all memory of the authentic, Alberti held that the authentic is irretrievably lost, for it was locked off from mankind by a faulty creation. The alternative creation myth that attempts to define an unpolluted writer will later parallel Alberti's attempt to create an artist similarly unpolluted. The former is conceived essentially as a messenger from God, the latter as a messenger from the humanist realm. Both are equally implausible postulates. But whereas the inflated claims of the writer-saint collapse when exposed to the reality principle, the unrealistic claims of the artists miraculously escape unscathed.

The Discourse on the Good and Happy Life

The "good and happy life" (variously phrased as *ad bene beateque vivendum* or *vivere bene e lodati*) appears frequently in Alberti's writings, as it is essential to the *societá natura e vera religione*. It designates a hoped for reconciliation between God and the world. It is in *De iure*, a text rarely studied, that Alberti comes closest to spelling out his vision of a successful union. Alberti here proposes two quasi-legal systems—one vertical, one horizontal. The former is the divine law which defines the relationships between good and evil, the latter is that of the bonds of kinship, which are enumerated as those of marriage, family, and friendship.

The good and happy life hinges on the proper implementation of the divine law, which differs from written law just as spirit differs from body.[12] The first has primacy over the second, but the latter sometimes forbids things demanded by the first. The Albertian judge, so we are led to understand, would never let that happen: "Divine things should be left to God and his ministers whereas human things only are to be weighed by a judge and handled through awards and punishments according to human laws. But the judge has to administer them mindful of God and as a very good priest of duty."[13]

Whereas divine law speaks in absolutes, human law knows many shades of grey (such as things that are good at first, but ultimately evil, and things that may seem evil but lead to a good end). Despite these complications, the true judge can never forget the primacy of divine law, which "has such a power and value that it orders one to act well and despise evil."[14] If the intactness of the divine law prevails, the bonds of kinship will also remain intact. In an ideal scenario the intersection is the locus of the humanist enterprise. In the fallen world, however, a dislocation has taken place. In *Discordia,* from *Intercoenales,* Alberti explains how the goddess Discord subverts the two systems: "She can subvert at will all human and divine laws, and even against the gods' wishes dissolve and destroy all bonds of kinship, marriage and friendship."[15]

De iure still needs to be investigated in the context of legal history by specialists of medieval and Renaissance law. For my purpose, it is enough to point out that a parallel exists between Alberti's concept of the arch-aesthetic realm and his concept of written law. Written law arose in response to mankind's defective human psyche, which "forgot" how to simulate properly and is under the sway of Discord. The more faulty the simulation becomes, the more laws are required *ad infinitum:* "For the Romans, twelve [laws] were enough for them to enlarge their republic. We, however, have sixty cabinets full of laws, and to this we add every day new laws."[16] The residual natural and divine law that still exists in mankind as conscience could perhaps be compared to the pre-Narcissistic realm that Baptista and Philoponius attempt to reintroduce into society, for it is this law that should guide man's actions, prior to any written law, for it alone "brings us closer to God."[17] Alberti's thesis is straightforward, yet by insisting on a trans-legal ethical system, he is consistent with his definition of a humanism that stands in naive and archaic contrast to *Realpolitik*. Alberti's ethical system must be seen within the context of other systems, such as the one devised by the archbishop of Florence, St. Antoninus (1389–1459), Alberti's contemporary and a legal theorist of repute. He envisioned a complex hierarchy of laws divided into seven categories, which were, theoretically at least, held to be capable of dealing with all possible contingencies occurring in secular society.[18] Alberti's schema is much less workable, but infinitely more powerful in its attempt to bond mythic and temporal time. Philoponius's twelve rings must be seen in this context; they are by definition "pure, simple, free of charge."[19] It is for this reason, as we have already seen, that Baptista gave "every artist copies of his great and worthy treatise."[20] Like all humanist texts, they instill in the readers "a zeal for a better life" (the vertical connection) and amuse them as well (the horizontal connection). "If a writer succeeds, by the force of expression, with variety and elegance of argumentation to give to the readers the zeal for a better life and at the same time to amuse them with friendliness and ease—this didn't occur too frequently at the time of the ancient Latin authors either—then without doubt, he must not be confused with the mass of contemporary writers."[21]

The Albertian writer must demonstrate that he has purged himself to qualify as spokesman for the good and happy life.

I have always held writing in the highest consideration, and to apply oneself to it I have accepted in my life anxieties of all types, great fatigues, unpleasantness, damages, dangers, torments, and misfortune unending, to the point that it seemed that I had dedicated myself to them completely. . . . I took upon myself poverty, enemies, and injuries, which were, as is well known, neither indifferent nor light.[22]

The writer, of course, cannot allow his otherness to manifest itself in his writings, for they should "not be employed to excite discord, or bring harm to others," Alberti holds, "but only to turn our affection, our senses, and our understanding towards a good and happy life."[23] This discourse on the good and happy life, held out as a counterbalancing vision in the temporal world, has, of course, few practitioners and is on the verge of dying out altogether.

Good literature, the noble arts, and the divine disciplines, have fallen so low as to prostitute themselves. And have you gone so far, O knowledge of things divine and human, custodian over good customs and glory, inventor and generator of everything that is high, you, who used to adorn the spirit of mankind, elevating his intelligence, confering praise, esteem and dignity, governing the state and guiding the world with the highest law and order?[24]

Alberti's polemic points to the belated and quixotic nature of his heroes, who are still fighting in the forlorn cause of "good literature, the noble arts, and the divine disciplines." They and they alone still point to the absolute, herald the exalted, elevate their intelligence, and stand guard over good customs and good arts; in short, they are perfect models for simulation. It is not "scholarship, but divine virtue" that will motivate them and lead them to a comprehension of "the essences and the causes of things, beauty and the pursuit of virtue and glory," all necessary for "the good and happy life."[25]

Mother Humanism

If there is an ideal representative of the discourse on the good and happy life, bringing about the artificially envisioned counter-creation myth, it is Baptista, in whom the jousting for position between humanist writer and society begins to be played out in earnest. As a counter proposition to the arch-aesthetic, Baptista hopes to defeat the fragmented society by an additive and agglutinative construction that unites cultural values in great density; he can penetrate the human psyche, paint, make music, excel in mathematics, and write, among other things. This synthetic identity is modeled on the principles inherent in the image of Mother Humanism, which is described in a piece called *Picture*, from *Intercoenales*. As mother of Peace, Happiness, Benevolence, and Contentment she demonstrates the seamless fusion of cultural attributes (see figure 7):

Figure 7
"Mother Humanism" (sketch by the author).

On the panel was the marvelous image of a woman with many different faces coming together on one neck: old, young, sad, happy, joyous, serious, humorous, and so forth. Similarly, the image had many hands extending from the shoulders. One hand held a quill, another a lyre, another a symmetrically shaped gemstone, another instruments used by mathematicians, and still another books. Above this picture was the title Mother Humanism.[26]

This description is startling. Multi-limbed Indian figures, known only vaguely from the tales of travelers, were often viewed as representing the devil.[27] More significantly, they were frequently employed in representations of Fortuna to symbolize her innate ambiguity (see figure 8). Alberti's Mother Hu-

Figure 8
Multi-limbed Fortuna in a fifteenth-century painting (British Library, London).

manism, however, triumphs as the ultimate warrior against
Fortuna, of which she is the counterimage; what Fortuna dis-
members, Mother Humanism reassembles. She embodies the
various aspects of human life (represented by the numerous
faces); she is a writer (symbolized by the pen); a Promethean
bringer of the divine light (symbolized by the gem);[28] a creator
of beauty (symbolized by the carefully crafted painting); an
organizer of human activities (symbolized by mathematical instruments); and finally a transmitter of texts (symbolized by
the manuscript).

The iconography of the individual elements, of course, was
not new. We only have to look at Andrea Bonaiuti's fresco *The
Triumph of St. Thomas of Aquinas,* painted in 1366, in the Spanish
Chapel of S. Maria Novella in Florence (figure 9). Bonaiuti
organizes knowledge into fourteen subcategories, seven sacred

Figure 9
Detail from Andrea Bonaiuti's "Triumph of St. Thomas of Aquinas"
(1366), in S. Maria Novella. (Art Resources)

and seven profane, each represented by a woman holding the appropriate object. Alberti, in creating his Mother Humanism, conflates in one image five of Bonaiuti's; the result is an oddly shaped being intended to demonstrate the principle of unification; it unites what is dispersed, much as does the figure of Baptista. Though Aristotle specifically condemns such grotesqueries, he does permit assemblage if the aims are benevolent or noble, as for example in the definition of a "great man." "Great men are distinguished from ordinary men in the same way as beautiful people from plain ones, or as an artfully painted object from a real one, namely, in that what is dispersed has been gathered into one."[29] As a literary topos, it can be found, for example, in Geoffrey of Vinsauf's description of Pope Innocent I and in de Lille's *Anticlaudianus*.[30]

In excellent lineage you compare with Bartholomew, in gentle heart with Andrew, in precious youth with John, in steadfast faith with Peter, and in perfect learning with Paul: all these qualities are found together in one.[31]

The skilled zeal of Nature brings together in one work the individual gifts she has bestowed here and there on others.[32]

Above all, it was the essential principle of hagiographic constructions. Already in the fourth century it was explained by a hagiographer that

No one should take offense if any of these deeds were done by some other saint since the holy apostle, through the mystery of the member saints united in one body, has so brought them into union that, by a comparison with a living body, we may harmonize the members, one with another, in turn. . . . Hence if any of those acts which we have written down were not of that man . . . nevertheless we should little doubt that they too belong to so great a man. The holy man himself teaches that, of all living things, there should always be attributed to one what was discovered in others.[33]

Alberti employed the hagiographic topos not only as a guiding principle in his theory of how to make works of art but also in developing his own synthetic literary ontology. Baptista is thus by no means to be construed as an emblem of pleasant universality but must be interpreted as making manifest the difficult battle against the centrifugality of society. While the world is dispersive, Baptista collects, and in collecting, saves.

Baptista and his Texts

A case where a hypothesized fusion of author and text is enacted by Alberti can be found in Baptista and *De pictura,* which as an ensemble constitutes an important thesis in Alberti's speculations. This constellation was constructed as a public *exemplum* that in the symbiotic interaction of its parts demonstrates permanence in a world continually in flux. In terms of Alberti's cosmology, this can be seen as an alternative to Neofronus (*Defunctus*) and the tragic death of the literary identity. Thus Alberti bares his chest, disingenuously informing the painter that the "learned and unlearned" will agree with him, knowing full well that they together will strive to separate writer from text (*Scriptor*).[34] Similarly, Alberti states that *De pictura* "will prove worthy in the ears of the *eruditi.*"[35] The author pretends that it is not his opponents who are blind to him but he who is blind to them.

Ironically and appropriately he trusts the painters more than his erudite readers, begging them as a reward for his labors to paint his portrait in their "historiae" and thereby proclaim to posterity that "I was a student of this art and they are mindful of and grateful for this favor."[36] The painting is more permanent than the text. Alberti should know, for Baptista is an idealized self-portrait barely hiding Alberti's vested interest in posterity. Like a genius loci dwelling in the *profugiorum* at the center of the city or like "Ennio, the poet, whose name hovers on the lips of cultured men," Baptista-Alberti, as painting, will live on in society.[37] (Little did Alberti know that it would be nineteenth- and twentieth-century scholars who would do him the honor.)

Whereas in *Philodoxeus* Alberti plants himself back in a classical age to establish himself as a myth, in *De pictura* he projects his myth into the future. In the first, the difference between protagonist and author is played up; in the second, the difference is played down. In the first, the author hopes that all will notice his claim to a higher identity; in the second, he hopes that it will remain a secret. (One should recall that Alberti wrote *De pictura* in 1436, shortly after the *Commentarium Philodoxeos Fabule.*)

With Baptista, Alberti has provided for history the necessary bipolar constellation of man and product—one that for him defines the essential characteristics of the humanist task, which, on one level at least, alleges to bypass the arch-aesthetic by placing therein an intact text-writer postulate without provoking critical rejection. The result, however, is as much a product of the arch-aesthetic as an attempt to bypass it. Both man and product are fiction—artifice. This circularity is only saved by the implication that by the time it is discovered—as scholars attempt to look behind the mask—Baptista, one of the *diispersimiles*, will have long since anchored his creator in the realm of immortality.

If Alberti had hoped that this would elevate *him* into the realm of immortality, earthly fame was slow in coming. After his death his modest legacy was squandered, his plan for an Alberti Foundation for the aid of poor students ignored, his tomb forgotten, and, worst of all, many of his texts irretrievably lost.[38] Only much later was Neofronus to emerge from the silence of Hades.

Versipellem

What is not and must never be evident in the Baptista-*De pictura* combination is Baptista's secret flaw. Irony, a potent counteragent, resides in his "house." In the *Vita*, we are told the following perplexing anecdote: "He [Baptista] was questioned by a mathematician why he harbored in his house double-tongued people (*bilinguem*) who could metamorphose themselves into different shapes (*versipellem*). He responded: 'Don't you know that the sphere touches the plane on only one point?'"[39] Because the image of the sphere touching the plane indicates instability and represents Fortuna, the retort to a mathematician signifies that the supposedly stable world of geometry is as much a phantom as the perfectability of human discourse. Alberti does not yet allow this hidden *terribilitá* to surface because he has first to let the humanist salvation myth play itself out. As we shall see in *Momus,* the "guest" in Baptista's house is Momus, the great artificer of metamorphosis and the cynic *par excellence.* Seemingly, Alberti planned them as a paired proposition and counter-proposition, much as the winged eye and the *quid tum* on the medallion. This, by the way, is one reason why we can never interpret Baptista as being identical with Alberti himself.

This pairing of mutually exclusive character propositions and the dynamic that develops between them could be viewed as the central dramatic event in Alberti's exposition. It builds from the rather simple confrontation between Leopis and Libripeta (*Scriptor*) through many intermediary stages to the complex and sophisticated pair of Baptista and Momus and to Alberti's own satire on his method in the Gelasto and Enopo pair. In the above quote Alberti foreshadows Momus's eventual ascendency—equivalent to the dubious ascendency of aesthetics—from the confines of Baptista's house, where ethics still attempts to bind aesthetics. As will be shown, Momus exposes the untenable artificiality of Baptista's synthetic unity. With Momus the Albertian autobiographical method is brought up to date, as the humanist vision finally comes face to face with the contemporary world in which any utopian potential is shown to be a pipe dream.

The Civic Functionary

In contrast with the distanced relationship of writer and society, the civic functionaries, representing the urban audience of the humanist writers, are trained in the practical wisdom of *astuzia* that places them *in media res.* They employ masking benignly and officially. The functionary—as we have seen with Giannozzo—is a man of experience, oriented toward the real world and adept not only at detecting deception but also at employing it.

At the beginning of book 1 of *Della Famiglia* we find an example of *astuzia* expressed by Alberti's deceased father Benedetto Alberti and recalled by Adovardo. Summarized, his arguments are as follows:

Watch over the family from all sides.

Use authority rather than power.

In every thought put the good, the peace, and the tranquility of the family first.

Know how to steer toward the harbor of honor, prestige, and authority.

Fill the young with good council.

Remain alert.

Be like a common father to all the young.

Benedetto Alberti, a "humanist" functionary, demonstrates *astuzia* by interlocking abstract morality with the practical realities of life, ethics with aesthetics. Even Jove, if he is to be an effective ruler, should do the same, but unfortunately Jove reads Momus's *tabella* "too late" (belatedness is the curse Alberti attaches to ethics). The text given to Jove is also a pragmatic blueprint, as opposed to the text on the good and happy life:

The prince must not do nothing, nor should he do everything either.

Whatever he does, he should not do it by himself nor should he do it with everyone.

He has to make sure that nobody is extravagantly rich and that not too many people are poor.

He has to help the good ones even if this is against their will.

He should not damage the evil ones unless he is forced to do so against his will (so that they do not become vindictive).

He has to be a good judge for the people.

He should abstain from reform except when he is forced to save the dignity of the state, or when reform offers itself as a secure opportunity of increasing his glory.

He must conduct himself magnificently in public and economically in private.

He has to fight against pleasures no less than he does against his enemies.

He should promote peace among his people, and gain glory and popularity for himself by acts of peace rather than with warlike enterprises.

He should listen patiently to the prayers of the humble people and should tolerate their problems with moderation if he wants the small people to support his luxury.[40]

Civic functionaries live in a realm that is neither entirely public nor entirely private. Therefore, "given the common treachery of mankind," Alberti writes in *De componendis cifris,* a treatise on coding, one must not only "discover the machinations and deceptions of others, but one must also cloak one's innermost thoughts."[41] In *Profugiorum ab aerumna* Agnolo, the civic humanist *par excellence,* explains that one must always keep in mind the destructive tendency of the masses. The sovereignty of one's thought must be guarded.

You can't show yourself to be free. Obey the power of the masses. For Euripides, the poet, the bad actions of the multitude appeared more powerful than fire itself, and more suitable for destroying and consuming things. And they say that the multitude is always undefeatable. . . . But how much, where and whom it is necessary to believe, necessity will teach you.[42]

And elsewhere it is affirmed that "One's domestic and private thought and life should not be exposed to the censure of the masses."[43] One fights *astuzia* with *astuzia,"* Giannozzo admits.[44]

This anxious awareness of public and private realms, which determines the existence of the functionary, mirrors an identical anxious state between being and image and shows that the civic functionary lives precariously close to the arch-aesthetic—so close in fact, that the two possible alternatives in Alberti's cosmology, saint and cynic, become ever more tempting as poles of refuge should things go wrong, as indeed they do for Benedetto Alberti. Benedetto, as described in *Intercoenales,* recants his "erroneous way of thinking" and accepts exile, complete with the change in mental states that it requires. Alberti shows him transformed from the patronal figure portrayed in *Della Famiglia* to an author type, renouncing *all* pecuniary ties with society in favor of the pure life of a humanist in exile. Just as the writers will have to face the loss of their text, the functionaries will have to face a separation from the city. In exile, Benedetto comes to realize that "From my youth on I have been susceptible to a certain erroneous way of thinking that led me to suppose unwisely that I truly possessed the things that most men say a man can have. I used to say 'my lands,' 'my possessions,' 'my riches,' according to the common habit of speaking among men. . . . But now I have the feeling that this very body in which I am trapped is not really mine."[45]

Operae Perdae

Albertian humanism, pointing out as well as struggling against the faulty creation, could be viewed as based on a sort of deism in which God, once having created the world, no longer interferes in its fate. Since meaning cannot be infused organically into life, texts as the potential embodiment of meaning are by definition the bizarre holdover from the Great First Cause.

Ideally the functionaries pave the way for the humanist reconquest of the memory of the originally benign creation. Hypothetically there was a time when Genipatro's writings, modeled on the principles of the good and happy life, found no resistance among the "first citizens," who frequently read and discuss his writings on how to live in a manner *bene e beato*.[46] In reality the functionaries cannot escape the impact of the arch-aesthetic and either succumb to it or flee (the topic of *Theogenius*). Thus Alberti's thought, by suggesting a cure while annulling it, points out that the humanist in essence speaks into the void and has no agent in the earthly realm and certainly no audience with power. The absence of an audience endangers the text-life of the writer on a fundamental level. The "plebians," of course, "can make only dreadful and obscene judgments . . . and [are] wholly negligent of those things that are absolutely necessary for the Good and Happy Life."[47] They are incapable of receiving the unmediated message.

Libripeta: Are you trying this on Tuscan soil? Ha, ha, ha.[48]

Agnolo: The multitude lives perpetually; they change progeny by progeny, their age flies away; they live on the earth tardy in wisdom, quick in dying and complaining in life.[49]

Without a local spokesman there is no one to uphold the high humanist ideals, which are soon forgotten. In *Profugiorum ab aerumna* Agnolo (Baptista's "father") prophesizes that Baptista's writings will fall on deaf ears, though they "are an ornament to the Tuscan language . . . and praise the value and glory of our fellow citizens."[50] He continues: "But I doubt, Baptista, that you will be able to act out your works, for there is so much envy and perverseness among mortals that divides this age of ours. . . . Oh, my fellow citizens, will you continue to offend him who loves you?"[51] And indeed, Baptista's *Della Famiglia* is not safe from the relatives who cause him, in a temporary fit of despair, to turn against his own work. Only the timely appearance of a "prince" saves the work from the hands of its own author: "He gave the three books of *Della Famiglia* to his relatives so they could read it. But he couldn't stand it that among all the lazy Albertis, only one bothered to read the title, though the books were being requested by others from outside. . . . Because of this insult he decided to burn the books, and would have done so, if just then some princes hadn't asked him for the books."[52]

In *De commodis litterarum atque incommodis* Alberti describes how the texts become mere objects of the marketplace. Book dealers are speculators in writers' souls.

Law, theology, natural philosophy and ethics, and all of the other forms of literature that is worthy, excellent, and suitable only for free men (oh, abominable crime!) first were set up for auction, then sold publicly. A large number of merchants, quick to present their offers, came from all parts. From the fields, from forests, from the serf lands, and from the dung heaps came a vast multitude. They were not really men, but, on the contrary, they were beasts, born for servile work, who, after having despised the countryside, made a sudden burst to put in sale and desecrate the discipline of writing. Oh the plague of literature! Those who should use the rake and pitch fork shamelessly manage books and writings![53]

As has already been pointed out, the "texts" of Alberti's authors, unlike those of the book dealers, are given to society free of charge. (One could compare this to having a pamphlet of Jehovah's Witnesses thrust into one's hand as one emerges from the subway.) *De pictura*, "handed down from the heavens and dug up from under the earth," stands outside the context of the marketplace and the relativizing effect of the money economy.[54] Baptista, by definition optimistic has a vested interest, being the teacher voice in *De pictura*. Thus, "in the future," there will be those—meaning of course those similar to him—who will see to it that his text is preserved: "There will probably be some who will correct my mistakes and who will be of far greater assistance to painters than I in this excellent and honorable art. I implore them, should they in the future exist, to take up this task eagerly and to readily exercise their talents on it and perfect this most noble art."[55]

In contrast to Baptista's necessarily hopeful frame of mind stands Neofronus's chagrin: "I am convinced that these times are exceedingly deplorable, so disgraced because there are so few men, truly erudite, who are capable of amending my writings. . . . Do you not remember what diligence, what sacrifice, and what constancy I employed in writing my works? . . . Oh yes, wasted . . . all wasted."[56] Naively believing that "posterity is grateful for one's lucubrations," Neofronus learns too late that he cannot prevent the destruction of his writings, which are ripped apart and used by his relatives as wrapping paper for the perfume that they find in his study. The perfume was "given to him" by Crantor. Crantor, of course, was a fourth-century Greek philosopher, whose famous work *On Grief* was described by Cicero as "not a large book but golden, to be learnt word by word."[57] The "gift," a self-fulfilling prophecy, both foreshadows and actually causes the destruction of Neofronus's work. On the level of allegorical signifiers, the clandestine presence of Crantor's perfume stands for a flaw in Neofronus's construction. While he did not use the perfume, neither did he comprehend its deceptive nature. Masks are more important than truth in the age of the arch-aesthetic.

Neofronus: I thought that my vigils would be richly rewarded and that my studies would be welcomed by future generations. In my madness, I envisioned my little treatises winning immortality. . . . My literary works, created by my own hands, elaborated with such care in the course of lucubrative vigils, were, in large part, already refined. They tore apart my works to use the sheets to wrap the perfume in!

Politropo: Oh! What a tremendous sin!

Neofronus: It seems I spent my whole existence producing only the most erudite of wrapping paper; I witness the humiliating descent of my studies, my vigils, and all my hopes.[58]

By demonstrating the vulnerability of the author-text constellation, Alberti set the stage for the planting of Baptista's
text *De pictura*—a perfume in its own right—in the heart of
society and for the entry of the painters and architects into the
vacuum created by the flight of the civic functionaries.

The Humanist and the Artist

So much scholarly attention has been focused on Alberti's differentiation between the architect and the craftsman that the
more important difference between the humanist and the architects and painters has fallen by the wayside.[59] As opposed
to humanists, who are fully aware of the dual-edged arch-
aesthetic, architects and painters must never gain access to
potentially paralyzing insights, question the stability of the
world, or suspect demonic dimensions. "We are obliged to the
architect for the stability, dignity, and glory of public things"—
a specious statement that seems to bestow on the architect
duties reserved for the Humanist.[60] Indeed, painters and architects are primed to bring the humanist dream into a civic
context. The Albertian humanist, "rejecting the patronage of
princes,"[61] speaking a language incomprehensible to the temporal world, and with only a narrow and fragile base of civic
humanism, turns to painters and architects as ultimate
implementors.

Like all functionaries, architects must practice with a certain
amount of *astuzia*. At the close of book 9 we read:

You should not run and offer your services to every man.

It is enough if you give honest advice and correct draughts.

You must take care to have the assistance of honest diligent overseers.

Concern yourself with none but persons of highest rank and quality.

Do not be carried away by a desire for glory. (Glory is reserved for
Alberti's humanist saints.)

Never make alterations without advice.

Unlike the civic functionaries, however, the architects and
painters are never made aware of the saint-cynic dilemma.
They thus belong to a special category of functionaries, primed

and groomed directly by the Albertian humanist to serve as his ultimate delegates. They are the implementors of an elaborately conceived literary strategy which places them in a privileged position. But in order for them to function within the strategy they must not be aware of its artifice. The humanist saints, the ultimate artificers in that they can create and conceal without being contaminated by the arch-aesthetic, create the ultimate illusion when it comes to defining the artists.

De pictura and *De re aedificatoria* are not so much theory relating to the practice of painting and architecture as the setting into practice of Alberti's cultural theory. For example, in order for the artist to perform his task, he must have absolute faith in the public domain, much as Benedetto had *before* his exile, when he was "never discontent with his private fortune and always willing to defend the public trust with the greatest vigilance and faith."[62] In *De re aedificatoria* the following words evoke his presence: "Without your generous wealth, you would not be able to honor yourself, your family, your descendants, or your city."[63] But Benedetto recants his "erroneous way of thinking" to take on the more exalted identity of exiled writer aspiring to sainthood.[64] To keep the artist from doing the same, he must be barred the way to transcendence; he must be prevented from undergoing painful transformations and must be protected from disillusionment with public life. He must be kept in blinders. Baptista, guardian of artists, cautions his charges against the seditious whisperings of the philosophers. Though Alberti himself is proud of his philosophical training,[65] the author of *De pictura* quietly advises the painter to "leave aside the disputes of the philosophers."[66] In *De re aedificatoria,* too, the author states: "I shall not discuss here those philosophical questions."[67]

Limits must be set on the development of the artist's critical faculties, resulting in a tremendous gulf between humanist and artist. Whereas the writer must continually struggle in the library, plow through "infinite books," ruin his eyes reading, spend long nights in thought, the *one and only* book the architect is advised to study, apart from *De re aedificatoria* itself, is *De pictura*—thus enclosing the artist in a clearly delimited and artificially controlled textual world. The architect should, of course, know geometry, mathematics, and a "little astronomy and oratory," but there is a noticeable sense of caution in Alberti's words:

I do not expect the architect to be a Zeuxis in painting, nor a Nicomachus at numbers, nor an Archimedes in the drawing of lines and angles. It is enough if he knows the *Elements of Painting*, which I wrote, be adept in mathematical things . . . as is necessary for the measuring of weights, surfaces, and solids. . . . These arts, together with study and diligence may serve the architect to obtain favor and deliver his name down to posterity.[68]

There is good reason why Alberti does not want the architect to be an "Archimedes in drawing." Archimedes, as he appears in *Profugiorum ab aerumna,* is so withdrawn from the public domain, that it becomes totally irrelevant for him. He is forced to live his obsession, like Theogenius and the exiled Benedetto, in meditative exile. He is forwarded as an *exemplum* not for the artist to follow, but for the writer "hearing and seeing nothing but himself."

Agnolo: Marcello, nearing Syracuse, ordered his army, despite the slaughter of such a noble land, to save Archimedes, the mathematician. . . . They found Archimedes absorbed by geometrical things, which he was drawing on the floor of his house. He was so removed from his senses that even the din of the weapons, the groans of the injured citizens, and yells of the dying multitude, who were killed by fire and collapsing roofs of the temples, didn't move him at all. It seems a miracle that such a din, such a thick fog of smoke and dust, didn't distract him from the investigations and reasonings to which he was devoting himself. . . .[69]

If the architect would be wise to that other world he would soon see through his activities on behalf of the patron. Thus we hear in *Theogenius* that man's insatiable greed causes him to "bore into mountains, build ships, rebuild valleys, and suspend granite from the ceiling, . . . all artifices that reflect our stupidity."[70] But in the preface of *De re aedificatoria,* architects in the patron's employment are praised when they "cut up rocks, bore through mountains, build ships, fill up valleys, and confine lakes."[71] The architect, who by his very nature legitimizes the powers of the establishment, can "perform works of great use and glory," and fulfill his function as long as he does not fathom the depths of society's evil or question the patron's motives.[72] He cannot leave society, even in imagination. He must fuse the artifact into the public realm without friction, and without having to overcome internal obstacles.

It is not surprising that Alberti never refers to his own architectural activity even in *De re aedificatoria,* where, given his autobiographical propensity, this would be not only natural but expected. Alberti's image of himself as a writer, would have made it implausible that he could also recognize himself as an artist under the limited terms of his own definition. Alberti knew all too well that he neither could nor wanted to aspire to the role of naive simulator.

The artists are barred not only from entry into mankind's subconscious, but also into their own. Whereas Alberti explores the psychological problems that arise in the mind of humanists in their ongoing struggle with and against society, nowhere in Alberti's so-called aesthetic treatises (themselves the product of an aesthetic) does he deal with the psychology of the artist. In fact, since collective criteria must structure the psyche of the civic artist, his private thoughts should not be too probing. Baptista, speaking as interlocutor for the prince in *De Iciarchia,* advises his nephews to temper their desire to excel if they want to be good citizens and, ultimately, good patrons in the style of Benedetto before his exile: "Don't trust your talent more than the judgment of benevolent ones, relatives, or those expert scholars in that which you are dealing, since with them rarely will it happen that you will regret it. It is not likely that the judgment of many good and experienced people could be fallacious."[73] Benevolent ones, however, don't exist: relatives are vindictive, and expert scholars are fakes. The writer himself, being exiled, is not in a position of power. Though Baptista's advice is artificial, its deceptive purpose is sanctified by its good intent. The artists must function within the larger context of the postulated myth of cultural continuity and more specifically within the patronage system.

The Albertian humanist, dealing with the night world (*Fatum et Fortuna* and *Somnium*) in which the turbulent workings of society are revealed, may on occasion reach for art as a palliative, but it is a different form of art from that practiced by public artists. Like wine and games, it is a temporary remedy for the anguish of the soul. Agnolo states: "And at times, such investigations being lacking, I built in my mind some very elaborate buildings, conceived with many different orders and numbers of pillars and with various capitals and unusual bases. I connected to these a convenient and graceful framing with wooden floors. And with similar occupations I occupied myself until sleep overcame me."[74] Art as palliative is an indulgence not permitted painters, architects, or sculptors. Metaphysical speculation, insight into man's soul, and understanding of the arch-aesthetic are anathema to their purpose. There is no need for them to be concerned with potentially rebellious thoughts. The architect's world has to be governed by rational discourse that upholds the fiction of a perennially stable society.[75] Agnolo seems to be addressing the artists in the following admonition: "When you don't see and don't hear the many things that can distress you, you see enough when you discern good things from bad things, worthy things from unworthy things, and you hear enough when you hear yourself in those things that are good for virtue and praise. The night has within itself its own pleasures."[76]

Indeed there is something inherently restrictive in Baptista's seemingly harmless assertion that the painter "has nothing to do with things that are not visible. The painter is concerned only with representing what can be seen."[77]

We should not interpret this in a negative light. On the contrary, Alberti is putting together the pieces of a powerful strategy, hoping to engage and ultimately work against the arch-aesthetic. The artists are planted in society as humanist seeds in a polluted soil. Seeing only the *superficie* of existence, they can inhabit the defunct patronly domain in lieu of the humanist writer and execute his intent.

Since the artists are kept from the dark side of life, Alberti can invite them to communicate openly. The unsuspecting artists, though maskless, serve as mask for the humanist. It is an excellent strategy that fools even the realm of *Realpolitik*. Practicing open, naive simulation in candid execution of their profession, the artists are perceived as no threat to society. All they need to know is that "if a man happens to think of anything new [in the arts], he likes to communicate and divulge it for the use of others, *as if coerced by nature* to do so. . . ."[78] And because "there is no one who does not think it an honor to express his opinion on someone else's work," the artist lives exclusively in the public eye.[79] Painting is in itself already so much part of all of mankind that it is intrinsically a public act: "You will not easily find anyone who does not earnestly desire to be accomplished in painting."[80]

Furthermore, Alberti conceals that his artists are actually in direct competition with the arch-aesthetic when he blithely tells the painter that "there is no need to fear that the judgments of censorious and envious critics can in any way detract from the merit of the painting."[81] Just ask Lepidus. Alberti encourages the painter to practice what he himself as a writer skillfully avoids, namely, open and direct communication. The artist is even admonished to take advice from the public, proving thereby that his work is performed within the limited boundaries of society's self-awareness.

> We will work out the whole painting and each of its parts by making sketches on paper and taking advice on it with our friends. . . . Friends should be consulted, and, while the work is in progress, any chance spectators should be welcomed and their opinions heard. The painter's work is intended to please the public. So he will not despise the public's criticism and judgment when he is still in a position to meet its opinion. They say that Apelles used to hide behind his painting, so that the viewers could speak more freely, and he could more decently listen to them enumerating the defects of his work.[82]

To close the circle, Alberti realizes that since the artist functions in the public realm, the art theorist is bound to the conditions of public communication as well. Thus, public texts such as *De pictura* are brought forward *as if* society were functioning properly. As a consequence, Alberti—in the authorial guise of Baptista—acts out the principle of open communication. Whereas in *Scriptor* the writer "discovers" the combined antagonism of "the learned and the unlearned," the author of *De re aedificatoria* and *De pictura* calmly points out that "the learned and the unlearned will agree with me (*doctis et indoctis consentibus*)."[83] In fact, all public artifacts, whether they be treatises, paintings, or buildings, are something in which "the learned and the unlearned both take delight."[84] In *De pictura* Alberti even bows in ironic courtesy to the hated *eruditi*.[85] By alleging congruence of author and society, Alberti masterfully implements his textual strategy.

The textual strategy inherent in the making of *De pictura* and *De re aedificatoria* must be totalizing for there is much at stake. Artists and architects must function less as servants of the corrupt patronage system than as delegates of the spiritual elite. Though they "deal only with those of the highest rank and quality," their ultimate patron is the Albertian writer.[86] If they follow him, they can attain what writers themselves cannot, namely "praise [from the learned and unlearned], riches, *and* endless fame."[87] (Ironically, Alberti the architect, as the delegate of Alberti the writer, has proven the effectiveness of this policy.)

It is tempting for me here to point out how closely related Alberti's thought is to our modern idea of the professional, who is expected to set aside his personal life and interests in the service of the public. This is parallel in a way to the Apollonian categories seen in *Oraculum,* where each person (representing a category) executes only his limited function. Clearly Alberti thought that society would function more smoothly if professional disinterestedness were meticulously adhered to. It is the contrivance of the private person behind the persona that allows the pernicious workings of the arch-aesthetic to disrupt the workings of society.

What is today a routine division of modern life was for Alberti a monumental discovery. In Alberti's scenario architects and painters are pressed into an elaborate ideology that relieves them of ultimate responsibility. This raises a question as to the ethical component of Alberti's counter-aesthetic. Painters and architects have to be above all moral; on this Alberti insists. After all, it links them with the humanistic ethical system. But since they do not set out to reveal the lack of ethics in the real world (something reserved for the saints and cynics) they need not concern themselves with the moral stance of others. Does it not represent an apologia for Alberti's own building activities in the service of Sigismondo Malatesta, who was infamous for his cruelty, perversion, and sadism? In grappling with this issue Alberti, theoretically at least, outfoxed the foxes, envisioning a two-tiered patronal system. The Albertian artists may owe their temporal existence to the patron, but their unquestioning and blind allegiance goes to the humanist cause, which is uncontestably anchored in the absolute.

From the point of view of Alberti's arch-aesthetic, the painter narrows the Narcissistic gap; image and reality come closer. The good artist, by means of perspective, will finally create the illusion of unity. It is, of course, Baptista who leads the way to a reunification of "image and being" and of "learned and unlearned."

He [Baptista] made some incredible things to be closed up in a small box to be seen through a small hole. Vast planes could be seen here, spreading around a huge sea, and far-off regions lost in the distance. He used to call these things demonstrations. They were such that the learned and the unlearned would affirm that they could not recognize it as having been made with a brush, but as true to nature.[88]

In this way the Albertian artists—textual fantasies of the Albertian writers—are the last holdout of the myth of intactness. Their simulation is carried on publicly and without deceptive intent. The learned and unlearned share a common ground in their antagonism to the true humanist conscience but by a clever artifice are led to accept the art of the humanist painters and architects who, unlike mankind at large, function *without* artifice. In essence Alberti's aesthetic theory is based on the ironic proposition that artists alone operate without deception.

The architects and painters present an ironic counter-image to the ambivalent world of the humanist functionaries. Whereas the world at large is adept at self-manipulation (Albertian humanists included), the Albertian artists manipulate at one remove. They are the only characters in Alberti's mental theater who do *not* speculate in aesthetics (a thesis that flies in the face of current scholarly opinion). In a way, we can visualize them as ideal functionaries who set forth from the humanist base camp alongside Theogenius's reflecting pool in the forest to enter the city, where they infiltrate the vicious political and temporal establishments with their "good art." Ostensibly they give their temporal allegiance to the prince, but their spirit, it is hoped, is under the control of the remote, exiled humanist.

The New—Artless—World

Momus opens with the creation of the world. Jove organizes the gods, builds a celestial dwelling, and leans back to "receive the just reward," a life without preoccupations, with the lesser gods and mankind singing his praises. Things do not go as planned. Prometheus steals the sacred fire—the art of simulation—entrusted to the goddess Fate, and gives it to mankind.

The sacred hearth came from the beginning of time. It had, among its other properties, one that was marvelous and unique, namely without the nourishment of any substance, and without support of any liquid it ignited itself, a perpetual flame. Whoever possessed of it became immortal and incorruptible. . . . The sacred fire was maintained among the threads of the material made by the god Virtue. From this sacred fire there derived the threads which were resplendent on the top of the forehead of all the gods. The power of those to whom it was given was that they could transform themselves according to their own talent into any desired figure. . . . When Prometheus stole a ray from the hearth, he was chained for this sacrilege to the Caucasian Mountains.[89]

As noble as the action of Prometheus may seem, it sets in motion an irreversible chain of events. Allegorically, it is equivalent to the moment in which Narcissus saw his image in the pool. The aesthetic age has dawned, but mankind's newly awakened simulative psychology lacks "any sort of regulation or law" and so the prerogative of transformation is soon abused.[90] Human beings quickly learn to copy the very visage of god.[91] The gods are unaware of the implications, but Momus realizes that the celestial order is about to be weakened (the theme of *Oraculum*). As a sign of skepticism Momus, when asked by Jove to contribute to the divine creation, gives the cockroach and the moth, alluding to Libripeta's subterranean world beneath the illusion of order. Momus's warnings are interpreted only as cynicism. To get rid of Momus the gods unite, exile him from the heavens, and force him to lead a life among mortals. Momus turns his exile into a triumphant demonstration of his complaint. Using his own ability to change form at will, he takes on myriad identities. He becomes a philosopher, a poet, and a woman; in fact, he is capable of a "hundred disguises."[92] He is a parody, a counter-image of Baptista: "Momus told [afterward] long stories of his exile [on earth] and of the jokes he played, and also of how he desired to experience all the principles and systems of human life so as to find the best, searching to unite theory with practice, diligence, and exercise, to become the most expert in all the arts."[93]

Momus (and we must not forget that Momus is Alberti's self-critical incarnation) joins the ranks of humans not to help them control their simulation capacity, but to increase it to its ultimate potential; he even teaches women how to use make-up, so that they too can become experts at masking and deception.

Momus has broken through all barriers of constraint, be they from society or from the humanist direction. He realizes that both attempt to control mankind's aesthetic obsession, if for different purposes. He therefore proposes simulation for the sake of simulation, which brings the humanist enterprise to a new extreme—the vagabond intellectual. The world of vagabonding is both artless and the highest form of art. There, simulation *qua* simulation reaches perfection as it is in the service of neither *Realpolitik* nor Albertian humanism. Even Baptista's art of geometry cannot compete: it requires disciplined artifice and is thus on par with a society that has transformed its own evil into a discipline.

Momus: There is this difference between the art of geometry and the art of vagabonding: the future geometrician needs an instructor. The art of vagabonding, however, requires no formal education. Geometry and the other arts require a period of study, fatiguing study, and the active exercise of rules well coordinated with application. They demand instructions of all types, none of which are needed in the art of vagabonding. The vagabond does not have to do anything except act according to his own convenience. He can laugh, accuse, rebuke at will all according to his individual talents, without any evil consequences. He can do what he wants without having his words and actions censured. Under the reign of evil princes, others escape and flee into exile, while you, O vagabond, animate the very fortress of the tyrant.[94]

Momus, a maskless vagabond *au nature*, the humanist dream out of control (in contrast to the artificially created maskless artists), can confidently live "in the theaters, loggias, and public buildings of all types" without experiencing the anxiety of the functionary and without needing blinders, an ironic shadow of Genipatro. The humanist spirit gone haywire has finally managed to infiltrate the defunct body of society. Animating "the very fortress of the tyrant," Momus, like the life-giving parasite that accompanies the shark, can succeed where Jove—not to mention all of the other humanist functionaries—failed.[95] "The vagabond can lead a life free of perturbation and can sleep peacefully, while others dream of flying over the earth, excavating the mountains, going to the edge of the earth and building structures to the sky."[96]

But let us go on with the story. Too late Jove sees that the world he created has gone awry and decides to create a better one (*novum quaerebamus exaedificare mundum*).[97] He begins with a great destruction of men and animals in order to clear the way for the new universe. The inhabitants of the earth, for a moment shocked into self-awareness, try to appease the gods by building a great theater "adorned with gold, gems, flowers, crowns and incense, alabaster panels, and mirrors, with statues of heroes between the columns."[98] The gods, flattered, relent, but still have not come up with a blueprint for a better world. (The theater will become important in the close of the work.) Jove calls a convention of all the gods. In the clamor of disparate voices three groups emerge. Parodying his own humanist program, Alberti describes mock-versions of his saint, cynic, and functionary, now all working at cross-purposes.

As the gods took sides, the passions degenerated into hostility and tumult, until finally there were at least three camps. On one side was Jove, outside of himself with a great desire to construct and collect, by good or bad means, a group of adherents, as many as possible, and organize them for the salvation of mankind.

Opposed to him was assembled a throng of common [gods] prejudiced to their own interests, but who attempted to mask that immoderate love of novelty that inflamed them with their zeal to demonstrate their obsequiousness toward the king of the gods.

In the middle there was a third group formed by those who believed heavily and dangerously that they could put themselves in charge of the ignoble and inconstant masses.[99]

In a bizarre turn Momus gives to Jove a *tabella*, a text—it is a functionary's text—as his contribution for the "redesigning of the new world" and even contrives to have Jove restore him to his "rightful" place, the one to which the humanist had aspired. Jove is fascinated by the knowledge Momus has gained while on earth and amazed to learn that human beings with all their sophistication fail to understand that they are indebted to His Supreme Sovereignty. Alberti, again elaborating ironically on his cosmological theory, has Momus tell Jove that there are three types of men: those who do not believe that the gods exist (the cynics and soldiers of fortune, *Virtus*), those who believe that the gods do not exist but that a belief in them must be maintained so that the populace can be controlled (corrupted politicians), and those who abuse their knowledge of the good arts in their vainglorious search for praise (false intellectuals).

As the honored confidant of Jove, Momus seems to have finally gained an audience with power, the ultimate dream of the false humanist. The other gods, who once ridiculed him, overwhelm him now with praise. Momus argues that his experiences have taught him how to cure the world of its ills. Jove need not destroy the entire earth but only the "perverse race of writers," together with their "schools, books, and libraries."[100] His *tabella*, presumably, would stand then in radiant isolation. It would help to construct a world without masks and without simulation, in which there would be neither art nor artifice.

Many other such pieces of advice were in the manuscript, but the most useful against the boring difficulty of government was that of all existent things one should make three piles. One pile should have what is good and desirable. In the second there should be that which is bad, and in the third, there should be all that which is by itself neither good nor bad. The distribution should take place like this. The gods Activity, Eagerness, Zeal, and Diligence, along with other similar gods, should fill their laps with objects taken from the first pile and, walking through the porticoes, theaters, temples, squares, and all other public places, should offer these things spontaneously to whomever they meet and to whoever shows that they desired these things. In the same way Envy, Ambition, Desire, Laziness, Sloth, and other goddesses of this kind, with their laps filled and open, should distribute willingly the bad things to those who desire them. Regarding the things that are neither good nor bad in and of themselves, but become good or bad on the basis of use, such as wealth, honor, and similar privileges searched for by man, these things should be left all to the decision of Fortuna. She should collect them with full hands and distribute them in the quantity she desires and to whom she likes the best.[101]

The Prophet Unmasked

The plan for a new world where being and image are identical is never implemented. Jove, prompted by Hercules and other gods jealous of Momus's learning, claims to have continued faith in the philosophers. He throws Momus's manuscript carelessly into the library, where it becomes just one of many rotting books. By implication, Jove has rejected the functionary's text because he aspires to the higher tone of the philosophers who flatter Jove with their expectations.

Momus: Some [of the philosophers] asserted that there must exist a single divine leader who regulates all things.

Others argued that there was a perfect correspondence of equal qualities and that thus the number of immortals corresponds to that of the mortals.

Others demonstrated that there existed one mind free of all material presence and of all contact and contamination with corruptible and material things, a mind that is mother and father of all divine and human essences.

Others affirmed that God must create a certain force that is infused in things, making them move, and which radiates in the spirit of men. However, this discordance of opinion among the philosophers was not such that it impeded them all from the single proposition, expressed in diverse ways, to oppose Momus most aggressively.[102]

Momus here exposes in an ironic mode the secret implicit in the humanist ambition to introduce an ideal world of proper correspondences between the divine and the earthly that affords total control and eliminates the ambiguity between word and meaning and the separation of being from image. Like the humanists, Jove too wants a world of total correspondences, where all contingencies are abolished. But only after he has realized the gap in congruences—which can only come about from the alienated perspective of exile—can he confront the falsity of these ideals. We can already anticipate that his aspirations, as articulated by the philosophers, will have to be challenged, and indeed that occurs at the end of *Momus*. But for the moment Jove, not satisfied with the functionary's text, searches for a real philosopher. Momus, now without his text, is unable to maintain control over the volatile gods and loses his exalted position. The ultimate separation of writer from text has now occurred. Momus is expelled once again, this time permanently—castrated and chained to a rock in the ocean with only his head above water. Once a free-roaming vagabond, he is now unable to move. Like the statue Apollo (*Oraculum*), he can neither simulate nor expose simulation, having been reduced to the static condition of mythic time.

Gods and mankind, for a moment united, celebrate his condemnation. Singing and dancing spread over the earth. Only Hercules knows that there is a hollowness to the festivities, but no one listens to his Laocoonian warning of impending doom. The jubilant gods take up residence in statues placed in the great and sumptuous theater constructed in their honor to celebrate the supposed unification; from the vantage point of their statues, the gods witness the "rites of purification." The theater, a microcosm of the heavens, caricatures of course the presence of mythic time on earth. At first everything goes well, and after the ceremony the gods laugh cynically at events surrounding the life of Momus. But when the nymphs of the winds attempt to enter the theater to participate in the festivities, the building collapses in an immense whirlwind of destruction. Because of the storm, in which many statues are damaged and gods injured, the gods retreat hastily and ignobly into the heavens. In the confusion Stupor, Pluto (God of Money), Night, and, fortunately, Hope are left behind on earth.[103]

Jove surveys the debacle. His feeble attempt to create a better world has resulted in disaster; the gods and mankind are more alienated from each other than ever. In the closing paragraphs he realizes that everything was prompted by his own incompetence. Wise now to the logic of alienation, as he is now permanently separated from the mortals (much as Momus is separated from his text), he decides too late to clean his long ignored library and finds Momus's *tabella* on good government. It is doubtful, however, that he will initiate improvements based on the principles it outlines now that the author is permanently severed from his text, much as God is from man.

The all-too-predictable failure of Momus results from an imbalance in Alberti's humanist system. The writer theoretically masks himself from the world, however benign the reason, while remaining on guard against his own masking that, as a genetic predisposition, poses an interior threat to his psyche. Alberti uncannily anticipated his dilemma in *Philodoxeus,* where an intricate system of semiotic pointing passes the hot potato from one authorial interlocutor to the other. Even the artificially contrived masklessness of Baptista results in an inner falsification. And so it is that Momus, a genius of "simulation and dissimulation" and an artisan of "many-tonguedness (*versipellem*)," exposes Baptista as a hagiographic phony.[104] It is Momus who is the mysterious inhabitant of Baptista's house in *Vita.* He is at once counter-humanist and humanist *par excellence.*

Momus: Feign and yet do not [appear to be feigning]. . . . The essential principle is this one only; namely, that there is no feeling that one cannot cover with perfection under the appearance of honesty and innocence. Adapting our words, we will brilliantly attain our image, and whatever particular externality of our persona, in a manner that seems to be similar to those who are believed to be beautiful and moderate. What a splendid thing it is to know how to hide the more secret thoughts with the wise artifice of colorful and deceptive fiction.[105]

This "wise artifice" that enables one to survive in the archaesthetic is the ultimate art. Momus, ironically, "simulating those who are believed to be beautiful and moderate" (like Baptista), comprehends that the discourse on the good and happy life is a sham, and passes himself off as "beautiful and moderate," fooling even Jove into allowing him to head the commission in charge of establishing a better world. His ironic playacting is so perfect that even the keen-eyed goddess Fraud considers him a disciple.[106] The total identification of Alberti's humanist enterprise with Fraud (equivalent to the totalizing mask inherent in the writing of *De pictura* and *De re aedificatoria*) closes the circle that began with Narcissus's alienation.

Exposed to irony, Alberti's humanist program collapses on its initial and seemingly unproblematic premise of the author in search of himself. The pardonable attempt to project an ideal model (*De commodis litterarum atque incommodis*) is itself revealed as the symptom of an incurable disease. The writer cannot find the authentic voice, because "mortal gods" cannot duplicate what is ultimately God's prize possession, ethics, and so even the effort to improve the world cannot escape the arch-aesthetic curse. There is no Archimedian point in the absolute. By implication, ethics and aesthetics do not interact according to the law of correspondences. Instead of pointing beyond itself to *autorità,* the text becomes a mere physical object, words on paper, another dusty *codex,* and worse, the *velum* on which is painted a deceptive discourse.

Peniplusius: The True One

Unlike Plato in the *Republic* Alberti never argues that power and knowledge should coalesce in one person. In fact, one might view Jove as a caricature of Plato's philosopher-king. The divergent aims of humanism and temporal power have to be made visible to prevent such a fusion from taking place under cover. Once their separate and antithetical natures have been accepted, contact can be made between the two, as Alberti charts out, in four ways: the writer-saint, the civic functionary, the artist or architect, and the cynic-vagabond. The first transcends the arch-aesthetic by embodying a supposedly uncontaminated realm of textual authority. The second compromises with the arch-aesthetic and employs artifice in an ostensibly benign way. The third is sent to infiltrate the power base, text in hand. The fourth is the uprooted vagabond living in public streets and for that very reason "invisible" in a world of mask makers.

An alternative to all these possibilities would be, of course, a miracle, which brings us to Peniplusius (Poor-Rich Man, i.e., poor in wealth, rich in virtue) and Megalophos (Grand and Plumed) and their competition for the last vacant seat in Caronte's boat, as described in the final pages of *Momus*. Peniplusius, a whimsical utopic afterthought, represents the impossible—as we now know—ideal scenario of the living text. He is "the true one" whom Baptista, Momus, Gelastus, and Philoponius had vainly tried to become. Caronte, seeking refuge in Hades and aware of the fate of the now textless Momus, recounts the remarkable tale of Peniplusius to Gelastus. Peniplusius, Caronte relates, was once among a group of shades whom he ferried across the river Styx; there was only one seat left, and Peniplusius successfully challenged the tyrant Megalophos for it. Such a power struggle, in which a humanist claimed the seat of honor over the representative of temporal government, would, of course, be inconceivable in real life. Peniplusius, first encountered in *Intercoenales*, had been immensely effective in his lifetime. His virtue had been recognized, his true leadership acclaimed, and his numerous efforts on behalf of the city acknowledged by all except Megalophos, whom he addressed thus:

Peniplusius: You have betrayed your function and behaved not as a king but as a tyrant. If you had procured your wealth for the state, then you would have accomplished your duty, but even then, no glory would have come to you. The merit does not belong to you, but to all the citizens, for they conquered wealth by wars or increased it by their own devices. I ornamented the capital and empire with monuments, and with my love I maintained peace and tranquility, and by my guidance I provide many subjects with fame and grandeur. All that we undertake in this field, however, is futile if we get carried away by the approval of the masses and want to be one with them.

I don't see why you should receive merit. You passed the night in sleeping if you were drunk or you passed it [merit] up for lust. I on the other hand was watching from my tower, protecting the city from fires, the citizens from the enemy and you yourself from the plots of your people. You passed by the laws, but I had to enforce them. Very often when you gave a speech, the people snickered, but everyone would listen to me with the greatest of attention when I gave a general order. In the battle you exhorted your soldiers, but I gave the signal for them to fight. Soldiers paid homage to you but they assaulted the enemy and they returned only when I blew my trumpet.

Finally, while everybody was flattering you, they were obeying me. Furthermore, you have caused laziness in citizens, and isn't this exactly the cause of many misfortunes and troubles which took place in the city, and isn't it the reason for all the envy, strife, and misfortune that has invaded public, private, religious, and lay life? For what purpose do you tell of your silly ostentations and other ignoble deeds of your rule? How could you boast of having built temples and theaters, when they were for your own glory and the survival of your name and not as ornaments of the city?[107]

Peniplusius prevails; "everyone obeyed him." The very spirit of social conscience, doing everything silently, effortlessly, and with modesty and strength, he is the *only* figure in Alberti's mental theater representing the successful bonding of mythic and historical time, a functioning of ethics in aesthetic time, and the impossible fusion of humanism with power. Peniplusius does not suffer, is never exiled, needs no text, and requires no legal system. He *is* the text, the icon come to life. This story, told in the darkening hours before the whirlwinds circle the earth, is accompanied by a Mephistolian laugh from the wings of Alberti's theater.

Postscript: Alberti as Architect

It is with some hesitation that I comply with the request of scholars and friends familiar with my work to attempt a comparison between Alberti's literary and aesthetic theories and his architectural projects. I hesitate because we move into an area where there is little historical evidence to sustain interpretation. Alberti rarely remarked on his projects in his writings, a circumstance that should not be taken lightly given his propensity for self-projection. Scholars have all too easily glossed over this by constructing precarious parallels between the built work and promising passages in *De re aedificatoria*. In actuality, the relationship between that text and the built work is far from clear and cannot be reduced to the simplistic equation of theory and practice. To take *De re aedificatoria* as the authentic voice of the author speaking in a theory mode is to read all too innocently (see "The Humanist and the Artist"). Nor are there many documents extant that would help us unravel Alberti's intent. The Rucellai facade, for example, is connected to Alberti by circumstantial evidence alone; for S. Sebastian there is only a letter; for S. Maria Novella and S. Pancrazio, merely a statement by Vasari; and it is still uncertain what, if any, Alberti's contribution was to Nicholas V's rebuilding projects at the Vatican.[1] When it comes to plans we are on even thinner ice; there is only one (showing only modest architectural skills) for a bath house that was never built.[2] Even the buildings yield few decisive cues. S. Andrea was begun *after* Alberti's death; and the Arco del Cavallo in Ferrara, attributed to him from circumstantial evidence, was moved from an as yet undetermined location. S. Francesco was never finished, and S. Sebastiano underwent mutations almost from its conception and was largely completed after Alberti's death.

For all these reasons investigations into Alberti's architecture can only exist in the realm of speculation. Scholars of Wölfflinian provenance can advantageously rely on their connoisseur's eye: "One look at the Volta del Cavallo," a scholar states, "is enough to convince one it is the work of Alberti, though there is no documentary evidence to prove it."[3] But if one wants to go beyond merely identifying Alberti's hand to arrive at a critical understanding of his thoughts on architecture, one arrives at a dead end, a circumstance which has led many scholars to clutch at Alberti's classicism, as it seems the most secure aspect of his work. But since the Renaissance is defined in these terms anyway, a tautological argument results that leads nowhere.

Alberti's cultural and aesthetic theories, ciphered as they are, might help in moving beyond the commonplace Renaissance themes of proportion, harmony, and classicism. For example, we would expect from earlier chapters that Alberti viewed each commission as a separate experiment in an overarching program. Keeping his literary works in mind, we would look for certain salient features such as distancing, social masking, irony, dual languages, medieval and classical elements in a dialectic, fragmentation, biographical notations, covert and overt meanings, an ecclesiastically styled skepticism toward the classical past, and last but not least context displacement, that is, the personalization of given public elements.

Let us then look at one of Alberti's earliest works, S. Francesco in Rimini, begun around 1448 and commissioned by Sigismondo Malatesta (figure 10). Whereas it is often held that Alberti was attracted to the court of Sigismondo because the vivacious and energetic ruler of Rimini had numerous humanists in his employ, it appears very likely that Alberti, as friend of Pius II, viewed Sigismondo with reservations similar to those of the pope, who openly denounced Sigismondo for his cruelty, sadism, greed, and sexual perversion.[4] It might seem strange that Alberti, the paragon of morality, would accept a commission from such a man. However, did Sigismondo, a sort of Megalophos, not epitomize the *civitas perversa* that figures so greatly in Alberti's writings, and would that not offer an opportunity to make manifest the dialectic between the humanist program and the frenzied world?

The assignment given to Alberti was to transform a humble Franciscan church into a structure *all'antica*. That it was a Franciscan church must have, more than anything, attracted Alberti to the commission, as Franciscan thought was an important component of his philosophy. But if he interpreted the structure as that "simple and unadorned flute" that, though costing much less than the ornate one, has a more beautiful

Figure 10
S. Francesco, Tempieto Maletestiano (Electa), Rome.

sound—which is how he saw his writings—how was he to ren-
ovate the structure without destroying its essence?[5] He solved
the problem by providing its dialectial opposite, a "classical"
neopagan realm (literally a defunct realm) of sarcophagi, each
framed by an arch. The old structure, visible through the
classical screen, appears untouched by the new, for churches,
Alberti explains, should not be "infected by the contamination
of secular life,"[6] and, in this case, so one could add, the contamination of Sigismondo's court. Creating a building that ne-
gates itself, Alberti invented a design where the old structure
haunts the new one, throwing the latter into doubt (figure 11).
The defunct society fails to bury the "pure and simple" that,
in dignified repose, still remains intact. As an ensemble, however, it is an anxious proposition, much as the one of Leopis
and Libripeta.

Figure 11
Side view of Tempieto Maletestiano (Electa).

Figure 12
The facade of the Rucellai Palace. (Sergio Anelli, courtesy of Elemond, Milan)

The Rucellai facade also deals with the problem of masking, though here enacted by Alberti for a patron Alberti admired (figures 12, 13). Even though the facade is an obvious expression of temporal society, which for Alberti is by its very nature masked, it is not a deception as it is employed in the context of a humanist functionary. Since the two right-hand bays were built in a second building phase and possibly not under Alberti's direct control, it has been argued that further expansion had been planned, but I find it unlikely that the carefully crafted unfinished edge of the facade, an architectural delight revealing the individual cross-sections of the various component parts of the facade (architraves, string courses, moldings, and arches) was accidental. One might conjecture that the incomplete facade may have been purposefully designed to evoke a state of ruin. Incompletion, facing the future, and fragmentation, facing the past, are the curses associated with the tem-

On Leon Baptista Alberti

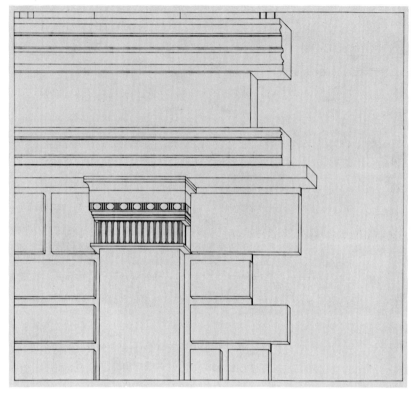

Figure 13
Detail of facade of Rucellai Palace (drawn by Lee Gray).

poral world. Just as Alberti's writings discuss this issue and indeed thematize it (see "Libri Disvoluti"), this facade presents this both-and situation as an architectural problem.

With the facade of S. Maria Novella (1458), Alberti again had to cope with the given, and again he saw this as an opportunity to express the dialectic of the spiritual and the temporal—in this case, in terms of earthly Fame and heavenly Glory (see "Philodoxeus" and "The Prince") (figure 14). When Alberti took over the commission, only the lower part of the facade with the six niches for sarcophogi had been completed. They were, so one might conjecture, the realm of earthly fame, but not that one alienated from eternal Glory as at S. Francesco. It is the Fame of the humanist city (Genipatro), interlocked by means of the new design with the realm of the eternal, that is represented by the pediment temple above; the facade is an ideogram of the ideal unification. We are reminded of a passage in *Della Famiglia* (see "Prince And His Ottimo Artefice"):

Glory springs up in public squares; reputation is nourished by the voice and judgment of many persons of honor, and in the midst of people. Fame flees from all solitary and private spots to dwell gladly in the arena [together with Glory] where crowds are gathered and celebrity is found; there the name is bright and luminous of one who with hard sweat and assiduous toil for noble ends has projected himself up out of silence, darkness, ignorance, and vice.[7]

At first glance the facade seems to express no more than the standard medieval topos differentiating Fame from Glory. This brings us to the entablature separating the two zones, a frieze ornamented with fifteen square panels. Recalling Alberti's historiography and the mediating role of the writers-saints, I am tempted to recognize this middle zone as their realm. Perhaps, in light of Alberti's autobiographical imagination, I can even be so bold as to suggest that the fifteen panels might stand for the fifteen letters of his name: BAPTISTA ALBERTI.

In S. Sebastiano (begun around 1460), in Mantua, Alberti could not establish this type of dialectic, as his assignment consisted of erecting a new building. The chapel was commissioned by Lodovico Gonzaga to house a relic of St. Sebastian, the patron saint evoked in times of plague. Is it coincidental

Figure 14
The facade of S. Maria Novella (adapted and redrawn by the author from Franco
Borsi, *Leon Battista Alberti* [New York: Harper & Row, 1977]).

that Alberti designed churches dedicated to St. Sebastian and St. Francis? Both figure prominently in his iconography of the saintly humanist, as they represent a state of protracted suffering, of enduring. At any rate, St. Sebastian's martyrdom, translated into the protracted suffering of the humanist saint, constituted a theme that greatly stimulated Alberti's autobiographic fantasy (see "The Twelve Rings").

It seems that only the lower part of the building was completed during Alberti's life. It had five openings, as can be seen on a photograph made before the addition of the stairs. Whether the upper part conforms to Alberti's original design is unknown. A plan drawn by a certain Antonio Labaccom, seemingly copied from the original, shows three entrances as opposed to the present five on the piano nobile (figure 15).[8] Therefore, instead of an awkward three openings on both levels, as some reconstructions have it, I see five on the ground floor and three on the upper (figure 16). Howard Saalman has convincingly argued that access to the chapel was not from the front but from the sides.[9] A classical precedent for this is the fourth-century Temple of Clitumnus near Spoleto, on the road between Rome and Urbino. It too has four pilasters on the facade. Alberti may well have known this building, as Nicholas V had completed a castle there.

The building's theoretical importance lies, however, not so much in the facade as in the volumetric organization of its parts. Much as in *Philodoxeus*, where Alberti gave the academicians what they wanted, and in *Vita St. Potiti*, where he gave the Vatican what it wanted while simultaneously developing his own ideology, this building also has two layers of meaning. One reading is intended to satisfy the patron; the other spells out the Albertian masterplan. For the patron Alberti designed a project that certainly appealed to Gonzaga's vanity, as it exalted him to the rank of king by alluding to the conflation of a king's two separate natures, the divine and the earthly (see "Writer-Saint"). Kings and bishops were considered *personae mixtae* (combining spiritual and secular) or *personae geminatae* (human by nature and divine by grace). Howard Saalman's research confirms my thesis that Alberti translated this image of theological duality into architectual form. The building is

Figure 15
The plan of S. Sebastiano, redrawn by author according to the measurements in the
Antonio Labacco sketch (drawn by Lee Gray).

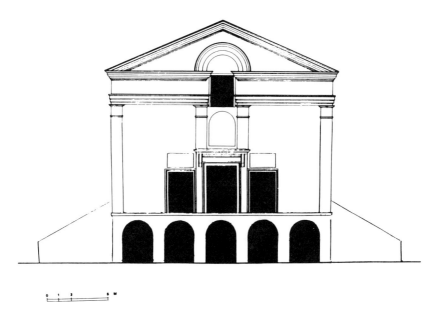

Figure 16
The facade of S. Sebastiano. (author)

actually a double chapel. The lower chapel, opening out onto
a piazza, is for the exhibition of the sarcophogi and relates to
the physical nature of the patronal family; the upper chapel,
an emblematic Greek cross, refers to his divine nature. Thus
the building bestows on the family of a onetime *condottieri* the
essential attributes of theologically defined kingship.

This, however, is only one reading of the architectural text;
we still have to discern the covert meaning. Much as the zone
on the facade of S. Maria Novella (according to my theory)
represents that of the mediating humanist saint, here too one
finds a third architectural element. Above the entrance portico
is a chamber where the relic of St. Sebastian was stored, an
idiosyncratic space largely ignored by historians. Obviously a
sacred realm, the room has a single window which opens onto
the piazza. It was from this window, equivalent to a divine eye
turned toward the secular, that on the appointed day the relic
was ritualistically exhibited for public adoration.[10] Furthermore, given Alberti's homonymic style, the building can be

read as symbolizing the crucification; the window then serves as the *speculum* into the divine heart.[11] A paradigm of the intact humanist realm, St. Sebastian could be equated with Philoponius, the ideal writer-saint and Albertian humanist *non plus ultra*, himself a *deus-homo* with two natures. The iconography and its homonymic conflation brings into focus the vanishing point toward which all of Alberti's thought strives, namely the miraculous interlocking of the terrestial realm with humanist sainthood.

Let us turn now to Alberti's last work, S. Andrea, also in Mantua (figure 17), designed in 1470 but begun after Alberti's death and not completed until 1702.[12] As is well known, this work shows Alberti's growing familiarity with classical forms and details. The interior draws on the volumetric monumentality of Roman structures and its facade brings to mind a Roman triumphal arch. These forms are often heralded as typical examples of Alberti's classicism.

What instantly disqualifies the building from being an ideal Renaissance church is that it is not freestanding but integrated into the urban fabric (figure 18). In fact, documents show that the building was started at the left-hand corner of the facade where it abuts the late-Gothic bell tower constructed in 1413.[13] No attempt was made to make the church appear to be freestanding. Presumably Alberti could have shifted the facade a bit or changed it in some way if he had wanted to create that impression.

In S. Francesco, Alberti, serving an evil patron, had to create a symbol of the defunct world opposing the primordially simple; in S. Andrea, working for a patron of moral stature whom he respected, Alberti had the opportunity to represent the positive aspect of his dialectic, rendering a microcosmic model of the intact realm. As there were no Roman ruins to speak of in Mantua, he compensated by delivering an "Etruscan temple," as he himself called the church. The structure thus imparted to Gonzaga historical legitimization and *grandezza* while at the same time affording Alberti a platform to stage a historical event within the given context. In S. Francesco the classical, representing the frenzied world, was not allowed to touch the sacred. Here, in a very different political setting, the

Figure 17
S. Andrea. (author)

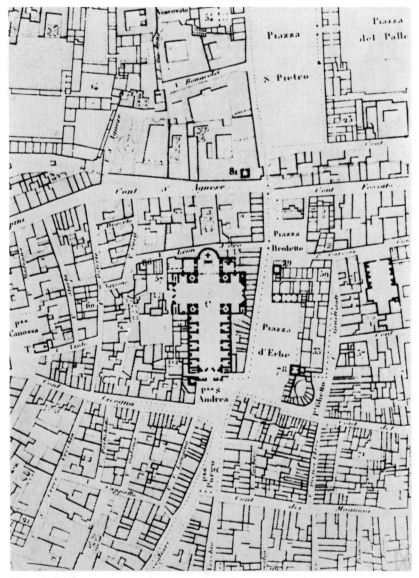

Figure 18
Site plan of S. Andrea. (Archivo del Stato, Mantua)

classical structure is interpreted as benign and as historically primary, with the city appearing to have built itself in its shadow. It thus demonstrates the successful interlocking—and not the dialectical opposition—of the spiritual and the temporal. As there were no other significant Roman ruins in the town there was no significant basis on which to contrast the real and the illusory. The substitution of the make-believe for the real was undetectable. The illusion was complete.

Alberti simulated the process of time. Ruins, as he would have known them from Rome, were frequently inhabited; bell towers were added or were incorporated into new structures (figure 19). Alberti evoked such an image by making the facade touch the bell tower, which, by means of a typical Albertian reversal, was meant to appear to have been constructed after the church. Furthermore, the building appears to have been nibbled into by the encroaching city, especially on the south, where a row of shops separated the wall of the nave from the Piazza dell'Erbe. The portico can also be read as an arcaded street, serving not only to provide axial entrance to the church but also to afford lateral access to an alleyway (now a courtyard) on the north side of the church. The building, therefore, reconstructs a simulated medieval context, demonstrating the ongoing presence of society's origins successfully embedded in the city (figure 20). In a sense, this could be viewed as the ideal humanist function implemented.

Alberti's "reconstruction" of the city of Mantua by means of a church projected backward in time (much as the "forgery" *Philodoxeus*) is equivalent to a miracle, for this ideal state could never come about naturally in chronological time, according to Alberti's cultural theory (see "Peniplusius, The True One"). But the process can be simulated as much as writer and text can be made to appear unified by means of a totalizing mask (see "The Humanist and the Artist"). Ironically, from an ecclesiastical point of view, S. Andrea was built to celebrate a miracle of its own: the liquification of the dried blood of Christ on Ascension Day. Beginning in 1401, when the vials were presented to the faithful, the church began to attract ever larger numbers of pilgrims; sometimes crowds of over 10,000 surged in, eager to benefit from the healing powers. Even Pius II, who

Figure 19
Jan Miel. *Porticus of Octavia.* ca. 1650. (Archives Photographiques, Paris)

Figure 20
Aerial photo of S. Andrea. (Giovetti, Mantua)

is said to have fallen ill while in Mantua, recovered after having prayed before the relics.[14] The contrast between the ecclesiastical miracle and Alberti's idea of a miracle is worth contemplating. The latter can, by definition, never occur in historical time, as it is the unattainable image of civic posterity. It can however be constructed as a "clever artifice" to simulate a version of historical time as it should have been.

Notes

Introduction

1. Heiner Mühlmann, *L. B. Alberti: Aesthetische Theorie der Renaissance* (Bonn: Rudolf Habelt Verlag, 1982).

2. Ibid., 14.

3. Giovanni Santinello, *L. B. Alberti: Una visione estetica del mondo e della vita* (Florence: G.C. Sansoni Editore, 1962), 157.

4. Ibid., 135.

5. Joan Gadol. *Leon Battista Alberti: Universal Man of the Early Renaissance* (Chicago: University of Chicago Press, 1969), 214. Gadol argues correctly that "no single work can serve to characterize in full the nature of his thought" (19, 213). Yet her practically exclusive focus on Alberti's aesthetics counters her intent. A discussion of what she calls Alberti's "humanistic" writings appears only in the last chapter and treats these texts quite summarily.

6. Ibid., 95.

7. Eugenio Garin, "Il pensiero di L. B. Alberti nella cultura del Rinascimento," *Accademia Nazionale dei Linei* 209 (1974): 21–22.

8. Ibid., 22.

9. Ibid., 23.

10. Eugenio Garin, "Il pensiero di L. B. Alberti: caratteri e contrasti," *Rinascimento* 12 (1972): 18.

11. Franco Borsi, *Leon Battista Alberti* (Milan: Electa Editrice, 1975), 7. "L'aura' nobilissima, lo schermo dialettico, le dotte citazioni, l'intento pedagogico caratteristiche communi a tutta l'opera albertiana e non solo a quella—perché i riferimenti alla cultura contemporanea sono stretti e molteplici—non possono eliminare un dubbio di fondo. E cioè, che al di là di tutto questo che ha dato origine alla monumentalità dell'Alberti e al suo cliché di uomo universale, fossero in fondo presenti una sostanziale dilacerazione, una sottile angoscia, una vena di pessimismo nella ormai constatata frattura tra cultura e realtà; una frattura ora conscientemente approfondita sul piano di una dolce evasione che prefigura i vantaggi, la *commoditas,* delle lettere, rispetto ai condizionamenti della realtà; ora invece tentata di superare o suturare attroverso tentativi di impegno concreto, di pratiche risoluzioni."

12. Lorenzo Begliomini, "Note sull'opera dell'Alberti: il 'Momus' e il 'De re aedificatoria,'" *Rinascimento* 12 (1972): 267–83. Begliomini argues that in contrast to the pair *De re aedificatoria* and *Della Famiglia* there are Alberti's less controlled works. "It seems that at certain moments he [Alberti] feels it necessary to experience liberty, to give vent to his feelings . . ." (268). "The problem of an Alberti 'of two faces (*della doppia faccia*),'" so he holds, "is inevitable" (267). Though Begliomini asks, "How can they be harmonized?" it is clear that once one begins with an artificial distinction not proved by Alberti's own statements, questions as to a "harmony" are equally misleading.

13. Anicio Bonucci, *Opere Volgari di Leon Baptista Alberti per la piu parte inedite e tratte dagli autografi* (Florence: Tipografia Galileina, 1843), volume 1, p. civ. In his *Vita anonyma,* for example, Alberti makes the following reference to his writings: "Fuerunt

qui ejus dicta, et seria, et ridicula complurima colligerent, quae quidem ille ex tempore, atque vestigio celerius ediderit ferme, quam praemeditarit."

14. Myron P. Gilmore, *The World of Humanism* (New York: Harper and Row, 1952), 204.

15. For Platonic and Aristotelian concepts of man and ethics see: Martha C. Nussbaum, *The Fragility of Goodness* (Cambridge: Cambridge University Press, 1986), 5ff.

16. Cecil Grayson, *Leon Baptista Alberti: Opere Volgari* (Bari: Gius, Laterza and Figli, 1966), volume 1, p. 140.

17. Giovanni Farris, *De commodis litterarum atque incommodis, Defunctus* (Milan: Marzorati, Editore, 1971), 210.

18. Eugenio Garin, "Intercenali Inedite," *Rinascimento* 12 (1965): 82.

19. For humanist reaction to the past, let it suffice to mention: Theodor E. Mommsen, "Petrarch's Conception of the 'Dark Ages,'" *Speculum* 17 (1942): 226–42; and Herbert Weisinger, "The Renaissance Theory of the Reaction Against the Middle Ages as a Cause of the Renaissance," *Speculum* 20 (1945): 461–67.

The Autobiographical Imagination

1. Giovanni Santinello, *L.B. Alberti: Una visione estetica del mondo e della vita* (Florence: G.C. Sansoni Editore, 1962), 21ff.

2. The scholar, in attempting to deal with Alberti's writings, must not freeze the author prematurely in a single position. One could compare the unsuspecting scholar to Andrew Berestov in Pushkin's *Tales of Belkin,* who discovers that Akulina, the peasant girl he loves, is actually a landowner's daughter Liza. But Liza, deceiving both her lover and her father, plays her two roles with equal aplomb: now she is archaic peasant girl, now powdered aristocrat. Andrei, who takes the world literally, fails to understand Liza's role playing. For him form and content coincide. He sees only "Akulina" and even continues to call her that, hoping thereby to enforce in her the identity of word and meaning. Liza-Akulina resolves things on a higher level: she enjoys living in both worlds, in contrast to Andrei's either-or proposition. Let us not make Andrei's mistake.

De Commodis Litterarum atque Incommodis

3. Giovanni Farris, *De commodis litterarum atque incommodis, Defunctus* (Milan: Marzorati, Editore, 1971), 56, 144. "Quare siquid fame et laudi consulendum putabunt pulchre domi sese occlusos detinebunt: resque omnes foris elegantes, amenas, admirationeque dignas omnino hi tales abdicabunt a se atque probscribent quo maiori, ut opus est, assiduitate ad literrarum cognitionem sese obfirment. . . . Velim tamen in eam partem nostra dicta prodesse studiosis ut cum sua prudentia et ratione cuncta que a me explicita sunt tenuerint, tum, me adiutore, siquid valeo, excitati diligentius, perspiciant litteras non ad lasciviam, non ad inanium caducarumque rerum expectationem conferre."

4. Not much is known about Carlo's life. See: Girolamo Mancini, *Vita di Leon Battita Alberti* (Rome: Bardi Editore, 1967), 25.

193

5. Farris, *De commodis litterarum atque incommodis, Defunctus,* 42, 44. "Tu semper aut gerendis negociis aut in litterarum cognitione versaris. Ego autem qui me totum tradidi litteris, ceteris posthabitis rebus, omnia posse libentius debeo quam diem aliquam nihil aut lectitando aut commentando preterire. . . . Nam prestantius sic esse recte opinantur ii qui laudem cupiant, quippiam etsi non omni ex parte perfectum atque absolutum conari, quam in litteris silentio consenescere."

6. Ibid., 144, 62.

7. Ibid., 62, 60.

8. Anicio Bonucci, *Opere Volgari di Leon Baptista Alberti per la piu parte inedite e tratte dagli autografi.* (Florence: Tipografia Galileina, 1843), Volume 1, p. xciv. In his *Vita anonyma,* Alberti makes the following reference to *De commodis litterarum atque incommodis:* "Eo tempore scripsit ad fratrem de Commodis literarum, atque Incommodis, quo in libello ex re ipsa perdoctus, quidnam de literis foret sentiendum, disseruit."

9. Farris, *De commodis litterarum atque incommodis, Defunctus,* 60.

10. Ibid.

11. Ibid., 48. ". . . ego esse litteras longe iucundissimas censerem. Dumque ceteris omnibus disciplinis illi cultum litterarum postponendum putarent, ego litteras rebus omnibus preponendas ducerem. Denique ita me cognitioni litterarum dedicaram omnino, ut nihil in litteris preclarum esse diceretur quod animo et voluntate non appeterem, quod laboribus, cura, atque vigiliis non prosequerer, quodve summa diligentia et observantia quantum possem non excolerem. Que posset enim apud me esse opinio aut institutum laudabilius non videbam. Excelsi quidem animi officium putabam labores, vigilias, omnesque reliquas studiorum curas et difficultates subire ac perferre vel sciendi causa, vel honoris et fame adipiscende gratia, quas me res posse litteris assequi existimabam."

12. Ibid., 148, 150, 118.

13. Ibid., 64.

14. Ibid., 116.

15. Ibid., 110.

16. Ibid., 42, 44. "Nihil mihi unquam pervestiganti in mentem subiit, quod ipsum a priscis illis divinis scriptoribus non pulchre esset occupatum, ut neque eam rem viro hac etate doctissimo quam iidem illi melius dicere, neque mihi similia illis apte et condigne agere relictum sit."

17. Ibid., 148, 150, 132.

18. Ibid., 142, 145, 74.

19. Ibid., 134.

20. Ibid., 138.

21. Ibid., 146, 148.

22. Ibid., 46. ". . . tum etiam quod fuerim materiam nactus non vulgarem neque satis ante hoc tempus explicitam, gratum tibi futurum arbitror."

23. See, for example, Boethius's *On the Supreme Good.*

24. Richard de Bury, *Philobiblon,* ed. Michael Maclogan, trans. E. C. Thomas (Oxford: Shakespeare Head Press, 1960), 109ff. See also *De librorum copia* by Petrarch, in Conrad H. Rawski, *Petrarch: Four Dialogues for Scholars* (Cleveland: Press of Western Reserve University, 1967), 30–55. The writer is also defined, in keeping with a longstanding medieval tradition, as a sage training himself in self-control, welcoming poverty, and resisting detractors. See: Beryl Smalley, *English Friars and Antiquity in the Early Fourteenth Century* (New York: Barnes and Noble, 1960), 52; and Ernst Robert Curtius, *European Literature and the Latin Middle Ages* (New York: Pantheon Books, 1953), 469.

25. Helene Wieruszowski, "Ars dictaminis in the Time of Dante," *Medievalia et Humanistica* 1 (1943): 105.

26. See for example: Thomas à Kempis, *Imitation of Christ,* trans. and introd. Leo Sherley-Price (New York: Dorset Press, 1952), 27f.

27. Lucia Cesarini Martinelli, "Philodoxeos Fabula, Edizione critica," *Rinascimento* 17 (1977): 147.

28. For the classical sources of this piece see Farris's introduction to *De commodis litterarum atque incommodis.* Farris, however, quotes from classical sources almost as if they were statements from Alberti.

29. Farris, *De commodis litterarum atque incommodis, Defunctus,* 136.

30. Ibid., 44. "Condant illi quidem historiam, tractent mores principum ac gesta rerum publicarum eventusque bellorum." Alberti is contrasting the interests of an older generation (*maturis et perfecte eruditis viris*) with those of a younger generation (*nobis . . . iuvenibus*). See also: Donald J. Wilcox, *The Development of Florentine Humanist Historiography in the Fifteenth Century* (Cambridge: Harvard University Press, 1969), 8. As Lauro Martines points out, all humanists, whatever their stripe, made candid alliances with power. Lauro Martines, *Power and Imagination: City-States in Renaissance Italy* (New York: Vintage Books, 1980), 199–200, 201. On the definition of *res gestae* see: F.P. Pickering, *Literature and Art in the Middle Ages* (London: Macmillan and Co., 1970), 197.

31. B. L. Ullman, "Leonardo Bruni and Humanistic Historiography," *Medievalia et Humanistica* 4 (1946): 49–50; Giuseppe Biasiaccia, "Past/Present: Leonardo Bruni's 'History of Florence,'" *Renaissance and Reformation* n. s. 9, no. 1 (February, 1985): 1–18.

32. Wilcox, *The Development of Florentine Historiography,* 8.

33. Farris, *De commodis litterarum atque incommodis, Defunctus,* 142.

34. Ronald G. Witt, *Coluccio Salutati and His Public Letters* (Geneva: Libraire Droz, 1976), 28–34. See also: Ernst Curtius, "Die Lehre von den drei Stilen in Altertum und Mittelalter," *Romanische Forschungen* 64 (1952): 66–69; Erich Auerbach, "Sermo humilis," *Romanische Forschungen* 64 (1952): 304–64 and vol. 66 (1954): 1–64; Peter Herde, "Politik und Rhetorik in Florenz am Vorabend der Renaissance," *Archiv für Kulturgeschichte* 47 (1965): 209.

35. See Petrarch's *De ignorantia.* The bulk of the text may be found in *F. Petrarch Prose,*

ed. F. Neri, G. Martellotti, P. G. Ricci, E. Carrara, E. Bianchi (Milan: Ricciardi, 1951 and 1955). For an analysis see Kenelm Foster, *Petrarch, Poet and Humanist* (Edinburgh University Press, 1984), 149–56.

36. On Augustinianism in early humanism see: David Gutierrez, *The Augustinians in the Middle Ages, 1357–1517* (Villanova: Villanova University, 1983); William Bouwsma, "The Two Faces of Humanism and Augustinianism in Renaissance Thought," *Itinerarium Italicum: The Profile of the Italian Renaissance in the Mirror of its European Transformations, Dedicated to Paul Oskar Kristeller,* ed. H. A. Oberman and T. A. Brady, Jr. (Leiden: E.J. Brill, 1975), 3–61; and Charles Trinkaus, "Erasmus, Augustine, and the Nominalists," *Archiv für Reformationsgeschichte* 67 (1976): 5–32.

37. Farris, *De commodis litterarum atque incommodis, Defunctus,* 102.

38. Ibid., 138.

39. Ibid. "Quis non ante oculos veluti pictam rem prospiciat casum atque perniciem disciplinarum et artium? Quis non condoluerit tantam iacturam, tantunque naufragium in litteris factum esse intuens."

40. Ibid., 140.

Philodoxeus

41. Martinelli, "Philodoxeos Fabula, Edizione critica," 111–234.

42. By the early fifteenth century Minerva would have been a well-known figure, particularly among Franciscan and Dominican theologians, who more than any others made frequent use of the classical pantheon in their studies. In one work she is compared to St. Thomas Aquinas, and in another she is used as a metaphor of the peace of Jesus. Smalley, *English Friars and Antiquity,* 211, 176. Minerva was often associated with Mary, as for example in the Dominican church Santa Maria sopra Minerva in Rome, which was built over a Roman temple to Minerva and which was during the fifteenth century one of the most important liturgical sites in Rome. Among the *literati* Minerva was associated with classical philosophy and learning, as can be seen in Richard de Bury's *Philobiblon* of the 1340s, (p. 102). Though Alberti, in *Commentarium Philodoxeos Fabule (Rinascimento* 17 [1977]: 145), defines Minerva in the more classical sense as the goddess of "the good arts, study and industry," the medieval associations cannot be brushed aside.

43. On the theme of the garden of love in Renaissance, see Paul F. Watson, *The Garden of Love in Tuscan Art of the Early Renaissance* (Philadelphia: Art Alliance Press, 1979).

44. L. Martinelli, "Philodoxeos Fabula, Edizione critica," 179. "Introivi domum: ausculto, tempto, aggredior, contemplor, revertor. Interea visus audire sum vocem, uti erat, Doxie; adsum, obsecro operam, dum alloquar. Ea negat illic solitario in loco atque abscondito id licere, quod, siquid velim, iubet suas ad fores ut veniam: ibi se adfuturam."

45. On Tyche, the Greek goddess of fortune, see: J. J. Pollitt, *Art in the Hellenistic Age* (Cambridge: Cambridge University Press, 1986), 2–6.

46. The linking of Fortune and Fame was to remain a constant postulate in Alberti's

thought. The Temple of Fortuna and the Chapel of Fame, so he holds in the later piece *Fama*, stand next to each other in the forum. He would also write a piece entitled *Fatum et Fortuna* that explores, in a highly original manner, the devastating consequences of this "marriage." In medieval literature Fame was much less widely employed than Fortune, but the linking of the two was increasingly accepted. B. G. Koonce, *Chaucer and the Tradition of Fame: Symbolism in the House of Fame* (Princeton, N.J.: Princeton University Press, 1966), 112.

47. L. Martinelli, "Philodoxeos Fabula, Edizione critica," 144. "Hec fabula pertinet ad mores: docet enim studiosum atque industrium hominem non minus quam divitem et fortunatum posse gloriam adipisci."

48. Howard R. Patch, *The Goddess Fortuna in Medieval Literature* (Cambridge: Harvard University Press, 1927). See also: Pickering, *Literature and Art in the Middle Ages*, 197.

49. Koonce, *Chaucer and the Tradition of Fame*, 22. On Fortune's role as distributor of fame and infamy, see Patch, *The Goddess Fortuna in Medieval Literature*, 60, 63, 89, 111ff., 144–45.

50. See, for example, the condemnation of earthly glory in *De republica*, vi. Cf. Macrobius, *Commentary*, II, 10–11. The continuity of pagan and medieval ideas on fame is discussed by Maria Rosa Lid De Malkiel in *La Idea de la Fama en la Edad Media Castellana* (Mexico City: Fondo de Cultura Económica, 1952), a useful summary of which appears in the review by N. R. Carier, *Speculum* 30 (1955): 656–66.

51. Pickering, *Literature and Art in the Middle Ages,* 181. See also: Steven Ozment, *The Age of Reform, 1250–1550* (New Haven: Yale University Press, 1980), 147–49.

52. Jacques Le Goff, *Time, Work and Culture in the Middle Ages,* trans. Arthur Goldhammer (Chicago: University of Chicago Press, 1980), 53.

53. Farris, *De commodis litterarum atque incommodis, Defunctus,* 48.

54. Ibid., 52, 50.

55. Ibid., 56. The double wedding was to become a typical resolution for Italian learned comedies. See: Douglas Radcliff-Umstead, *The Birth of Modern Comedy in Renaissance Italy* (Chicago: University of Chicago Press, 1969), 30.

56. Francesco Petrarch, *Petrarch's Secret or the Soul's Conflict with Passion,* trans. W. H. Draper (Westport, Conn.: Hyperim Press, 1978) 181–82.

57. Hans Baron, "Franciscan Poverty and Civic Wealth," *Speculum* 13, no. 1 (January 1938): 2ff. David Marsh points out several connections to Petrarch, in particular its principle subject—the humanist's struggle to achieve glory. David Marsh, "Petrarch and Alberti," *Renaissance Studies in Honor of Craig Hugh Smyth* (Florence: Giunti Barbèra, 1985), 363–75. See also Giovanni Ponte, "Il petrarchismo di Leon Battista Alberti," *Rassegna della letteratura italiana* 62 (1958): 216–22.

58. Giovanni Boccaccio, *Amorosa Visione,* introd. Vittore Branca (Hanover: University of New England, 1986).

59. Averroes and others had long since pointed out that the two systems of power in the Christian world were not conducive to a smooth functioning of society, for invariably each sent out conflicting directives. Averroes, whose opinions Alberti would certainly have known (having studied law at Bologna, a hotbed of Averroistic philos-

ophy), tried to show that in Arabic philosophy no such division between spiritual and temporal power existed and that consequently all members of the social hierarchy, from the lowest to the highest, could work in unison toward common goals. Alberti might be suggesting something very similar.

Leopis-Alberti

60. Martinelli, "Philodoxeos Fabula Edizione critica," 147. "Tamen, ne meas lucubrationes perderem, adieci prohemium in quo et studia et etatem et reliqua hec de me omnia aspersa esse volui, ut, siquando libuisset, nostram liquido esse—quod fecimus—vindicaremus." Though the *Commentarium* deals only with this particular play, Alberti's remarks reveal much about his literary method.

61. Ibid., 146–47. "Idcirco hanc in eo quo tum eram constitutus merore incommodorum meorum et acerbatis illorum . . . consolandi mei gratia fabulam scripsi . . . Defendite vestrum Leonem Baptistam Albertum studiosis omnium deditissimum; defendite, inquam, me ab invidorum morsibus, ut, cum per otium licuerit, bona spe et vestra approbatione confirmatus possim pacato animo alia huiusmodi atque non invita Minerva longe in dies maiora edere, quibus et delectari et me amare vehementius possitis."

62. Ibid., 149. ". . . hec est fabula, Philodoxios hec dicitur fabula. Quid conspectatis? Quid pendetis? Fabule nomen est. Hem, iam nunc video: amplius me vobis notum voltis. Dixero: sum catus demens et inscitus sapiens. Hoc habetis iam nomen: Lepidus. Ha, ha, he, et vos lepidi estis!"

63. One such professional forgerer was a certain "Fulgentius," who wrote numerous works in a classicizing mode. See: Smalley, *English Friars and Antiquity*, 230–39. Leonardo Bruni did something of the opposite; he once held that his translation of Polybius's *De bello Italico adversus Gothos* was a work of his own hand. See: B. L. Ullman, "Leonardo Bruni and Humanistic Historiography," *Studies in the Italian Renaissance* (Rome: Edizioni di storia e letteratura, 1955), 324–25.

64. Martinelli, "Philodoxeos Fabula, Edizione critica," 146–147. ". . . tum et ea eloquentia est, quam in hunc usque diem docti Latinis litteris omnes approbarint atque usque adeo esse antiqui alicuius scieptoris existimarint, ut fuerit nemo qui non hanc ipsam summa cum admiratione perlegerit, multi memorie mandarint, non pauci in ea sepius exscribenda plurimum opere consumpserint. . . . Quam ego fabulam cum eo placere et passim a studiosi expeti, quo vetusta putaretur, intelligerem, rogantibus unde illam congessissemus per commentum persuasimus ex vetustissimo illam esse codice excerptam. Facile omnes adsentiri: nam et comicum dicendi genus et priscum quippiam redolebat neque difficile creditu erat adolescentem pontificiis scriptis occupatum me ab omni eloquentie laude abhorrere." Despite Alberti's statement, the play was often held to be classical. The German humanist Albert von Eyb, chamberlain to Pope Pius II, so esteemed the play that he published passages from it in his rhetorical work *Margarita poetica* (1475), erroneously attributing it to onetime secretary of the Florentine republic Carlo Marsuppini of Arezzo. Eyb thought the play worthy to be placed beside works of Plautus and Terence. See: Radcliff-Umstead, *The Birth of Modern Comedy in Renaissance Italy,* 30, 31. See also: George E. Duckworth *The Nature of Roman Comedy* (Princeton: Princeton University Press, 1952), 397–98.

Intercoenales

1. The two groups are in H. Mancini, *Opera inedita et pauca separatim impressa di Leon Battista Alberti* (Florence: G. C. Sansoni, 1890), 122–224; and in E. Garin, "Intercenali Inedite," *Rinascimento* 12 (1965). Some of the dialogues have been published as separate pieces, such as *Defunctus*, published and translated into Italian by G. Farris in *De commodis litterarum atque incommodis e Defunctus* (Milan: Marzorati, 1971). Until recently, the only English translations were of *Religio, Virtus,* and *Fatum et Fortuna:* "The Italian Philosophers; Selected Readings from Petrarch to Bruno," *Renaissance Philosophy,* vol. 1, ed. and trans. Arturo Fallicio and Herman Shapiro (New York: Modern Library, 1967), 27–39. For an entire translation see: David Marsh, *Leon Battista Alberti Dinner Pieces* (Binghamton: Medieval and Early Renaissance Studies, 1987).

Garin argues that this work reflects Alberti's "anguish" and that it is almost "contemporary," reflecting "a bitterness, at times morose and almost desperate" (Eugenio Garin, *Portraits from the Quattrocento,* New York: Harper and Row, 1972, 120). Garin's attempt to project a modern *Angst* onto Alberti is an exaggeration. As I point out, Alberti's interlocutors cannot be taken as literal expressions. Apart from Garin's bold attempt to crack the shell of Alberti's mystique, there are only a few studies of this important work. One is David Marsh's "Alberti as Satirist," *Rinascimento* 23 (1983): 198–212.

In some sense the additive structure of *Intercoenales* was typical of late medieval and early Renaissance storytelling. Poggio Braciollino's *Facete,* for example, written during the same decade, is also a collection of numerous tales and fables. In content, however, the works are very different. Many of Poggio's stories are baudy and indecent, and indeed, papal humanists had a reputation for Boccaccian storytelling. *Intercoenales,* though "humorous and witty," was written, so Alberti himself explains, not simply for pleasure but as a "bitter emetic to cure the sick." Mancini, *Opera inedita,* 122. See also Robert J. Clements and Joseph Gibaldi, *The Anatomy of the Novella* (New York: New York University Press, 1977), 36–61.

2. Not all the pieces are equally important to my discussion. Some, like *Pertinacia* (Defiance), are in imitation of Aesop's fables, which in Alberti's time had just been rediscovered; others, like *Bubo* (The Horned Owl), are allegorized political debates. On Horatian aspects of some of the pieces see: Marsh, "Alberti as Satirist," 198–212.

Apollo and Virtus

3. Mancini, *Opera inedita,* 151–54. The piece bears similarities to Lucian's dialogue *Vitarum auctio,* which was translated from Greek into Latin by Rinuccio Aretino around 1440. See: D. F. Lockwood, "De Rinucio Aretino graecarum litterarum interprete," *Harvard Studies in Classical Philosophy,* no. 24 (1913): 52–109.

4. Macrobius, *Commentary on the Dream of Scipio,* trans., introd., and notes by William Harris Stahl (New York: Columbia University Press, 1952), 87–92.

V. Zoubov points out several similarities in phrasing between Macrobius's *Saturnalia* and Alberti's *De re aedificatoria.* V. Zoubov, "Leon Battista Alberti et les Auteurs du Moyen Age," *Medieval and Renaissance Studies* 4 (1958): 245–66.

5. Macrobius, *Commentary on the Dream of Scipio,* 90.

6. Charles du Cange, *Glossarium mediae et infimae Latinatis* (Bologna: Forni Editore), vol. 6, p. 52.

7. Mancini, *Opera inedita*, 151.

Philargirus: Oro, Apollo, fave: hoc plaustrum rusticanis instrumentis onustum dono affero. Divitem me esse affecto.

Apollo: Interdiu omne id ferramentorum genus defodiens habeto. Vespere tamquam in speculo ipsum te in illis conspectato.

Philargirus: Hos ego semper labores fugiendos duxi.

Apollo: Nullum ergo dedecus vereare.

Procer: Oro, Apollo, fave: has gemmas atque nummos dono affero. Invidiam metuo.

Apollo: Eas tu pecunias inter bonos distribuito.

Procer: Non novi.

Apollo: Plusquam duo te una spectent oculi caveto.

Procer: Haud quidem licet.

Apollo: Da operam ut plures tibi similes adsint.

Procer: Durum.

Apollo: Ergo ne metue invidiam.

8. Eckhard Kessler, *Das Problem des Fruehen Humanismus* (Munich: W. Fink, 1968), 114ff.

9. Mary E. Barnard, *The Myth of Apollo and Daphne from Ovid to Quevedo: Love, Agon, and the Grotesque* (Durham: Duke University Press, 1987), 53–54.

10. Mancini, *Opera Inedita*, 154.

Penus: O Apollo fave. Quandoquidem nihil habeo praeterea quae dono dedam; Apollo tuae sunt partes efficere ut possim re multo plura afferre quam ipse modo pollicear. Si tu me divitem feceris, tripodes argenteos, candelabra aurea, atque smaragdis onusta dono afferam. Quid respondes? Apollo obmutuit! Ipsi quoque dii nos egenos adeo spernunt! At unum hoc iterum atque iterum precor, obtestorque, Apollo, gratis datam nequeo paupertatem ferre.

Apollo: Eam tu arbori, infelicissime, suspendito.

The tree on which the Poor Man is told to hang himself is undoubtedly the same tree of judgment that figures in *Religio*, a subsequent dialogue featuring the cynic Libripeta. As David Marsh points out, Alberti may also be referring to the tree which Timon the misanthrope offered as a gibbet to Athenian suicides. The Poorman's speech seems to recall one made by a priest addressing Chronos in the opening of Lucian's *Saturnalia*. David Marsh, "Petrarch and Alberti," *Renaissance Studies in Honor of Craig Hugh Smyth* (Florence: Giunti Barbèra, 1985), 373.

11. Mancini, *Opera inedita*, 158–66.

12. Ibid., 163.

13. Ibid., 132–36. It should also be noted that Alberti here portrays Virtue as one individual as opposed to the six Cardinal Virtues of Christian theology. The image of one Virtue was always considered pagan in the Middle Ages. Filarete gives himself credit for having been the first to reestablish a unified goddess of Virtue, whom he takes as a model for his own life (Filarete means "Lover of Virtue"). See E. F. Rice, ed., *Medieval and Renaissance Studies of T. E. Mommsen* (Ithaca: Cornell University Press, 1959), 176. Mommsen, however, makes no mention of Alberti's dialogue. See also G. Sasso, "Qualche osservazione sul problema della virtù e della fortuna nell'Alberti," *Il Mulino* 2 (1953): 600–18; Howard R. Patch, *The Goddess Fortuna in Medieval Literature* (New York: Octagon Books, 1967). The figures of Virtue and Mercury were probably inspired by Martianus Capella's *The Marriage of Philogy and Mercury*. See: Bernardi

Perini, "La 'Philogia' del Petrarca, Seneca e Marziano Capella," *Atti e Memorie dell'Accademia Patavina di Scienze, Lettere ed Arte* 83 (1970–71): 147–69.

This piece has had an unusual history, as it was discovered only recently that it was authored by Alberti. See E. Garin, "Il pensiero di L. B. Alberti nella Cultura del Rinascimento," *Accademia Nazionale dei Lincei,* no. 209 (Rome, 1974): 28.

14. Jaroslav Pelikan, *The Growth of Medieval Theology (600–1300),* vol. 3 of *Christian Tradition: A History of the Development of Doctrine* (Chicago: University of Chicago Press, 1978), 181.

15. Though Virtus's protégés are from the classical world, such a collection of honoraries was a typical late medieval device. On the lowest zone of the Campanile in Florence, for example, are depicted the first horseman, the first navigator, and the first navigator of the air (Daedalus) as well as Euclid, Pythagoras, Orpheus (father of poetry), and other fathers and benefactors of society. See: Jean Seznec, *The Survival of the Pagan Gods* (Princeton: Princeton University Press, 1953), 30–31.

16. Mancini, *Opera inedita,* 133–34. "Idcirco Plato philosophus contra nonnulla de deorum officiis cepit disputare. At illa excandescens: Apage te hinc verbose, inquit, non enim decet servos deorum caussam suscipere. Ceperat et Cicero orator plura velle suadere, at ex turba armatorum erupit Marcus Antonius praepotens latera illa sua digladiatoria ostentans, gravissimumque pugnum in os Ciceronis injecit: hinc ceteri amici mei perculsi metu fugam sibi propere consuluere: neque enim Polycletus peniculo, aut Phidias scalpro, aut Archimedes oroscopo, aut reliqui inermes adversus audacissimos armatos, eosdemque praedis atque homicidiis et assuetos bello ad sese tuendos valebant."

17. Ibid., 134.

18. Ibid.

19. Ibid., 135. "Ego et nuda et despecta excludor." Alberti credits this work to Lepidus. In fact, it is a type of apologia for Lepidus's "failure" as a writer, which shall be discussed elsewhere.

20. Ovid, *Metamorphoses,* trans. Rolf Humphries (Bloomington: Indiana University Press, 1955), 7.

21. Richard de Bury, *Philobiblon,* ed. Michael Maclagan, trans. E. C. Thomas (Oxford: Shakespeare Head Press, 1960), 102.

22. C. Grayson, *Opera Volgari,* vol. 1, p. 132. "Pertanto troppo mi piace la sentenza d'Aristotile, el quale constitui l'uomo essere quasi come un mortale iddio felice, intendendo e faccendo con ragione e virtù."

Blindness and Insight

23. Mancini, *Opera inedita,* 125.

24. Ibid. Leopis states: "Ego quidem apud meos libellos occupatus enitebar aliquam de me famam proseminare literis." Alberti seems to have imitated Lucian's employment of "Lycinus" in his own invention of "Leopis," which resembles Alberti's assumed name Leo. See David Marsh, "Alberti as Satirist," 202.

25. The character Libripeta is also Lucianesque and seems to draw on some themes from Lucian's "Remarks Addressed to an Illiterate Book-Fancier." The differences should also be noted, for Alberti does not copy Lucian blindly, in literary style or in character types. Libripeta not only undergoes an important transformation (*Somnium*) but belongs to a larger spectrum of characters.

26. Mancini, *Opera inedita*, 125.

27. Ibid.

28. Ibid. Libripeta states: "Ah! ah! eh! ridiculum hominem! isthoc ne tu in agro etrusco id tentas, qui quidem tam undique opertus est caligine omnis ignorantiae, cujus et omnis humor est penitus absumptus aestu ambitionum et cupiditatum, quemve qui colunt multo in dies impetu invidiae perturbantur."

29. Ibid. Libripeta states: ". . . nam est quidem ad vituperandum pervigil et admodum severus censor vulgus. . . ."

30. Ibid.

Leopis: O literatorum alumne. . .

Libripeta: . . . inprimisque metue ipsum me ad quem plus accessit auctoritatis, quam palam omnibus detraxerim, quam si per quam multos collaudassem.

The distinction Alberti makes between the *vulgus* and the learned was a common one. Petrarch, for example, in *De remediis* (II, praef.) insists that the treatise was intended as much for the *vulgus* as for the *docti*. Alberti transforms this topos into a theoretical postulate that makes both enemies of the writer.

31. Giovanni Ponte argues that Libripeta is Niccolò Niccoli, the noted humanist, who was the center of numerous invective battles (Ponte, "Lepidus e Libripeta," *Rinascimento* 12, 1972:237–66). Indeed there are many similarities, as Ponte points out: Libripeta, who appears in several dialogues, is a learned scholar, cynic, and bibliophile. However, Libripeta is rigorously antireligious, as this quote demonstrates. Niccoli, by contrast, was known for his piety. Libripeta, though partially inspired by the figure of Niccoli, is not so much a real person as an authorial stance that Alberti himself creates for his literary ontology.

32. Mancini, *Opera inedita*, 129–31.

33. Ibid., 131. Libripeta states: ". . . vestrasque, o religiosi, jejunas precationes aspernabitur. Praeterea an tu deos nobis homunculis persimiles arbitraris? Ut veluti imprudentes atque incauti homines extemplo consilium captent, atque item extemplo pristina consilia mutent? Profecto in tanta rerum administratione nihil esse diis laboriosius audio ab his qui literas profitentur; deos ordine paene aeterno orbem agere. Quae quidem res dum ita sit, insani vos quidem longe diliratis, si existimatis deos . . . vestris verbis aut persuasionibus, ad novas alias res agendas animum aut operam divertere."

34. Ibid., 129.

35. Ibid., 130. Libripeta states: "Tu ni te ipsum multis vigiliis lectitans conficeres, Leopide, haud palleres, minimeque esses crudus. . . ."

36. Ibid., 131. Leopis states: "Quae abs te dicta sunt, Libripeta, in disputationis locum ita accipio ut apud me tamen semper haec mens et opinio sit de diis, ut censeam preces bonorum et vota superis esse non ingrata."

37. For Heraclitus see Epistles 2; 7.10; for Crates, 7, 17, and 23; and for Diogenes, 42. Works on classical cynicism are too numerous to list. See: Abraham J. Malherbe, "Self-Definition among Epicureans and Cynics," *Jewish and Christian Self-Definition*, vol. 3, ed. Ben F. Meyer and E. P. Saunders (Philadelphia: Fortress Press, 1982), 54–55. See also: Donald R. Dudley, *A History of Cynicism*, (London: Methuen & Co., 1937).

38. E. Garin, "Intercenali Inedite," *Rinascimento* 12 (1965): 25–29.

39. Macrobius, *Commentary on the Dream of Scipio*, 90. Among the precedents should be listed Lucian's *Dream* (Somnium), *True History* (Vera historia), and *Icaromenippus*. The nightmare, reported by the chronicler John of Worchester, was illustrated in the Oxford MS., Corpus Christi College, 157, ff. 382–83. A reproduction may be found in Jacques Le Goff, *La Civilisation de l'Occident médiéval* (Paris: 1964), 117–18. See also: Jacques Le Goff, *Time, Work and Culture in the Middle Ages,* trans. Arthur Goldhammer (Chicago: University of Chicago Press, 1980), 57.

40. There are numerous "dreams" in late medieval literature, whether in works by such well-known authors as Chaucer or by obscure theologians such as Pierre Ceffons, a Cistercian monk of the mid-fourteenth century. See: Beryl Smalley, *English Friars and Antiquity in the Early Fourteenth Century* (New York: Barnes and Noble, 1960), 258. See also: Giovanni Boccaccio, *Amorosa Visione*, introd. Vittore Branca (Hanover: University of New England, 1986), xii–xiii; J. A. MacCulloch, *Medieval Faith and Fable* (London: George G. Harrap, 1932), 183–200.

41. Antonio Pucci, *Centiloquio*, in *Delizie degli eruditi toscana* (Florence: 1785), 4: canto 31; also Villani, *Cronica,* bk. 8, ch. 70. See also Samuel Y. Edgerton, Jr. *Pictures and Punishment: Art and Criminal Prosecution during the Florentine Renaissance* (Ithaca: Cornell University Press, 1985), 66.

42. Garin, "Intercenali Inedite," 25. Descriptions of dream journeys can be found throughout the Middle Ages. There is the *Roman de la Rose* by Guillaume de Lorris, composed around 1220, a work known by both Dante and Petrarch, and Brunetto Latini's *Tesoretto,* begun in 1262.

43. Garin, "Intercenali Inedite," 27.

44. Ibid. Mario Martelli discusses this passage as a possible source for Ludovico Ariosto's *Orlando Furioso*. Martelli, "Una delle 'Intercenali' di Leon Battista Alberti fonte sconosciuta del 'Furioso,'" *Bibliofilia* 66, no. 2 (1964): 163–70. Alberti, in suggesting an age guided by the "good arts" giving way to one guided by "stupidity," seems to transpose the medieval view that an "ancient" time of rational faith has been replaced by a new age given over to "credulity."

45. The medallion has been discussed by Renée Neu Watkins in "L. B. Alberti's Emblem, the Winged Eye, and His Name Leo," *Mitteilungen des Kunsthistorischen Institutes in Florenz* 9, Hft. 3/4 (November, 1960): 256–58. Watkins, not aware of the source, agrees with Edgar Wind's conjecture that *Quid tum?* should read as *quid tunc*. Edgar Wind, *Pagan Mysteries of the Renaissance* (New Haven: Yale University Press, 1958), 11. *Quid tum?* also appears twice in the dialogue *Vaticinium* as Philargirus "discovers" that money destroys contractual relationships rather than cements them. See: Mancini, *Opera inedita,* 163.

46. Garin, "Intercenali Inedite," 28–29. Libripeta states: "Egi gratias atque ut primum in adversa ripa constiti, intueor prata quedam amplissima, ubi pro cespite atque foliis herbarum surgebant come barbeque hominum, capillique mulierum, atque crines iumentorum; nec non et iube leonum, ut eiusmodi pilis nihil posset in prato non

opertum conspici. Enim vero, superi boni, quantum illic numerum somniatium pers-
pexi, nescio quas radiculas effodientes, quas qui edunt et vafri et docti cum minime
sint / videntur. Multam illic consumpsi operam. Sed me ingens copia pediculorum,
que ex prato convolabat, pene exedit, ut soa fuga salus mihi foret petenda. Iccirco
conieci me in pedes, atque unde sese mihi exitus obtulit, inde me vesanum tanta ex
peste eripuerim, fata hanc nobis cloacam prebuere."

47. Ibid., 26.

48. Ibid., 25.

49. Ibid., 28. ". . . tua omni ex maxima bibliotheca, quam occlusam detines. . . ."

50. This definition comes from Lepidus's introduction to *Philodoxeus*. See: Lucia Cesarini Martinelli, "Philodoxeos Fabula, Edizione critica," *Rinascimento* 17 (1977): 149.

51. Garin, "Intercenali Inedite," 41. Lepidus states: "Juvat his quas a te didici rebus,
me apud te non ignarum videri." This statement comes from *Fama*, in which another
debate between Lepidis and Libripeta is described. Libripeta tells of a "battle" that has
just taken place in the temple of Fame. A group of writers approached this temple,
near that of Fortune (let us recall *Philodoxeus*), in the hope that they might gain access
and thus posterity. They brought a bull into the temple but unable to bring him into
the sanctuary proper they cut the animal up into pieces so that each could carry a
part to the altar. This dismemberment (equivalent to the fragmentation of the literary
enterprise) provoked the gods to anger. They attacked the writers, who beat a hasty
retreat. Libripeta, who had carried the belly of the bull, is covered with its malodorous
contents. Lepidus, on hearing of the events, advises Libripeta to take a bath.

52. Garin, "Intercenali Inedite," 25.

53. Ibid., 29. Lepidus states: "I ergo iam nunc, atque te lotum redde. Ego ad meos
quos tu dictitas insanos et indoctos, redibo." A similar ending can be found in *Fama*.

54. Garin, "Intercenali Inedite," 34–41.

55. In the Middle Ages Phoebus was often portrayed as a type of Christ figure in
combat with the devil. Alberti defines his Phoebus as having no such militant characteristics. See: Mary E. Barnard, *The Myth of Apollo and Daphne from Ovid to Quevedo:
Love, Agon, and the Grotesque* (Durham: Duke University Press, 1987), 61–67.

56. Garin, "Intercenali Inedite," 35. Cynicus states: "Id ego curabo, O Phebe, qui in
omnibus hisce notus et hosce ferme omnes ad unguem novi."

57. The employment of beasts to depict vices is a common theme in late medieval
literature. A striking example is the painting by Cola di Rienzo, who organized a coup
d'état in Rome against the Colonna family in 1347. Cola drew paintings on the walls
of public buildings to express his political views. One such painting is described by his
anonymous biographer: "On the upper right [of the painting] were four rows of
different animals with wings who were holding horns to their mouths and blowing as
if they were winds who made the sea rage and endangered the foundering ship. In
the first row were lions, wolves, and bears. The inscription said "These are the powerful
barons and evil leaders." In the second were dogs, pigs, and roebucks. The inscription
said, "These are the bad councillors, followers of the nobles." In the third were lambs,
dragons, and foxes. The inscription said, "These are the plebians, robbers, murderers,
adulterers, and plunderers." In the fourth row, on top, were hares, cats, goats, and
monkeys. The inscription said, "These are the false officials, judges, and notaries."

See: *The Life of Cola di Rienzo*, trans. and introd. John Wright (Toronto: Pontifical Institute of Medieval Studies, 1975), 34–35.

58. Garin, "Intercenali Inedite," 41.

The Lost Garland and the Newfound Wisdom

59. Ibid., 29–34.

60. Ibid., 33. Lepidus states: "Ex his ego sum qui cum litteris delecter, tum semper studuerim, servata dignitate, ut essem ipse mecum et apud familiares meos festivitate et risu non vacuus."

61. Ibid. "Nam ita fato quodam meo evenit, ut ex eo die quo in lucem veni, nulla ne minima quidem res mihi ex animi mei sententia successerit. Mirum ut omnia preter spem nobis, atque contra quam instituerim, cadunt. Si amicos officiis et beneficiis paro, inimicos excipio. Si studiis bonarum artium gratiam sector, invidia rependitur. Si neminem ledendo rem meam pacate et modeste agere enitor, obtrectatores, delatores, occultos inimicos nequissimosque proditores offendo, qui instituta consiliaque mea omnia perturbent. Denique quicquid aggredior, quicquid enitor, omne secus accidit quam studuerim."

62. Ibid., 34.

Lepidus: . . . Itane repente, itane coronam ipsam a me diripuisti, etiam usque irritata eam dilaceras dentibus, tum et pessundas?

Invidia: Quid tibi nominis?

Lepidus: Mihin? Lepido.

Invidia: Tu Lepidus? Quin immo mordax et asper atque irrisor? Abeamus, virgo. Nam hoc toto in foro reperies neminem corona dignum.

63. Grayson, *Opere Volgari*, vol. 2, p. 122. "Quinci saremo in ogni officio d'umanità e culto di virtù ben composti, e ben serviremo alla naturale società e vera religione, e preporrenci in ogni nostra vita esser constanti e liberi." *Società naturale* is yet another reference to the intact garden that represents the mythic conception of social harmony.

64. As quoted by Manfredo Tafuri in "Discordant Harmony from Alberti to Zuccari," *Architectural Digest*, nos. 5–6 (June 1979): 36.

65. Farris, *De commodis litterarum atque incommodis, Defunctus* (Milan: Marzorati, Editore, 1971), 154–249.

66. Ibid., 228. Neophronus receives an oration spoken by an evil-minded bishop with the obvious intent to ironize Neofronus's life. It begins with the following words: "O hominum, inquit, prudentissime, o justissime, o felicissime Neophrone, quanti te in vita fecisse decuit, cujus memoriam non paribus, sed meritis laudibus concelebramus? . . . Oh! virtutem egregiam. . . ."

67. Ibid., 211, 203.

68. Ibid., 155.

69. Ibid., 194.

70. Ibid., 228, 188, 158, 236. "Itaque apud mortales ipsa etiam gravitas ac virtus insania est?" (188). "An tu ignorabas hominum vitam his animi motibus nunquam esse vacuam" (158).

71. Ibid., 236.

72. Ibid., 246.

73. Perhaps Alberti's interest in the Italian grammar reflects in *praxis* his interest in finding the autobiographical "grammar" that links mythic time with historical time. By finding a grammar in the *volgare* Alberti is showing the links that society has to its metaphysical past.

The Mendicant Exile

74. Mancini, *Opera inedita*, 126–28.

75. Ibid., 127. ". . . qui sese ob meritum literarum ditioribus praeferri cuperet. . . ."

76. Ibid., 126.

77. Ibid. "Erat istiusmodi fortuna adolescenti gravis quidem, sed illud longe gravius quod impiissimi adolescentis affines summopere elaborabant. . . ."

78. Ibid.

79. Ibid. "Nam is relictus puer, patre defuncto, sine ullis parentibus, proscriptus a patria, conjunctissimisque ab affinibus non modo bonis omnibus paternis spoliatus, sed etiam a domestica suorum familiaritate et convictu exclusus atque omnio ita abjectus fuit, ut apud extraneos sibi esset mendicandum."

80. For a description of the Alberti family exile see: Girolamo Mancini, *Vita di Leon Battista Alberti* (Florence: G. C. Sansoni, Editore, 1882); Susannah Kerr Foster, *The Ties that Bind: Kinship Associations and Marriage in the Alberti Family 1378–1428*, Ph.D. diss., Cornell University, 1985; and Randolph Starn, *Contrary Commonwealth: The Theme of Exile in Medieval and Renaissance Italy* (Berkeley: University of California Press, 1982), 109–10.

81. F. P. Pickering, *Literature and Art in the Middle Ages* (London: Macmillan and Co., 1970) 186–92. See also the hagiography of St. Oria described in Simina M. Farcasiu, "The Exegesis and Iconography of Vision in Gonzalo de Berceo's 'Vid de Santa Oria,'" *Speculum* 61, no. 2 (1986): 305. See also Baptista's description of the city in *De Iciarchia*. Grayson, *Opera Volgari*, vol. 2, pp. 285–86.

82. Mancini, *Opera inedita*, 129.

83. Mancini, *Opera inedita*, 127–28, 129. "Itaque tantis calamitatibus actus ac devictus adolescens incenso amino indignatione et iracundia haec in verba prorupit. Quid ego Superos in me fore propitios sperem, qui quidem me reipsa sentio egregie esse per- petuam ad miseriam natum? . . . Obsecro, o pissimi Superi, ne quis posthac pupillus commodiorem sibi, quam ipse pertulerim, fortunam obtigisse gaudeat, nullam pupilli apud suos cives humanitatem inveniant, nullam inter suos affines pietatem comperiant, nullam apud conjunctissimos fidem sentiant, nullam apud fratres caritatem reperiant:

sed contra adsint pupillis omnia plena odii, insidiarum, inimicitiarum, calamitatum et miseriae."

84. See also Calvin B. Kendall, "Bede's 'Historia ecclesiastica': The Rhetoric of Faith," *Medieval Eloquence,* ed. James J. Murphy (Berkeley: University of California Press, 1978), 170.

85. George Holmes, *Florence, Rome and the Origins of the Renaissance* (Oxford: Clarendon Press, 1986), 47.

86. Starn, *Contrary Commonwealth,* 132–36.

87. Ovid, *Metamorphoses,* trans. Rolf Humphries (Bloomington: Indiana University Press, 1955), 7.

88. Giuseppe Corsi, *Rimatori del Trecento* (Turin: Unione Tipografico-Editrice Torinese, 1969), 215–23.

89. Starn, *Contrary Commonwealth,* 124–25. Alberti makes a very similar statement in *Theogenius.* Grayson, *Opera Volgari,* vol. 2, p. 79.

90. Starn, *Contrary Commonwealth,* 138–40.

91. Ibid.

Intact Wisdom

92. Mancini, *Vita di Leon Battista Alberti* (Rome: Bardi Editore, 1967), 369. "Ti esorto ad imitare come fai l'avo il padre, uomini ragguardevoli ed illustri per le altre virtu e per la cognizione delle lettere, affinchè la patria possa gloriarsi d'aver posseduto in una sola primaria famiglia tali cittadini insigni per virtù e meriti ereditari verso la repubblica." The thesis of a higher parental order so deeply ingrained in the medieval Christian mind begins already as a topos in antique classical literature. See: Ernst Robert Curtius, *European Literature and the Latin Middle Ages* (New York: Pantheon Books, 1953), 131. Already Aristotle had advocated such rhetorical heightening of an individual's identity by exaggerating his good lineage. "We must prove that our hero's noble acts are intentional," Aristotle insists in *Rhetorica* (1367b). This can be done by pointing to his lineage and the excellence of his education: "Good fathers are likely to have good sons and good training is likely to produce good character" (1367a). The vehemence of the break that leaves Philoponius "a mendicant" has Franciscan overtones. In fact, Alberti's own hagiography of St. Potiti, which we shall consider later, describes a Franciscan rejection of the biological father in favor of a mendicant existence.

93. Mancini, *Opera inedita,* 143. "Pro Deum! quantis et quam variis vita hominum morbis refertissima est. . . ."

94. Giovanni Farris, *De commodis litterarum atque incommodis, Defunctus,* 42, 146.

95. Grayson, *Opera Volgari,* vol. 2, p. 274. "Dirà quello da' suoi piccini nati in casa babbo: 'costui è mio figliuolo.' E io dirò: 'vero; ma tu lo facesti simile agli altri animali nati con due piedi, io lo feci simile per virtù a uno dio terrestre.' Voi giovani, a chi diresti che costui così ornato da me fusse più obligato, al babbo o a me vero e ottimo padre?"

96. Mancini, *Opera inedita*, 126.

97. Grayson, *Opera Volgari*, vol. 2, pp. 347–65.

98. For examples in the classics we need only think of Virgil's famous picture of the storm in the *Aeneid* (1.106–7) and Ovid's description of a storm at sea in *Tristia* (II. 1–36). "Shipwrecks" were topoi commonly employed in painting in the Middle Ages. In 1335 Cola di Rienzo, before his coup d'etat, painted on the side of a building the floundering ship of Rome surrounded by the already destroyed ships of Babylon, Carthage, Troy, and Jerusalem. See: *The Life of Cola di Rienzo*, trans. John Wright (Toronto: Pontifical Institute of Medieval Studies, 1975), 32–35. Also see: Curtius, *European Literature and the Latin Middle Ages*, 129. On medieval ship imagery see: Howard R. Patch, *The Goddess Fortuna in Medieval Literature* (Cambridge: Harvard University Press, 1927), 101–7.

99. Grayson, *Opera Volgari*, vol. 2, p. 350. "Quo quidem miserrimo statu, quid putatis, viri optimi, pro vestra prudentia, quam assiduas mortes hinc superarimus, hinc expectarimus; omnis que paulo maior volvebatur unda, nostram ad necem intumuisse arbitrabamur. Mirum tamen ut in hoc tanto vite discrimine spes animum, animus vero ipse sese non deseruerit atque semper ea fortitudine fuerit, ut de salute nobis continuo quippiam bene polliceretur. Ac sepius id ipsum mihi admiranti et vix fieri posse credenti, ut solem lucemque hanc essem amplius revisurus, in mentem redit spem unam esse in terris deam que miseris sit comes relicta. Nam 'hec dea, cum fugerent scelerata numina terras, ex diis invisa sola remansit homo. Hec facit ut videat cum terras undique nullas, naufragus in mediis brachia raptet acquis. Carcere dicuntur clausi sperare salutem, atque aliquis pendes [sic] in cruce vota facit.' Nos igitur nimirum dea hec ipsa, que miseros et ceteris a diis desertos malisque oppressos numquam destituit, minime passa est tantis ingruentibus in nos malis succumbere."

Philoponius and the Twelve Rings

100. Mancini, *Opera inedita*, 224–365.

101. Ibid., 226.

102. Ibid., 224–25. Genius states: "Oh rem intolerabilem! Si quando ille quidem ad fontem sacrum Heliconam appulit, quod etsi male plerumque vertit, facit tamen et lubens et frequens; illic primum, uti solent qui se tibi totos dicarunt, rem divinam facturus, cum sese in fontem spectarit, oculosque subinde ad coelum sustulerit, frondesque ex fonte infusas degustarit, illico ut posteritatem pro more acclamare orsus est, praesto sunt Invidia, accurrit Calumnia, acri infestoque impetu incessunt, lacessunt, perturbant distrahunt. Tum et saevissima dearum Paupertas, oh! te miserum, atque iterum miserum, Philopone! quam vario laedendi genere, quantis injuriarum modis prosequitur! hoc testor: vidi equidem iratam deam cum hunc a religione tui neque vi, neque verbis posset avertere, rem dictum incredibilem!"

103. Ibid., 227. Philoponius states: "Negabitisne me ante diem trigesimum plus triginta eduxisse calculos raros et spectatos? At vos adeo inde recensete quae nobis praemia sint relata. Deduxi unos atque alios tersos atque expolitos, in variasque facies redactos. Hos, qui modestiores erant, vix despiciebant, non aperte vituperabant, sed mussantes ajebant: enimvero hi nihil ad verteres uniones tum et multa desunt: atque abibant. Reliquos vero quid memorem, quotiens et duris a temporibus et malis ab hominibus, ne deorum quempiam offendam, nobis datum est ut poenituerit, cunctis injuriam

detestantibus: quo fit ut vos, quorum ductu in tantas offensiones inciderim, merito odisse oportuerit."

104. Ibid., 225. Minerva states: "Oh! te ridiculum, Geni! Dolesne in Philopono quod ad virtutem faciat? An te illud fugit quod vulgo inprimis fertur: scilicet ut fulvum spectatur ignibus aurum tempore sic duro est inspicienda virtus?"

105. Ibid., 225–26. Philoponius states: "Apage si es malam tu quoque in rem veterator, piget auscultasse. Romanae turres et vos valeatis amici qualescumque sitis, tuque Minerva, vale: horsum hinc juvat effugere." There are some similarities here to Ovid's *Tristia* (II. 33–34).

106. Garin, "Intercenali Inedite," 43–54.

107. Ibid., 43–44.

108. Ibid., 44.

109. Ibid., 53, 54. Philoponius states: "O mi suavissime, specimen humanitatis, quam apud me maximi momenti et ponderis tua hec fuere verba! Tu, homo salis suavitatis leporisque refertissimus, ita ab iracundia ad equaminitatis [sic] modum deflexisti animum meum. . . . Taceo admodum et maximam per te egritudinis levationem accepisse fateor, et congratulator et gaudeo."

110. Ibid.

111. Ibid., 53. ". . . ita meam omnem ad me totum considerandum cogitationem et mentem vertisti, ut quanto magis magisque cogito, tanto perevestiganti et cogitanti mihi homo sese nemo offert, quem cum diligentius pensitem pre me esse fortunatum dicam. . . . Itaque sic statuo prudentis esse, se velle eum esse qui sit. Quam ad sententiam, superi boni, quos et memoria et mente celeres et mirificos ipse mecum discursus nunc primum feci!"

112. Ibid.

113. Ibid., 49.

114. Smalley, *English Friars and Antiquity,* 168, 267. Perhaps there is a connection here with Apuleius's *Golden Ass.* The narrator describes how, after having been transformed into an ass for his youthful transgressions, and after suffering inumerable torments, he is finally returned to human form by the goddess Isis. His elaborate ritual of purification ends when he receives twelve sacred shawls and a religious habit. Much as does the shorter and more somber *Anuli, The Golden Ass* ends with Apuleius elevated to a higher mental and spiritual state. He "no longer needs to fear the envy and slander of others and can perform his task as advocate with a noble head." Apuleius, *The Golden Ass,* trans. W. Adlington, rev. S. Gaselee (New York: G. P. Putnam's Sons, 1922), 581ff. The twelve rings also bring to mind the six crowns that Cola di Rienzo received in his famous, short-lived assumption to power.

115. Mirella Levi d'Ancona, *The Garden of the Renaissance: Botanical Symbolism in Italian Painting* (Florence: Leo S. Olschki Editore, 1978), 307–8.

116. This symbol, which appears on the famous medal by Matteo de' Pasti commemorating Leon Baptista Alberti, has been discussed by Renée Neu Watkins in "L. B. Alberti's Emblem, the Winged Eye, and His Name Leo," 256–58. Watkins refers to

Anuli, but her description of the events that take place in the dialogue is wrong and the quotation taken out of context.

117. Mancini, *Opera inedita,* 229–30, 231. *"Concilium:* Corona et laetitiae et gloriae insigne est; oculo potentius nihil, velocius nihil, dignius nihil; quid multa? Ejusmodi est ut inter membra primus praecipuus, et rex, et quasi deus sit. Quid quod deum veteres interpretantur esse quidpiam oculi simile, universa spectantem, singulaque dinumerantem? Hinc igitur admonemur, rerum omnium gloriam a nobis esse reddendam Deo; in eo laetandum totoque animo virtute florido et virenti amplectendum praesentemque, videntemque nostra omnia et gesta et cogitata existimandum. Tum et alia ex parte admonemur pervigiles, circumspectosque esse oportere, quantum nostra ferat animi vis, indagando res omnes quae ad virtutis gloriam pertineant, in eoque laetandum si quid labore et industria bonarum divinarumque rerum simus assecuti. . . . /

Spes: Favete superi. Oh! laetum augurium. Cedo hunc anulum primum. Da tu manum, Philopone, porrige digitum, quem in nuptiis solent; ego tibi hoc anulo spondeo secundis te usurum fatis. Viden in platano sublimem purissimam palumbem subingemiscentem et alis admodum erga nos gestientem plausum atque misericordiam? Proculdubio, neque enim me usquam artes hae, quas a matre didici, fefellere; proculdubio hinc tibi spondeo fore ut propediem summa illa et potentissima, quae Jovis optimi maximi rem moderantur, fata erga te propitia sint si qua fortassis usquedum neglexere. Oh! te felicem. Tu, Minerva, fave."

118. Ibid., 235.

119. A plane tree appears in Antonello da Messina's (1430–79) *St. Sebastian Martyred* (Dresden Gemälde Gallerie).

120. Mancini, *Opera inedita,* 234. Genius states: "Non possum non facere quin maxima exclamem voce: volo me audiat supremum aethera profundumque oceanum. Oh! tempora, oh! tempora, tam nullos reperiri. Sed nolo tristi omine prospera istius auspicia contaminare."

The Writer-Saint

1. For a discussion see: Glending Olson, *Literature as Recreation in the Later Middle Ages* (Ithaca: Cornell University Press, 1986), 24–25.

2. Ibid., 34.

3. Ibid., 75–77.

4. Thomas Aquinas supported the recreational aspect of literature as long as it furthered the joyous contemplation of God. Ibid., 223–24.

5. Hieronymo Mancini, *Opera inedita et pauca separatim impressa di Leon Battista Alberti* (Florence: G. C. Sansoni, 1950), 122–23.

6. Eugenio Garin, *Leon Baptista Alberti: Intercoenali inedite* (Florence: G. C. Sansoni, 1965), 24.

7. John Freccero, "Petrarch's Poetics," *Literary Theory / Renaissance Texts,* ed. Patricia Parker and David Quint (Baltimore: Johns Hopkins University Press, 1986), 21.

8. Cecil Grayson, *Leon Baptista Alberti: Opere Volgari* (Bari: Gius, Laterza, & Figli, 1966), vol. 2, p. 241. Baptista states: "L'opera dello ingegno e intelletto hanno in sè molta parte di divinità." The role of Baptista shall be explained in the next chapter; he is a continuation of the Philoponius theme. Heroic sentiment was an essential part of early Renaissance thought. Trinkhaus describes the humanists as "alive, actively assertive, cunningly designing, storming the gates of heaven." Charles Trinkahaus, *In Our Image and Likeness* (Chicago: University of Chicago Press, 1970), xxi. However, it should be noted that nowhere in the writings of Petrarch, Salutati, Valla, Manetti, Poggio, and Bruni does one encounter such a rich and forceful exploration of the spiritual will to define oneself as immortal and godly.

9. Giuseppi Martini, *Leon Battista Alberti: Momus O Del Principe* (Bologna: Nicola Zanichelli Editore, 1942), 4. "Qua nimirum intelligimus rara eo sapere omnia divitatem, quo illuc tendant, ut unica, atque egregie sola, a caeterorumque coetu et numero segregata habeantur."

10. Ibid., 4. "Hinc fortassis illud est quod si quos praestare ingenio et prae caeteris eo a multitudine deflectere animadvertimus, ut sint illi quidem suo in laudis genere singulares ac perinde rari, hos divinos nuncupemus proximeque ad deos admiratione et honoribus prosequamur natura edocti."

11. Joan Gadol, for example, wants to place Alberti in the Neoplatonic camp of Marcilio Ficino (1433–99). Joan Gadol, *Leon Battista Alberti: Universal Man of the Early Renaissance* (Chicago: University of Chicago Press, 1969), 231. The connection between Alberti and Ficino is still far from clear. However, since Ficino's earliest philosophical woɪk was written in 1454, by which time Alberti had long since established his own theory, I would think that Ficino might have been influenced by Alberti rather than the other way around. The essential difference between the two is that Ficino, for the most part, lacked the sense of irony so typical of Alberti.

12. G. Pico della Mirandola, *De hominis dignitate,* ed. Eugenio Garin (Florence: Vallecchi, 1942), 266–68.

13. Ernst H. Kantorowicz, *The King's Two Bodies: A Study in Medieval Political Theology* (Princeton: Princeton University Press, 1957), 59.

14. Ibid., 46.

15. Ibid., fig. 20.

16. Giovanni Orlandi, *Leon Battista Alberti: l'Architectura—De re aedificatoria* (Milan: Edizioni il Polifilo, 1966), 545. "His de rebus velim quidem templo tantum adesse pulchritudinis, ut nulla species ne cogitari uspiam possit ornatior; et omni ex parte ita esse paratum opto, ut qui ingrediantur stupefacti exhorrescant rerum dignarum admiratione, vixque se contineant, quin clamore profiteantur, dignum profecto esse locum deo, quod intueantur."

17. Giovanni Farris, *Leon Baptista Alberti De commodis litterarum atque incommodis, Defunctus* (Milan: Marzorati Editore, 1971), 148, 150. "Quibus omnibus rebus si diligentissimam abhibueris operam, adolescens, comperies litteras esse voluptuosissimas, utillimas ad laudem, ad gloriam, atque ad fructum posteritatis et immortalitatis accommodatissimas."

18. Grayson, *Opere Volgari*, vol. 2, p. 135. "Come la mano compremendo radolca e prepara la cera a bene ricevere l'impressione a sigillo della gemma, così le lettere adattano la mente ad ogni officio e merito di gloria e immortalità."

211

19. Ernst Breisach, *Historiography: Ancient, Medieval, and Modern* (Chicago: University of Chicago Press, 1983), 147. For a discussion of the stages by which Petrarch restricted the *De viris illustribus* to purely Roman subjects, see T. E. Mommsen "Petrarch's Conception of the 'Dark Ages,'" *Speculum* 17 (1942): 228f. See also: Wallace K. Ferguson, *The Renaissance in Historical Thought: Five Centuries of Interpretation* (Boston: Houghton Mifflin, 1948); and Beryl Smalley, *English Friars and Antiquity in the Early Fourteenth Century* (New York: Barnes and Noble, 1960). *De viris illustribus*, it should be added, was modeled on classical works such as Plutarch's *Lives* and medieval ones such as Vincent of Beauvais's *Mirror of the World* (ca. 1250).

20. E. F. Rice, ed., *Medieval and Renaissance Studies of T. E. Mommsen* (Ithaca: Cornell University Press, 1959), 173.

21. Ibid., 174.

22. Petrarch admitted that he left out "doctors, poets, and philosophers." See: H. J. Erasmus, *The Origins of Rome in Historiography from Petrarch to Perizonius* (Assen: Royal Van Gorcum, 1962), 8.

23. Mancini, *Opera inedita*, 127.

24. Farris, *De commodis litterarum atque incommodis, Defunctus*, 86. "Quod si tandem preter mores, preter veterem bonorum consuetudinem quispiam iuste opulentus erit futurus ex doctrina, is plane sit cui fortuna facilior, scientia profundior, auctoritas prestantior, amicorum observantia cultior longe quam ceteris atque amplior fuerit, cuius item facundia, facilitas, ingenium, versutia, calliditas acceptior atque ad hominum aures et opinionem accommodatior. Talem enim hunc esse litteratum oportet, ut dum ei non dubitet civitas universas fortunas commendare suas, tum frequentissimos questus et premia porrigere assuescat. At vero in eo quidem gradu claritatis perpaucissimi reperientur."

25. The dialogues of Bruni and Poggio are known to have been conceived as propagandizing the flourishing culture of Florence. See David Marsh, *The Quattrocento Dialogue* (Cambridge: Harvard University Press, 1980), 25.

26. A. S. Piccolomini, *Opera omnia* (Basel, 1571), 454, as qtd. in: Nancy S. Struever, *The Language of History in the Renaissance: Rhetorical and Historical Consciousness in Florentine Humanism* (Princeton: Princeton University Press, 1970), 40.

27. Lauro Martines, *Power and Imagination: City-States in Renaissance Italy* (New York: Knopf, 1979), 202.

28. Grayson, *Opera Volgari*, vol. 2, p. 122. "Questo intelletto, questa cognizione e ragione e memoria, donde venne in me sì infinita e immortale se non da chi sia infinito e immortale?"

The Five Ages of History

29. There are many parallels between Alberti's historiographic pattern and his five Psalms, which still await poetic translation.

30. B. L. Ullman, "Leonardo Bruni and Humanistic Historiography," *Medievalia et Humanistica* 4 (1946), 58.

31. *Hesiod: The Homeric Hymns and Homerica* (New York: Macmillan and Co., 1964), 11–15. Also *Hesiod*, trans. Richmond Lattimore (Ann Arbor: University of Michigan Press, 1959), 41–43.

32. Breisach, *Historiography: Ancient, Medieval, and Modern*, 85. Augustine, basing himself on Revelations 5:1, held that there were six ages: Adam, Noah, Abraham, David, the Babylonian Captivity, Jesus Christ, and Christ's Second Coming. See also: F. P. Pickering, *Literature and Art in the Middle Ages* (London: Macmillan and Co., 1970), 173–79.

33. Joseph Ratzinger, *The Theology of History in Saint Bonaventure* (Chicago: Chicago University Press, 1971).

34. On the spiritual tradition and its heretical leanings see Steven Ozment, *The Age of Reform, 1250–1550* (New Haven: Yale University Press, 1980), 73–134.

35. John F. D'Amico, "Paolo Cortesi's Rehabilitation of Giovanni Pico della Mirandola," *Bibliothèque d'Humanism et Renaissaice* 44, no. 1 (1982): 37–51.

36. Ozment, *The Age of Reform*, 150–55.

37. On the development of the Cathari see: Martin Erbstösser, *Heretics in the Middle Ages* (Erfurt: Druckerei Fortschritt, 1984), 86–95.

38. Though Alberti's position consistently fails to refer to the Church—except where absolutely necessary—the anti-republican political implications of his thought would have found favor in the Church. Ozment, *The Age of Reform*, 135–37.

The Winged Eye—Quid Tum?

39. The date of 1438 proposed by Renée Neu Watkins, "L. B. Alberti's Emblem, the Winged Eye, and His Name Leo," *Mitteilungen des Kunsthistorischen Institutes in Florenz* 9, Hft. 3/4 (November 1960): 256, is based rather weakly on a passage in the so-called *Vita anonyma* of Alberti, written in that year: "In Venice he would paint friends that were in Florence and whom he had not seen for a year. And he used also to ask children if they could immediately recognize people in the portrait that he was making. If they said no, the picture was without art. He would sketch the faces of his relatives and his own face so that whoever went to visit him could easily recognize him." Translated from: Anicio Bonucci, *Opere Volgari di Leon Battista Alberti* (Florence: Tipografia Galileina, 1843), cii. Other scholars give the date as between 1446 and 1450.

40. Biblioteca Nazionale di Firenze II.IV.38, mentioned by Hubert Janitschek, "*Kleinere Kunsttheoretische Schriften*" *Quellenschriften für Kunstgeschichte,* 2 (Vienna: 1877).

41. Watkins, "L. B. Alberti's Emblem," 256.

42. Mancini, *Opera inedita*, 233–34. "Pegaseum esse in vitae cursu labilique aetate qua rapimur; properantibus enim ad pegae vitae melioris, nobis utendum alis erit, ne undis immergamur. Alae hominum ingenii vis animique dotes sunt, quibus ad coelos usque rerum congitione pervadimus, et pietate virtute que superis jungimur."

The Humanist Drama

1. Giovanni Farris, *Leon Baptista Alberti: De commodis litterarum atque incommodis, Defunctus* (Milan: Marzorati Editore, 1971), 104–6.

2. Ibid., 90.

3. Caroll William Westfall, *In this Most Perfect Paradise* (University Park, Pa.: Pennsylvania State University Press, 1974), 19.

4. If a close communication between the two existed, it was certainly omitted in Manetti's *Vita Nicholas V.* Manetti went to great length, so it seems, to omit any mention of Alberti.

St. Potitus

5. For a discussion refer to: Cecil Grayson, *Opuscoli inediti di L. B. Alberti: "Musca," "Vita S. Potiti"* (Florence: Leo S. Olschki, 1954).

6. The life of St. Potitus was often linked with that of St. Ephysius, as the bodies of both were transported to Pisa in 1088. See: George Kaftal, *Iconography of the Saints in Tuscan Painting* (Florence: G. C. Sansoni, 1952), 346–47. The two saints were depicted in 1391–92 on frescos by Spinella Aretino in the Camposanto of Pisa. The representation of St. Potiti, however, has been lost. See A. Lasinio, *Pitture a fresco del Camp Santo di Pisa* (Florence: 1832), p. 596, fig. 334.

7. Alberti in his introduction addressed to the curia makes it clear that he does not want to be responsible for the changes typical of this *scribendi genere.* "Since I must bow to your [Dati's] wishes, tell me whose life I should describe first and I will strive to the best of my ability to satisfy your expectation. You shall, as they say, 'superintend' my work: and as soon as I write something, you will see it and correct it. Then in truth, it will be that what you order and judge to be done will be done." Grayson, *Opuscoli inediti,* 64.

8. Ibid., 35.

9. Ibid., 68. "At Potitus plenus deo eas omnes patris rationes refellebat tanta eloquentia tantaque scripturarum memoria, ut omnium disertissimus videretur, multa insuper de Christi religione disserens." The combination of the maturity of age and youth is a commonplace from the classics. See: Ernst Robert Curtius, *European Literature and the Latin Middle Ages* (New York: Pantheon Books, 1953), 99. Saints, especially those of the Franciscan and Dominican Orders, were frequently praised for their eloquence. St. Bernardine of Siena (1380–1444) is even said to have devoted himself to the research of ancient manuscripts. See "Vita Ambrosii Traversarii" (Munich: W. Fink, 1968) in Lorenzo Mehus, *Historia litteraria Florentina.*

10. Grayson, *Opuscoli inediti,* 72. "Ego secus gloriam dixero non dignosci, non approbari a stulta multitudine. . . ."

11. Ibid., 69. ". . . etenim pulchrius intra feras belluas versari arbitrabatur quam intra crudeles, nefarios immanesque homines, quorum nulla pene urbs non refertissima est. . . ."

12. Curtius, *European Literature and the Late Middle Ages*, 428. Miracles in which the saint forces men of evil to behave foolishly and ineffectively were typical of *vita sancti*.

13. Grayson, *Opuscoli inediti*, 65. "Potiti adolescentis vitam non iniuria primam esse voluisti, qua meas vires periclitarer. Est ea quidem adolescentis constantia et miraculorum multitudine singularis, in qua colenda qui se exerceat multam dicendi materiam inveniat multamque sibi attentionem comparet."

14. Ibid., 71.

15. Ibid., 72. "Verum hoc quoque ne tacerem commonuit adolescentis Potiti vita, qui quantum interesset et hodiernam inter et priscam Christi disciplinam per id fantasma quasi per picturam intellexit. Demonis namque illusiones, hoc est rerum caducarum possessiones, primo hominis effigiem habuisse quasi non esset alienum ab humanitate bonis terrenis perfrui, deinde supra hominem crevisse hoc est fastu et superbia intuisse, postremo divitiis et opum copia in belluas nostros supremos clericos verti vidit."

Baptista

16. Grayson, *Opere Volgari*, vol. 2, p. 116. "Odiano chi non esca di vita con animo invitto e nulla perturbato. Uomini prestantissimi! Uomini rari!"

17. Anicio Bonucci, *Opere Volgari di Leon Battista Alberti* (Florence: Tipografia Galileina, 1843), vol. 1, xcviii. "Vixit cum invidis et malevolentissimis tanta modestia, et aequanimitate, ut obtrectatorum, aemulorumque nemo tam etsi erga se iratior, apud bonos et graves de se quidpiam, nisi plenum laudis, et admirationis auderet proloqui."

18. There has been a long debate about the authorship of the *Vita anonyma*. Today scholars seem to be in agreement that it was indeed Alberti's. I agree, for there are many similarities in vocabulary and thought between this piece and Alberti's other writings. For a discussion of the *Vita anonyma* and the questions surrounding its authorship consult Riccardo Fubini and Anna Menci Gallorini, "L'autobiograpfia di L. B. Alberti. Studio e edizione," *Rinascimento* 12 (1972): 21–78. The authors elaborate on the attribution of the text to Alberti based on overwhelming philological and textual evidence.

Unfortunately, the work is often seen as autobiographical. Of course here, as elsewhere, there are many autobiographical elements. These elements, however, are arranged and explicated in a hagiographic manner that denies the pure empiricism of self. To see *Vita anonyma* as an autobiography is to misinterpret the thrust of the work, which I hold has been designed as a platform for the interlocutor Baptista. *Vita anonyma* is not then an autobiography as much as a character description. The consistencies between *Vita anonyma* and the figure of Baptista as described or as participating in his other writings would support this conclusion. David Marsh in "Petrarch and Alberti," *Renaissance Studies in Honor of Craig Hugh Smyth* (Florence: Giunti Barbèra, 1985), 363–75, pointing out that this piece "can scarcely be read as mere autobiography," also observes that "its motif of repeated illness also closely parallels the sufferings of the enamored student Friginnius in Alberti's *Amores*" (p. 366. The *Vita* appears to be a fragment of a larger text. However, I believe that this is only an illusion, for the organization follows the principles of writing outlined in *Cynicus*, a dialogue from *Intercoenales*. I shall discuss this point in chapter 7.

19. Bonucci, *Opere Volgari*, 1, xcvii–c.

20. Ibid., civ.

21. Ibid., cvi.

22. Ibid., cviii.

23. Ibid., xc. "Omnibus in rebus, quae ingenuum et libere educatum deceant, ita fuit a pueritia instructus, ut inter primarios aetatis suae adolescentes minime ultimus haberetur." Though the definition of Baptista is highly inventive, there can be no doubt that in the early Quattrocento there existed a great fascination with child prodigies. In fact, we have a contemporary description of such a prodigy that in its schematic form shows several parallels with Alberti's definition of Baptista. In 1445 a boy wonder, a certain twenty-year-old Fernando of Cordova, was in Navarre impressing the Scholastics at the university there with his learning. He traveled throughout Italy, performing at numerous universities, and even appeared in Rome before 1445. Whether Alberti met him or not cannot be ascertained. As Alberti's Baptista was already created by 1438, it is unlikely that Fernando was Alberti's model. However, it is interesting that the contemporary description of him lists those very attributes Alberti claims for Baptista. He was skilled in music, mathematics, fighting, horsemanship, debating, and even painting. See: Lynn Throndike, *University Records and Life in the Middle Ages* (New York: Columbia University Press, 1944), 341–43.

24. Bonucci, *Opere Volgari*, 1, xcii. "Armorum praeludiis adolescens claruit. . . . Numulum argenteum manu tanta vi emittebat, ut qui una secum afforent in templo, sonitum celsa convexa tectorum templi ferientis numi clare exaudirent."

25. Ibid., cxii. "Ex solo intuitu plurima cujusque praesentis vitia ediscebat."

26. Ibid., xc–xcii. "Ferrariensibus ante aedem, qua per Nicolae Estensis tiranni tempora maxima juventutis pars ejus urbis deleta est, o amici, inquit, quam lubrica erunt proximam per aetatem pavimenta haec, quando sub his tectis multae impluent guttae. . . ."

27. Ibid., xc. "Ingenio fuit versatili, quoad nullam ferme censeas artium bonarum fuisse non suam."

28. Ibid., xcii, xciv. ". . . ut per aetatem coepisset maturescere, ceteris omnibus rebus posthabitis, sese totum dedicavit studiis literarum; dedit enim operam juri pontificio, jurique civili, annos aliquot. . . ."

29. Antonio Degli Agli (ca. 1400–77), the Florentine prelate, wrote a *vita* in 1475 taking up many themes of Alberti's *Vita* (1438): youthful poverty, abdominal pains, numerous worries, family problems, dedication to learning, an interest in painting, sculpture, and theater, temptations of the flesh, and false accusations. It is quite likely that Antonio would have known Alberti, as both were closely associated with the curia. Any literary connections remain conjecture. Nelson H. Minnich, "The Autobiography of Antonio Degli Agli (ca. 1400–77), Humanist and Prelate," *Renaissance Studies in Honor of Craig Hugh Smyth* (Florence: Giunti Barbèra, 1985), 178–91.

30. For a discussion of brief medieval hagiographies, see: Ernst Breisach, *Historiography, Ancient, Medieval, and Modern* (Chicago: University of Chicago Press, 1983), 98.

31. Bonucci, *Opere Volgari*, 1, xcvi, xcviii, c ". . . quandoquidem sibi secus, quam caeteris auctoribus non licuerit; cuique enim ajebat ab ipsa natura vetitum esse meliora facere sua, quam possit facere. . . . Bonis et studiosis viris fuit sommenfatus. . . . Illis libris illecti, plerique, rudes concives studiossimi literarum effecti sunt."

32. Grayson, *Opere Volgari*, vol. 2, p. 138. "Vorrebbesi tesé, Battista, esser laggiù a quel

nostro Gangalandi co' cani, o alle colline o a' piani, ed essercitarsi qualche ora, e poi ridursi agli studi delle lettere e a filosofia come è tua usanza, Battista."

33. Bonucci, *Opere Volgari*, 1, c. Alberti has the following to say about *Della Famiglia:* "Cum libros *De Familia* primum, secundum atque tertium suis legendos tradidisset, aegre tulit, eos inter omnes Albertos, alioquin ociosissimos, vix unum repertum fore, qui titulos librorum perlegere dignatus sit, cum libri ipsi ab exteris etiam nationibus peterentur; neque potuit non stomachari, cum ex suis aliquos intueretur, qui totum illud opus palam, et una auctoris ineptissimum institutum irriderent. Eam ob contumeliam decreverat, ni principes aliqui interpellassent, tris eos, quos tum absolverat, libros igni perdere."

34. Ibid., cvi. "Ceteris in rebus mediocritatem approbabant. Unam excipiebat patientiam, quam aut nimis servandam, aut nihil suscipiendam statuebat, ajebatque per sapius graviora ob patientiam tollerari, quam ob vehementem acrimoniam tullissemus."

35. Grayson, *Opera Volgari*, vol. 1, p. 320. "Mai si nostro officio con opere lodatissime palesarli mendaci e fitti."

36. Ibid., vol. 2, p. 277. Baptista states: "Ma niuna dissimilitudine, niuna disgregazione e alienazione d'animi e voluntà mai sarà da natura maiore quanto de' buoni virtuosi mansueti contro a' viziosi ambiziosi rapaci."

37. Bonucci, *Opere Volgari*, 1, cii. "Facile, inquit, patiar, te, quod voles, mentiendo ostendere qualis quisque nostrum sit: tu istiusmodi praedicendo efficis, ut te isti parum esse modestum sentiant, magis quam me tua isthac praesenti ignominia vituperes."

38. Ibid., cvi–cviii. "In jurisconsultum perfidum, qui altero humero depresso, altero sublato deformis incederet: aequa, inquit, istic nimirum iniqua sunt, ubi lances in libra non aeque pendant."

39. Ibid., cviii. "Tuta ab hostium injuriis civitate, cum facinorosum concivium haberi coepta esset ratio: nonne, inquit, istuc fir percommode, ut imbre sedato, tecta resariciantur."

40. Ibid., cx. "Obtrectatores fallaces, ambiguos et omnes denique mendaces, ut sacrilegos, et capitales fures ajebat esse plectendos, qui veritatem judiciumque, religiosissimas, ac multo rarissimas res e medio involent."

41. Ibid. "Ambitiosi domum spectans: turgida, inquit, domus haec suum propediem efflabit herum, ut evenit quidem: nam ob alienum aes ipsarum aedium fortunatissimus dominus in exilum secessit."

42. Ibid., cxii. "Extant ejus Epistolae ad Paulum Physicum in quibus futuros casus patriae annos integros ante praescriptserat; tum et pontificum fortunas, quae ad annum usque duodecimum essent affuture praedixerat, multarumque reliquarum urbium, et principum motus ab illo fuisset enunciatos, amici et familiares sui memoriae proderunt."

Agnolo and Giannozzo

43. *Profugiorum ab aerumna* continues the long tradition of investigations into man's *melancholia*, from Boethius's *Philosophiae Consolationis* to Petrarch's *Secretum and De remediis utriusque fortunae*. Alberti admits that "many of our important Latin authors

and many Greeks" wrote on similar subjects. Grayson, *Opera Volgari*, vol. 2, p. 160. Though Alberti makes good use of these and other works, he claims that his approach to the subject is different.
Agnolo di Pandolfini also appears in the dialogue *Vita civile* by Matteo Palmieri. For a discussion see: Claudio Finzi, *Matteo Palmieri dalla 'Vita civile' alle 'citta' di vita'* Universita 'di Roma Facolta' di scienze politiche, N. 47. 1984).

44. Grayson, *Opere Volgari*, vol. 2, p. 124. Agnolo states: "Dicono: ama la patria, ama e' tuoi sì in far loro bene quanto e' vogliano. Ma e' dicono ancora che la patria dell'uomo si è tutto el mondo, e che 'l savio, in qualunque luogo sarà constituto, farà quel luogo suo; non fuggirà la sua patria, ma addotterassene un'altra, e quivi arà bene assai dove e' non abbia male, e fuggirà sempre essere a sé stessi molesto. E lodano quel detto antiquo di quel Teucer, uomo prudentissimo tanto nominato, qual dicea che la patria sua era dov'egli bene assedesse."

45. Ibid., 159.

46. Ibid., 135. "Un ricordo non voglio preterire, che a ogni ottima instituzione, a ogni bene adotta ragione del vivere, a ogni culto e ornamento dell'animo nostro molto e molto gioverà darsi alle lettere, alla cognizione e perizia de' ricordi e ammonimenti quali e' dotti commendorono alla posterità."

47. Ibid., 108–9. Niccolo states: "Voglio inferire che a Battista, qual sempre v'appella padre, e védevi e odevi con avidità e volentieri, e' vostri ragionamenti saranno, come e' sono a me, [Niccola] accettissimi e gratissimi."

48. Ibid., 144–45. Agnolo states: ". . . tanto può l'invidia in questa nostra età fra e' mortali e perversità. . . . O cittadini miei, seguirete voi sempre essere iniuriosi a chi ben v'ami? Tu, Battista, seguita con ogni opera a diligenza esser utile a' tuoi cittadini."

49. Ibid., 107. "E certo questo tempio ha in sé grazia e maiestà: e, quello ch'io spesso considerai, mi diletta ch'io veggo in questo tempio iunta insieme una gracilità vezzosa con una sodezza robusta e piena, tale che da una parte ogni suo membro pare posto ad amenità, e dall'altra parte compreendo che ogni cosa qui è fatta e offirmata a perpetuità. Aggiungni che qui abita continuo la temperie, si può dire, della primavera: fuori vento, gelo, brina; qui entro socchiuso da'venti, qui tiepido aere e quieto: fuori vampe estive e autunnali; qui entro temperatissimo refrigerio."

50. Ibid., 109.

51. Ibid., 108. Niccolo states: "E riferiscovi quel ch'io intesi spesso da lui, che due soli uomini gli paiono ornamento della patria nostra, padri del senato e veri moderatori della Repubblica: l'uno si è Giannozzo degli Alberti suo, uomo tale per certo quale e' lo espresse in quel suo terzo libro *De Familia,* buono uomo e umanissimo vecchio; l'altro siete voi [*Agnolo*], quale e' compari a Giannozzo in ogni lode." The dialogue opens on a rhetorical level, as Agnolo points out that Niccola "does not report his real opinions and judgments but only attempts to lure Agnolo into the discussion (p. 110). Such recantation devices were typical in Renaissance dialogues. For a discussion refer to: David Marsh, *The Quattrocento Dialogue* (Cambridge: Harvard University Press, 1980), 30f.
Regarding the absence of Baptista in the dialogues Alberti may have had Petrarch's *Secretum* in mind. In Petrarch's dialogue, which also is on the theme of psychic stress, Truth accompanies the disputants as a silent witness. Though he doesn't speak, it is the voice of Baptista that summarizes the arguments at the beginning of books 1 and 2. For Petrach's *Secretum*, see Francisco Rico, *Vida u orba de Petrarca: I. Lectura del "Secretum"* (Padua: Editrice Antenore, 1974); Adelia Noferi, *L'esperienza poetica del*

Petrarca (Florence: G. C. Sansoni, 1962), 236–84; Francesco Tateo, *Dialogo interiore e polemica ideologica nel* Secretum *del Petrarca* (Florence: G. C. Sansoni, 1965), 15–19.

52. Grayson, *Opera Volgari*, vol. 1, p. 63. "... tutti e' mortali sono da essa natura compiuti ad amare e mantenere qualunque lodatissima virtù."

53. Ibid., 108.

54. Bonucci, *Opere Volgari*, 1, civ–cvi. "Domum vetustam, obscuram et male aedificatam, in qua divertisset, tritavam atque idcirco nobilissimam aedium appellabat, siquidem caeca et incurra esset."

Theogenius, Genipatro, and Microtiro

55. Alberti paints a particularly embittered and cynical portrait of humanity in *Theogenius*. See in particular Grayson, *Opera Volgari*, vol. 2, pp. 92–94.

56. Ibid., 66. Theogenius states: "A Genipatro viveno più e più figlioli, e' libri suoi da sé ben composti ed emendatissimi, pieni di dottrina e maravigliosa gentilezza, grati a' buoni e a tutti gli studiosi, e quanto dobbiamo sperarne immortali."

57. Ibid., p. 55.

58. Ibid. "Tanto t'affermo, io scrissi questi libretti non ad altri che a me per consolare me stessi in mie avverse fortune."

59. Ibid., p. 88. "E quanto pronto vediamo ora niuna, come dicea Mannilio poeta, segue mai simile a una altra ora, non agli animi degli uomini solo, quali mo lieti, poi tristi, indi irati, poi pieni di sospetti e simili perturbazioni, ma ancora alla tutta universa natura, caldo et dì, freddo la notte, lucido la mattina, fusco la sera, testé vento, subito quieto, poi sereno, poi pioggie, fulgori, tuoni, e così sempre di varietà in nuove varietà."

60. Ibid., 95–96.

61. Ibid., 96. Microtiro states: "Maravigliomi e di me fo coniettura quanto io in me tutto el dì soffero, né vedo in che modo possa non molto nuocermi la malignità de' perfidi e iniquissimi uomini, quali ottrettando, inculpando, insimulando, e con quanta possono opera, cura, industria, con ogni loro studio, assiduità e diligenza, con ogni arte, con ogni ingegno, con ogni fraude, mai restano infestissimi e molestissimi fare e dire e pervestigare cose per quali a me ne conseguiti povertà, odio, invidia, inimicizia, mala vita e grave infamia. Pessimi uomini, quali in molti modi benificati da me, impiissimi godono per loro fraude e nequizia vedermi pieno di indignazione, suspizione, sollicitudine e paura, ed estremo pericolo d'ogni mia fortuna e salute."

62. Ibid., 103. "Quale animo sendo, come affermava Eraclito, purgato da ogni crassitudine e peso della terra, fugge da questo carcere come saetta e vola in cielo. E credo io troveresti uscito di vita niuno qual volesse ritornarci. . . ."

Gelastus and Enopus

63. Giuseppe Martini, *Leon Battista Alberti: Momus o del Principe* (Bologna: Nicola Zanichelli, 1942).

64. Ibid., 179–80. "Ego, a patria exul, aetatis florem consumpsi continuis peregrinationibus, assiduis laboribus; diutinam per egestatem, perpetua cum inimicorum tum et meorum iniuria vexatus, pertuli et amicorum perfidiam et affinium praedam et aemulorum calumnias et inimicorum crudelitatem; fortunae adversos impetus fugiens, paratas in ruinas rerum mearum incidi. Temporum perturbationibus et tempestatibus exagitatus, aerumnis obrutus, necessitatibus oppressus, omnia tuli moderate ac modice, meliora a piisimus dis meoque fato sperans quam exceperim. Atqui o me beatum. Modo mihi ab cultu et studiis bonarum artium quibus semper fui deditus, feliciora rependerentur! Sed in litteris quid profecerim, aliorum sit iudicii."

65. Ibid., 180. "Nam unde gratia debebatur, inde invidia redundavit, unde subsidia ad vitam expectabantur, inde iniuria, unde boni bona pollicebantur, inde mali mala rettulerunt. Dices: ea fuere quidem eiusmodi ut hominibus evenire consueverint, et te meminisse hominem oportet."

66. Ibid., 167. "'Trita haec sunt quae Gelastus confabulatur, deque tota istorum re nihil est quod probem quam personatum Gelastum hunc: nam ei profecto nihil fieri potest similius.' Audit et alios Charon dicentes fuisse bene doctum Gelastum in vita et prudentem, alios contra fuisse quidem stultum et procul dubio delirasse cum ceteras ob res, tum quod tantis iniuriam offensionibus lacessitus seque dignitatemque suam neglexerit per animi pusillitatem. Neque probare illius vitae rationem, qui perseveravit omnibus aeternum prodesse cum se multi in dies lacesserent et laederent. Non illis quidem cum Oenope rem fuisse, qui se ad propulsandas vindicandasque iniurias magis quam ad firmandam insolentium temeritatem fortem esse ostenderet nimis ferendo."

Libris Disvolutis

67. Bonucci, *Opere Volgari*, 1, civ.

68. Grayson, *Opera Volgari*, vol. 2, p. 161.

Terminus a Quo

1. Giuseppe Martini, *Leon Battista Alberti: Momus o Del Principe* (Bologna: Nicola Zanichelli, 1942), 68.

2. C. Grayson, *Leon Battista Alberti: On Painting and On Sculpture, The Latin Texts of "De Pictura" and "De Statua"* (New York: Phaidon, 1972), 62. The entire passage reads: "Quae cum ita sint, consuevi inter familiares dicere picturae inventorem fuisse, poetarum sententia, Narcissum illum qui sit in florem versus, nam cum sit omnium artium flos pictura, tum de Narciso omnis fabula pulchre ad rem ipsam perapta erit? Quid est enim aliud pingere quam arte superficiem illam fontis amplecti?" It is worthwhile to note that Plotinus condemned that which Alberti glorifies, namely the equation of art and simulation, despite the fact that there is an undeniable Neoplatonic element in Alberti's theory: "Whoever throws himself upon them (beautiful simulacra) urged by the desire to touch real things, is like him who wanted to seize his beautiful reflection floating on the water and—this is what the legend means in my opinion—fell into the profound abyss and disappeared. Plotinus, *Enneadi* (Bari, 1947), 107. Whereas for Plotinus the tale of Narcissus signifies that representation is a dangerous illusion in and of itself, Alberti employs the tale on a smaller scale to represent an original aesthetic impulse.

3. Cecil Grayson, *Leon Baptista Alberti: Opera Volgari* (Bari: Gius, Laterza, and Figli, 1966), vol. 2, p. 131. "... e interverracci che simulando diventerremo quali vorremo parere." Alberti also suggests that the following should be inscribed in a public temple: "... talis esto, qualis videri velis. ... Giovanni Orlandi, *Leon Battista Alberti: l'Architettura—De re aedificatoria* (Milan: Edizione il Polifilo, 1966), 611.

The Human Prerogative

4. Martini, *Momus*, 164–66. Prometheus was frequently considered a type of sculptor, a creator of the human race, by medieval and Renaissance thinkers. See Olga Raggio, "The Myth of Prometheus," *Journal of the Warburg and Courtauld Institutes* 21 (1958): 47ff.

5. Grayson, *On Painting*, 58. For a discussion of the Christian concept of the division of the ways see: E. Rice, ed., *T. E. Mommsen: Medieval and Renaissance Studies* (Ithaca: Cornell University Press, 1959), 175ff.

6. Grayson, *On Painting*, 58.

7. Ibid., 102.

8. The advantages of a "masked" life are so great that even Charon, later on in the story, decides to apply a mask to protect himself.

The Lost Ointment

9. Hieronymo Mancini, *Opera inedita et pauca separation impressa di Leon Battista Alberti* (Florence: G. C. Sansoni, 1890), 143–46.

The Art of Simulation

10. Mancini, *Momus*, 13. "... proxime ad hos accedebat ut belle dea Fraus fecisse videretur quod muliebres mortalium adiecisset delitias, artesque fingendi, risumque, lachrymasque."

11. G. Orlandi, *De re aedificatoria*, 23, [I,2].

12. Ibid., 65, [I,9].

13. Ibid., 443, [VI,1]. "... et qui forte per haec tempora aedificarent, novis ineptiarum | | deliramentis potius quam probatissimis laudatissimorum operum rationibus delectari. ..."

14. Grayson, *On Painting*, 120. "Hinc nimirum studia hominum similibus efficiendis in dies exercuere quoad etiam ubi nulla inchoatarum similitudinum adiumenta in praestita materia intuerentur, ex ea tamen quam collibuisset effigiem exprimerent."

15. Cosimo Bartoli, *Opuscoli Morali di L. B. Alberti*, (Venice: Francesco Franchesi, 1568), 370. "Era costume de nostri antichi, e principalmente di coloro che per la intera cognitione e disciplina delle buone arti e per la religione de loro santissimi costumi erano eccellentissimi, di lodare quei loro cittadini che ne erano degni, e a quali si

trouauano obligati, di fare immortali, per quanto ei poteuano con ogni loro studio e diligentia, i nomi de gli homini eccellenti, e di metterli ancora ne loro scritti. Noi possiamo conietturare, che eglino usassino di far questo, parte per riconoscere con iustitis, e con equità i meriti, alla quale virtù erano del tutto inclinati: parte ancora per instigare e confermare con piu uehementia gli studiosi giouani, allo esercitio della virtù, accioché ei diuenissino in quel modo, più utili alla patria, e più famosi appresso de posteri: parte ancora perché ei consumassino lo otio, del quale sorse abbondauono, in quello esercitio di lodare l'un l'altro grato, e in uero accetto a tutti. Et possette tanto appresso di loro lo studio di celebrare, e publicamente e priuatamente, le lodi de gli huomini grandi, che non solo si faceuano le publiche orationi ne mortorii, o si metteuano in scritto, come si fa ancor hoggi, presa tal lodi e delle attioni humane, furono alcuni che gli chiamarono Dii. Alcuni altri ui accommodarono oltra di questo alcune loro fauolose inuentioni, da non si potere in maniera alcuna credere, solo per soiare e esaltare la virtù."

16. Ibid.

17. Ibid.

18. Orlandi, *De re aedificatoria*, 629.

19. Ibid. 653ff.

20. Grayson, *On Painting*, 62.

21. I am basing this partially on Steven Ozment's excellent description of the play. Steven Ozment, *The Age of Reform, 1250–1550* (New Haven: Yale University Press, 1980), 88. The argument, almost a topos, can be found in several contexts. I mention, by way of example, the statement prepared by the Second General Conference of Latin American Bishops at Mediellìn, Columbia, in the fall of 1968: ". . . *Less human:* the oppressive structures that come from abuse of ownership and of power and from exploitation of workers or from unjust transaction. *More human:* overcoming misery by the possession of necessities; victory over social calamities; broadening of knowledge; the acquisition of cultural advantages. *More human also:* an increase in respect for the dignity of others; orientation toward the spirit of poverty; cooperation for the common good; the will to peace. *More human still:* acknowledgment, on man's part, of the supreme values and of God who is their source and term. *More human finally,* and especially faith, the gift of God, accepted by men of good will and unity in the charity of Christ, who calls us all to participation, as sons, in the life of the living God who is the father of all men." Second General Conference of Latin American Bishops, *The Church in the Present-Day Transformation of Latin America in Light of the Council* (Washington, D.C.: National Conference of Bishops, 1979), 28. It is clear that the progression reverses the topos of "history" to arrive at the authority of the Church.

Civitas Perversa

22. On medieval concepts of art, see: Rosario Assunto, *Die Theorie des Schoenen im Mittelalter* (Köln: DuMont Buchverlag, 1963).

23. *Civitas perversa* was a term coined by the Augstinian bishop Otto of Freising and contrasted with *civitas Christi*. See: Ernst Breisach, *Historiography: Ancient, Medieval, and Modern* (Chicago: University of Chicago Press, 1983), 143.

24. See: "Apollo and Virtus."

25. Giovanni Farris, *Leon Baptista Alberti: De commodis litterarum atque incommodis, Defunctus*, (Milan: Marzorati Editore, 1971), 244. Grayson, *Opere Volgari*, vol. 1, p. 285–86. "E ben sai, in tanta diversità d'ingegni, in tanta dissimilitudine d' oppinioni, in tanta incertitudine di volontà, in tanta perversità di costumi, in tanta ambiguità, varietà, oscurità di sentenze, in tanta copia di fraudolenti, fallaci, perfidi, temerarii, audaci e rapaci uomini, in tanta instabilità di tutte le cose, chi mai si credesse colla sola simplicità e bontà potersi agiugnere amicizia, o pur conoscenze alcune non dannose e alfine tediose? Conviensi contro alla fraude, fallacie e perfidia essere preveduto, desto, cauto; contro alla temerità, audacia e rapina de' viziosi, opporvi costanza, modo e virtù d'animo; a qual cose i' desidero pratico alcuno uomo, da cui io sia più in fabricarmi e usufruttarmi l'amicizie, che in descriverne e quasi disegnarle fatto ben dotto."

26. Eugenio Garin, *Leon Baptista Alberti: Intercenali Inedite* (Florence: G. C. Sansoni, 1965), 26. Libripeta states: "Minime; verum, o rem incredibilem, pro undis infiniti hominum vultus volvuntur, at ex his videres alios vultus pallentes tristes valitudinarios, alios hilares venustos rubentes, alios oblongos macilentos rugosos, alios pingues tumidos turgidos, alios fronte aut oculis aut naso aut ore aut dentibus aut barba capillo aut mento prolixo prominenti ac deformi: horror, stupor, monstra." D. W. Robertson writes of the medieval idea that "a man corrupted in some way by . . . sensuality might exhibit animal characteristics, or even plantlike features." Robertson, *A Preface to Chaucer* (Princeton: Princeton University Press, 1962), 154. On Petrarch and the grotesque, see: Mary E. Barnard, *The Myth of Apollo and Daphne from Ovid to Quevedo: Love, Agon, and the Grotesque* (Durham: Duke University Press, 1987), 99ff.

27. Grayson, *Opere Volgari*, vol. 2, p. 92. "Nè trovasi animale alcuno tanto da tutti gli altri odiato quanto l'uomo."

28. Ibid. "Gli altri animali contenti d'un cibo quanto la natura richiede, e così a dare opra a' figliuoli servano certa legge in sé e certo tempo: all'uomo mai ben fastidia la sua incontinenza. Gli altri animali contenti di quello che li si condice: l'omo solo sempre investigando cose nuove sé stessi infesta. Non contento di tanto ambito della terra, volle solcare el mare e tragettarsi, credo, fuori del mondo; volle sotto acqua, sotto terra, entro a' monti ogni cosa razzolare, e sforzossi andare di sopra e' nuvoli."

29. Ibid., 93–94.

30. Mancini, *Opera inedita*, 129.

31. Garin, *Intercoenali Inedite*, 35–36. In his critique of money and its impact on human consciousness Alberti is taking up a favorite theme of many late thirteenth- and fourteenth-century poets who portrayed the evils generated in the wake of the rising mercantile mentality in Italy. Anonimo Genovese states, "Every man is in the market"; Niccolò de' Rossi (d. ca. 1438) writes how "Money makes the man . . . the world and fortune [are] ruled by it." Chroniclers often spoke of "new men" and "new citizens." See Lauro Martines's excellent discussion, *Power and Imagination: City-States in Renaissance Italy* (New York: Vintage Books, 1980), 83ff. Alberti may allow his uncle Giannozzo to be guided by a civic mercantilism (*Della Famiglia*), but when it comes to the Albertian humanist writer-saints, they are to live a Franciscan life: "Observe in these considerations how the writer compares with other social classes. The masses consider them ridiculous; all mock them, and many despise them, and this especially when they are not rich. Those then who accidentally are rich know, however, that those who are honored occupy themselves not with writings but with wealth, and not with manly excellence (*virtus*) but with fortune. In fact, they draw attention to those . . . conceding their place or expressing respect if the splendor of gold and togas does not first strike their eye. With gold lacking, and toga put aside, everyone immediately ignores you. So it is. Those who put on very rich clothing are received with honor by the masses;

the very wealthy are considered most worthy of honor and reverence." Money destroys the relationship between God and man (*Religio*) and interjects an intermediary zone of aesthetic distance that relativizes and "forgets." In *Intercoenales* Alberti describes how Apollo, when asked by the priests which god is the supreme one, responds that it is Mammon (The Syrian God of Money); consequently, priests, forgetting their real duties, "are devoted to money."

32. Garin, *Intercoenali Inedite*, 41.

33. Ibid., 37. "Moribus et vita fuere huiusmodi, temulenti et contumaces, crudeles, inexorabiles. Domestico in magistratu considendo dicendoque iure, pupillos, viduas imbecillioresque quosque cives expilarunt. In officio gerendo, non libertatem tutati, sed pro intoleranda libidine omnia suo arbitrio gessere; cives cunctos, qui libertatis cupidi videbantur, odere. Pueros impuberes virginesque ingenuas constuprarunt. Eos qui sese tantis sceleribus, aut vetando, aut oppugnando obiecerant, mulctaverunt, in exilium, in carcerem pepulerunt." In a similar vein Alberti writes in Psalm 5 (Mancini, *Opera inedita*, 34–35):

Petulcum os et duri invidia oculi, fronsque omni turpitudine obscena,
Refertum vitio pectus, impia mens, perversum ingenium, et efferatus animus,
Quid vobis cordi injuriae, proditio, scelus, crimen, calumnia semper atque mendacium est?
Vos ne non poenitet usque sordidissimi, justorum adversus vos odia irritare?
Fiant Arabum vobis aromata teter odor, et sapiat mel hyblaeum amaros cineres.
Gemmae inter vestros digitos fiant atrae, et vestris in palmis lilia nigrescant.
Ager vobis vere non virescat, et poma in hortis vestris acerba cadant.
Putrescat vobis aurum in leves pulveres, sintque vestri omnes conatus frustra.

Is it possible that Alberti is describing his patron Sigismondo Malatesta? Pope Pius II writes the following of Sigismondo: "Sigismondo Malatesta was an illegitimate member of the noble family of the Malatestas and had a great spirit and a powerful body. He was an eloquent and skillful captain. He had studied history and had more than an amateur's knowledge of philosophy. He seemed to be born to do whatever he put his hand to. But he was so ruled by passions, and abandoned himself to such an uncontrollable greed of money, that he became a plunderer and a thief to boot. He was so dissolute that he raped his daughters and sons-in-law. When a boy, he often acted as the female partner in shameful loves, and later forced men to act as women. He had no respect for the sanctity of marriage. He raped virgins who had vowed themselves to God as well as Jewesses, killed young girls, and had young boys who rebelled against him brutally whipped. He committed adultery with many women whose children he held at baptism, and murdered their husbands. His cruelty was greater than any barbarian's and he inflicted fearful tortures on guilty and innocent alike with his own bloody hands. He rarely told the truth, and was a master of pretense and dissimulation, a traitor and a perjurer who never kept his word." Pius II, *I Commentarii* (Siena, 1972), vol. 1, pp. 186–87 (Taken from Franco Borsi, *Leon Baptistas Alberti* [New York: Rizzoli, 1980], 127).

34. Grayson, *Opere Volgari*, vol. 2, p. 96. Farris, *De commodis litterarum atque incommodis*, 190. "Hoc tibi persuadeas velim, in animis atque mentibus hominum ita hanc labem manasse, ita longe lateque diffusam esse ut nulla eorum meditatio, nullus discursus, nullum judicium, nulla institutio, nulla opinio mortalium sit ab imperio stultitie libera."

35. A. Bonucci, *Opere Volgari*, 1, xcviii. "Vixit cum invidis et malevolentissimis tanta modestia, et aequanimitate, ut obtrectatorum, aemulorumque nemo tam etsi erga se iratior, apud bonos et graves de se quidpiam, nisi plenum laudis, et admirationis auderet proloqui."

False Intellectuals

36. Martini, *Momus*, 92. "Haec ut homines dinoscerent et profiterentur, viri docti et in gymnasiis bibliothecisque, non inter errones et crapulas educati, effecere dicendo, monendo, suadendo, monstrando quid aequum sit, quid deceat, quid oporteat, non popularium auribus applaudendo, non afflictos irridendo, non maestos irritando, fecere, inquam docti ipsi suis evigilatis et bene diductis rationibus, ut honos dis redderetur, ut cerimoniarum religio observaretur, ut pietas, sanctimonia, virtusque coleretur."

Philosophers

37. Grayson, *Opere Volgari*, vol. 2, p. 119.

38. Ibid., 115. "E' me gli pare vedere disputare con una maiestà di parole e di gesti, con una severità di sentenze astritte a qualche silogismo, con una grandigia di sue opinioni tale che t'aombrano l'animo, e parti quasi uno sacrilegio stimare che possino dicendo errare."

39. Ibid., 118. "Così questi filosofi, medicatori delle menti umane e moderatori de' nostri animi, vorre' io m'insegnassero non fingere e dissimulare col volto fuori, ma entro evitare le perturbazioni ed espurgare dall'animo con certa ragione e modo quello che essi giurano postersi."

40. Bonucci, *Opere Volgari*, 1, cx. "Cum intueretur levissimos et ambitiosos aliquos, qui se philosophari profiterentur, per urbem vagari, et se oculis multitudinis ostentare: ecce nostros caprificus ajebat, qui quidem infructuosissimam, et superbam isthanc solitudinem adamarint, quae publica sit."

41. Martini, *Momus*, 164.

42. Grayson, *Opere Volgari*, vol. 2, p. 117. ". . . se questi uomini dotti ed essercitatissimi, inventori, defensori e adornatori di queste simili sentenze più tosto maravigliose che vere, o non poterono secondo noi altri men dotti, o forse, secondo voi prudentissimi, non seppero nulla stimare le cose caduche e poco temere le cose avverse, noi altri e d'ingegno e di condizione e di professione minori e in ogni grave cosa più deboli, chente potremo?"

43. Garin, *Intercoenali inediti*, 24. "Quod si supinam te aliorum pericula sollicitam reddunt, vultures quidem, que ab ipso sub stellis ethere exsangue aliquod pervestigant cadaver, admonuisse decuit. Namque illis quam nobis omnis est casus longe periculosior."

44. Ibid., 38. "*Philosophi:* Vestre, o Mercuri, sumus delitiae, tuque, Phebe, favete, nam celitum dignitatem et numen apud ignavos mortales omnibus nostris in litteris tutati sumus, in omnique nostro instituto degende vite, ab omni corporis et humanarum rerum commertio, supera et divina spectantes, alieni fuimus, ut vestre iam sint partes id providere: ne denuo ad ullam carnis molem nobis invisam retrudamur. / *Cynicus:* O gentem petulcam, improbam, insolentem! Num dispudet etiam diis legem indicere? Idne ita vobis licere arbitramini, quod tanta fueritis tamque insigni imbuti arrogantia, dum vitam inter homines agebatis, ut non modo privatis civibus populisque regibusque, sed vel orbi terrarum et ipsis astris, et universe nature legem sitis ausi inconsultissime inscribere? Unum admoneo, o Phebe, si hos auscultes sophistas, in eam procacitatem

proruent ut coram non te esse deum contendant (p. 40). *Mercurius*: Insaniunt. Mereri enim se de diis grandia autumant: multum attulisse mortalibus luminis ad bene beateque vivendum, deos fecisse ut vereantur. Quid multa? Alii leonem, alii elephantum, alii aquilam, alii cete et grandia nobiliaque huiusmodi suis animis condicere corpora protestantur."

45. Grayson, *Opere Volgari*, vol. 2, p. 110. "E questi filosophi con loro parole credono spegner quello che con effeto tanto può per sua natura in noi. Questo donde e' sia non so: pur lo sento in noi mortali esser fisso e quasi immortale. E quale e' sia per sé tanto veemente e tanto ostinato, vi confesso, Agnolo, non lo so: ma che e' sia, lo sento e pruovo, e duolmi."

The "Holy" Disciplines

46. Boccaccio's defense of poets can be found in his *Genealogy of the Gentile Gods*. For brief summary of Boccaccio's arguments see: *Classical and Medieval Literary Criticism*, ed. Alex Preminger, Leon Golden, O. B. Hardison, Jr., and Kevin Kerrane (New York: Frederick Ungar, 1974), 449. Alberti is not against poetry in and of itself. After all, he wrote poems. He is only pointing out that poets have fallen from their archaic mission.

47. Garin, *Intercoenali inedite*, 39. "Cave, Phebe, hos qui adsunt deputes tanto fuisse ingenio, ut veteres illos imitari potuerint, qui de vobis diis ludicra finxere; sed a veteribus auctoribus, verisculos unos itemque alteros deflorarint, quos tanto in honore haberi volunt ut Museum Orpheumque longe sibi postponendum asseverent."

48. Farris, *De commodis litterarum atque incommodis*, 44. ". . . tantum aures ad cognoscendum nimium delitiosas porrigunt: quasi doctis sat sit non pectus sed aures eruditas genere."

49. Ibid., 42.

50. Grayson, *Opere Volgari*, vol. 1, p. 287. "Ma non ciascuno dotto in lettere saprà porgere la sua virtù con modo e dignità a farsi valere a benivolenza e amicizia, né saprà quello scolastico dove e quanto l'assiduità, lo studio, el beneficio, in questo più che in quello ingegno, luogo e tempo giovi e bene s'asetti; quale cognizione dico, e tu non credo neghi, essere necessaria."

51. Farris, *De commodis litterarum atque incommodis*, 134. "Sunt ergo magna ex parte ut vides litterati apud omnes ordines, apud plebem usque adeo ridiculi, ab omnibus irrisi, a multis despecti, atque id quidem potissimum ubi non fuerint valde locupletes. Tum qui (quod rarissime evenit) fortassis fuerint fortunati, sciant illi quidem non litteris, sed divitiis, non virtuti eorum sed, fortune honores tribui. Et enim animadvertant quot assurgant, cedant, aut dignentur, nisi eorum oculos toge aurique splendor prius perculserit. Desit aurum, dependatur toga, ignorabere. Equidem ita se res habet, qui ditissimi, iidem honoribus et observantia, dignissimi putantur, ut nemo tametsi prudens, peritus, atque rerum preclarissimarum scientia atque sapientia excultissimus vir sapiens habeatur, nisi auri atque divitiarum suffragio quicquam ex se possit in vulgus proferre, quod laude aut admiratione dignum putetur."

52. Garin, *Intercoenali inedite*, 39. "*Scriptores:* Non eadem nobis atque his fuit in studiis litterarum opera et cura. Vestra enim, o dii, gesta tradidimus litteris, et temporum versiones, et volubilitatem fortune descripsimus, ut qui nos legerint, et doctiores et prudentiores fiant. / *Cynicus:* Hi quidem omnium sunt qui pre ferant si eorum scripta

perlegas, nihil scisse vacuum mendacio dicere. Finxere principes invictissimos, contiones habitas, superatos montes et maria, denique debellatas gentes, que hostem nullum viderunt. Alia ex parte reclusi bibliothecis, bene meritorum famam rodendo voluere putari vulgo litteratissimi, et tanta flagrant invidia, ut preter se alios litteratos haberi nullos cupiant. Et in hac levitate gloriantur posteris immortalitatem sui nominis reliquisse.

Phebus: Hos ego, etsi leves fuerint, quia tamen id egere ut in vita fuisse videantur, laudandos censeo. Estote iccirco mures. Vos vero proximi."

53. Grayson, *Opere Volgari,* vol. 1, p. 82.

54. Bonucci, *Opere Volgari,* 1, cx. "Obtrectatores fallaces, ambiguos et omnes denique mendaces, ut sacrilegos, et capitales fures ajebat esse plectendos, qui veritatem judiciumque, religiosissimas, ac multo rarissimas res e medio involent."

55. Garin, *Intercoenali inediti,* 39. Cynicus states: ". . . tametsi ipsi nequiores estis, qui vestras primas laudes in eo posuistis, quod applaudendo et assentando gratiam inire, obtrectando vero atque maledictis quemvis trahere in odium atque invidiam, sitis docti?"

56. Farris, *De commodis litterarum atque incommodis,* 44. "Num parum commode Isocratem illum rhetorem imitabimur, qui Busiridem, nequissimum tirannum, laudasse ac Socratem, optimum et sanctissimum philosophum, conditis orationibus vituperasse fertur."

57. Mancini, *Opera inedita,* 153–65.

58. Ibid., 165.

59. Ibid.

60. Garin, *Intercoenali inedite,* 11. "Une quidem erant ex ebore, in quibus gemmarum ornamenta et omnis antiquitatis memoria miri artificis manu insculpta pulcherrime aderant, quas profecto ipse deum rex posset, dignitate servata, inflare; sed in illis hoc aderat vitii, quod sonitum referebant penitus nullum."

61. Farris, *De commodis litterarum atque incommodis,* 52. "Multas preterae dicendi rationes que ad motus animorum valent ac denique plures argumentandi modos abiiciat, ne videatur producere disciplinas ad contemptum et litteras velle despiciendas tradere."

62. Ibid., 44. "A nobis magnis vigiliis non prisce imprimis eloquentie et elegantie expetenda laus est, ad quod etsi viribus totis iam diu contenderimus nunquam tamen ne mediocriter quidem assequi potuimus."

63. Garin, *Intercoenali inedite,* 46. "Hinc fiebat, certandi studio vicendique cupiditate, ut suo etiam maximo cum discrimine quisque eorum ceteros omnes in calamitatem cadere elaboraret. . . . Qua ex re que acerbissime inter eos iniuriarum et vindicte contentiones, que gravissime discordie, que pernities et interitus facile subsecuti sit, non recenseo: res ante oculos versatur miseranda et collugenda."

64. Ibid., 28. ". . . tua omni ex maxima bibliotheca, quam occlusam detines, adeptus es."

65. Mancini, *Opera inedita,* 152.

Libripeta: O Apollo fave. Hos libros dono affero. Aveo videri literatus.

Apollo: Sis, atqui ut sis noctesque diesque assidue lectitato. Quam ob rem te laudent praebeto; id cum desit, multos ipse collaudato.

Libripeta: Taedet, longeque malo videri quam esse.

Apollo: Omnium ergo literatorum obtrectator esto.

66. Garin, *Intercoenali inediti*, 32. "Ain vero? Mihin isthunc parum cognitum reris, qui quidem ex me genitus sit et apud me educatus, ut omnes quas ipsa novi artes egregie didicerit atque ad unguem teneat: detrahere omnibus, facta dictaque improbare omnium, inque triviis bonis atque pravis, doctis / atque indoctis succenseri, vera falsaque promiscue ad ignominiam decantare: hec enim omnia egregie et perquam belle novit, me magistra et instructrice."

67. Mancini, *Opera inedita*, 141. "Tum umbre inquiunt: Id quidem genus mortalium pessimum est, etenim suspiciosi, callidi, invidique apud vos dicuntur, nam perversa natura et deprivatis moribus praediti, cum nolint nare, cum suis paleis gaudent nantibus esse impedimento. Suntque his persimiles alii, quos vides, ut altera manu utrem interdum, aut tabulam ab aliis furtim et injuria rapiant: alteram illi quidem enim manum musco et limo, qua quidem re evenire fluvio molestius nihil potest, implicitam atque occupatam sub undis habent. Ac est quidem genus id impedimenti ejusmodi, ut manibus semel in gluten actus perpetuo inhaereat: vos vero istos ipsos estis avaros, cupidosque nuncupare soliti."

68. Garin, *Intercoenali inedite*, 64. ". . . ex suoque quisque sensu non ex re ipsa, ut par esset, aliorum scripta reprobat, studiosorumque nemo est cui certa et non reliquorum iudiciis repugnans sententia adsit. Alios enim nihil ni corturnatum ampulosumque delectat; alii quicquid accuratius editum promitur, durum id et asperum deputant. Alii flosculos et lautitiem tantum verborum rotundosque periodos lectitando libant et olfaciunt. . . ."

69. Guglielmo Gorni, "Storia del Certame Coronario," *Rinascimento* 12 (1972): 135–82.

70. Ibid., 168. "E forse sarebbe chi vuj giudicherebbe né interj huomminj, dove non proibissti in tempo quello che vedevj et per vostra divina sapienza conoscievj essere dannoso."

71. Ibid. "Et chi diciesse una et un'altra libra d'argiento troppo essere premio alle fatiche di qualunque studioso, qual di costoro ciertatorj, mentre che'ssi exceritò in questo ciertame, non pospose ogni sua privata chura et domesstica faccienda, qual di loro non expuose più et più vigilie in elimare et esornare suo poemj? Se in voj sono ingiegnj divinj, et potete estempore et subito podurre ottimj vostrj poemj, meritate biasimo chè non conventisstj, dove dificultà potavate aonesstare simile principiata consuetudine in la patria nostra, qual da voi era state troppo commendata."

72. Ibid.

73. Garin, *Intercoenali inedite*, 42–43. Libripeta states: "Eam ob rem placuit bovem eo ipso in templi vestibulo mactare frustrisque precium distribuere, ut singulas singuli partes in sacellum deportarent; pauci integrum aliquod membrum, quisque tamen honestam sibi partem sumpsit; ego ventrem, qui humi relictus esset, in gremium recipio. . . . At sacerdotes indignum facinus profanari templum acclamarunt. Confestim plebs tumultuans undique in nos irrupit. . . ."

74. Ibid., 63–65.

75. Ibid., 63–64. "Siquidem ut nunc id ita est, ut videre videor, neminem tantisper

tinctum litteris, qui etsi intervallo maximo speciem sit aliquam eloquentie conspicatus, quin idem illico eam de sese spem suscipiat ociosus, ut propendiem summum in oratorem evasurum se confidat."

76. Ibid., 64. "At enim varia res est eloquentia. . . ."

77. Ibid. "In aliorumque scriptis pensitandis ita sumus plerique ad unum omnes fastidiosi, ut ea Ciceronis velimus eloquentie respondere, ac si superiori etate omnes qui approbati fuere scriptores eosdem fuisse Cicerones statuant. Inepti!"

78. For a discussion of the impact that the discovery of Cicero's manuscript had on fifteenth-century thought see: David Marsh, *The Quattrocento Dialogue* (Cambridge: Harvard University Press, 1980); and M. L. McLaughlin, "Histories of Literature in the Quattrocento," *The Languages of Literature in Renaissance Italy* (Oxford: Clarendon Press, 1988), 63–80.

79. Garin, *Intercoenali inedite*, 64. "Cum autem sibi ad rem tenendam plus quam oscitans opinabatur adesse negocci intellexit, tum omni librorum copia contendit, ac si ipsis libris, non acerrimo nostro studio, dicendi simus rationem adepturi. Cumque sese eloquentie locos satis preter ceteros quisque tenuisse opinetur, fit inter nos ut non consequenda ipsi laude, sed in aliis carpendis et redarguendis fatigemur."

80. Ibid., 24. "Bubulus limoso in litore inter palustres herbas proiectas capram quandam, que maceriem vetustissimi cuiusdam scrupeum supra saxum collapsi templi consederat, his verbis admonuisse ferunt: 'Io, quenam te isthuc temeritas, o lasciva, rapuit, ut herboso spreto litore isthec, ardua et penitus invia affectes? An non prestare intelligis dulci et succoso gramine exsaturari, quam aspera continuo rudera et amarum alte caprificum sitiendo carpere? Velim tibi quidem consulas ut, quanto deinceps cum periculo verucas istas ipsas ambias, non peniteat.' Bubulis aiunt capram huiusmodi verbis respondisse: 'He, en. An quidem, gravissima et tristissima mollipes, tu ignara es, ut os ventri, ori pedes operam sedulo suppeditent. Mihi autem non bubulus, sed capreus stomachus est. Tibi quidem, si que ipsa carpo, eo sunt ingrata quo datum est eadem ut nequeas attringere, mihi tue isthec ulva eo non grata est, quo passim vel desidiosissimis omnibus pecudibus pateat.' Equidem, mi Poggi, huc ipsum nobis, dum his conscribendis intercenalibus occupamur, evenire plane sentio: ut sint plerique, qui nostrum cupiant uberioribus et commodioribus in campis eloquentie ali et depasci . . . qui quidem, si capram hanc nostram audierint, nihil erit quod nos, uti arbitror, reprehendendos ducant."

81. Farris, *De commodis litterarum atque incommodis*, 138. "Quis non condoluerit tantam iacturam, tantunque naufragium in litteris factum esse intuens: posteaquam in has ipsas morum tempestates et procellas incidimus. . . ."

82. Ibid., 136–38. "Ex quo effectum est ut cum sanctissime pene omnes discipline istac hominum fece replete dehonestateque sint, tum idcirco nobilissimi et prestantissimi, qui litteris affici olim consueverant, admodum dedignentur. . . . Nam aut gibbi, aut strume, aut distorti et comminuti, stoldi, hebetes, inertes, atque rebus aliis obeundis invalidi et incompotes omnes ad litteras deportantur."

83. Ibid., 138.

84. Ibid. "Quis non ante oculos veluti pictam rem prospiciat causum atque perniciem disciplinarum et artium? Quis non condoluerit tantam iacturam, tantunque naufragium in litteris factum esse intuens. . . ."

85. Grayson, *Opere Volgari*, vol. 2, p. 6.

Burchiello sgangherato sanza remi,
composto insieme di zane sfondate,
non posson piu' le Muse far lellate,
poiché per prora sì copioso gemi.

The sonnet, of which this is the first stanza, is thought by scholars to describe the poet Domenico di Giovanni (1404–48), nicknamed "Burchiello." See Guglielmo Gorni, *Leon Battista Alberti rime e versioni poetiche* (Milan: Riccardo Ricciardi Editore, 1975), 4–5. It seems that Alberti forwards Burchiello as a negative exemplum of literary demise. See also Renée Neu Watkins, "Il Burchiello 1404–1448: Poverty, Politics and Poetry," *Italian Quarterly* 14, no. 54 (1970): 21–57.

Nature as Patron

86. See in particular book 2. Alberti uses the term "nature" in several different ways, not only in the manner discussed here. For a discussion of some of these uses (limited to *De pictura*) see Ivan Galantic, *The Sources of Alberti's Theory of Painting* Ph.D. diss., Harvard University, 1969.

87. Mancini, *Opera inedita,* 125.

88. Bonucci, *Opere Volgari,* 1, xciv.

89. Mancini, *Opera inedita,* 244.

90. Grayson, *Opere Volgari,* vol. 2, p. 182.

91. Grayson, *On Painting,* 36. "Quibus quidem cognitis, quoad ingenium suppeditabit, picturam ab ipsis naturae principiis exponemus."

92. Ibid., 38. "Sphaerica superficies dorsum sphaerae imitatur."

93. Orlandi, *De re aedificatoria,* 811. "A pertissimis veterum admonemur, et alibi diximus, esse veluti animal aedificium, in quo finiundo naturam imitari opus sit." The relationship between nature and mathematics is one of the themes of IX,5.

94. Ibid., 819. "Tum et contra nusquam pari apertiones numero posuere; quod ipsum naturam observasse in promptu est, quando animantibus hinc atque hinc aures oculos nares compares quidem, sed medio loco unum et propatulum apposuit os."

95. Grayson, *Opere Volgari,* vol. 2, p. 57.

96. Ibid., 57–58. "Qui colonne fabricate dalla natura tante quante tu vedi albori ertissimi. Qui sopra dal sole noi copre ombra lietissima di questi faggi e abeti, e atorno, dovunque te volgi, vedi mille perfettissimi colori di vari fiori intessuti fra el verde splendere in fra l'ombra, e vincere tanto lustro e chiarore del cielo; e da qualunque parte verso te si muove l'aura, indi senti venire a gratificarti suavissimi odori. . . . E questo qui presso argenteo e purissimo fonte, testimone e arbirro in parte delli studi mei, sempre m'arride in fronte, e quanto in lui sia, attorno mi si avolge vezzeggiando, ora nascondendosi fra le chiome di queste freschissime e vezzosissime erbette, ora con sue onde sollevandosi e dolce immurmurando bello m'inchina e risaluta, ora lieto molto e quietissimo mi s'apre, e soffre ch'io in lui me stesso contempli e specchi."

97. For the nature topos see: Ernst Robert Curtius, *European Literature and the Latin Middle Ages* (New York: Pantheon Books, 1953). See also Barnard, *The Myth of Apollo*

and Daphne from Ovid to Quevedo, 102. Boccaccio in *Amorosa Visione* places a dreamer together with the goddess Philosophy in the glorious setting of "fragrant cedars" and "tall grasses," but when the thoughts of the dreamer are less than pure, he suddenly awakens and looses her. Alberti's forest exemplifies no such ambiguities. Giovanni Boccaccio, *Amorosa Visione,* introd. Vittore Branca (Hanover: University of New England, 1986), 198–207.

98. For a discussion see: Roger D. Sorrell, *Tradition and Innovation in Saint Francis of Assisi's Interpretation of Nature,* Ph.D. diss., Cornell University, 1983, 83–91.

99. Grayson, *Opere Volgari,* vol. 2, p. 119.

100. Grayson, *Opuscoli inediti di L. B. Alberti: "Musca," "Vita S. Potiti"* (Florence: Olschki, 1954), 72. "Alii enim questibus inserviunt, alii militie insudant, alii litteris et vigiliis marcescunt, omnes ut fama clariores in hominum ora quam gloriosi in dei conspectum veniant."

101. Bonucci, *Opere Volgari,* 1, cxiv. "Vere novo cum rura et colles efforescentes intueretur, arbustaque, et plantas omnes maximam prae se fructum spem ferre animadverteret. Vehementer tristis animus reddebatur, hisque sese castigabat dictis: 'nunc te quoque, o Baptista tuis de studiis quidpiam fructum polliceri oportet.'"

102. Ibid., c. "Suas inventiones dignas, et grandes exercentibus condonavit."

The Belated Aesthetic

103. Orlandi, *De re aedificatoria,* 443.

104. Ibid., 447. ". . . ut hoc audem dicere: nulla re tutum aeque ab hominum iniuria atque illesum futurum opus, quam formae dignitate ac venustate."

105. Ibid., 449. "Illis, ni fallor, abhibita ornamenta hoc contulissent, fucando operiendoque siqua extabant deformia, aut comendo expoliendoque venustiora, ut ingrata minus offenderent et amoena magis delectarent. Id si ita persuadetur, erit quidem ornamentum quasi subsidiaria quaedam lux pulchritudinis atque veluti complementum. Ex his patere arbitror, pulchritudinis quasi suum atque innatum toto esse perfusum corpore, quod pulchrum sit; ornamentum autem afficti et compacti naturam sapere magis quam innati."

106. Farris, *De commodis litterarum atque incommodis,* 46.

107. Grayson, *On Painting,* 78–80. ". . . in pingendis regibus, si quid vitii aderat formae, non id praetermissum videri velle, sed quam maxime possent, servata similitudine, emendabant."

108. Orlandi, *De re aedificatoria,* 813. "Hoc si persuadetur, haud erit quidem prolixum ea recensere, quae adimi augeri mutarive praesertim in formis atque figuris possint." Alberti's aesthetics is least applicable to sculpting in stone, which, as he argues in *De statua,* is a process of removal, a restriction, for the artist can aspire only to an imitation of "the real natural object." (Grayson, *On Painting,* 118, 120). We are told that the sculptor can aim at a *simulacrum,* but precisely how this is to be achieved in a substance such as stone is not explained. Baptista, it is important to observe, never sculpts anything from stone. He prefers to model with clay and wax. Agnolo states: "Io non potrei dipingere né fingere di cera uno Ercole, un fauno, una ninfa, perché non sono

essercitato in questi artifici. Potrebbe questo forse qui Battista quale se ne diletta e scrissene." Grayson, *Opera Volgari*, vol. 2, p. 118. Since "sculpting in wax proceeds by adding and taking away," something you cannot do in stone, it is closer to the aesthetics of simulation discussed in *De pictura* than is carving into stone.

109. Grayson, *On Painting*, 98.

110. Bonucci, *Opere Volgari*, 1, c. "Ignarum se multis in rebus simulabat, quo alterius ingenium, mores peritiamque scrutaretur."

111. Grayson, *On Painting*, 98. ". . . sed ne a natura quidem petita uno posse in corpore reperiri, idcirco ex omni eius urbis iuventute delegit virgines quique forma praestantiores, ut quod in quaque esset formae mulierbris laudatissimum, id in pictura referret."

112. Ibid., 104.

113. Ibid., 68.

114. Ibid.

115. Ibid., 78.

116. Ibid., 80.

The Prince and His Ottime Artefice

117. Grayson, *Opere Volgari*, vol. 2, p. 286. "Dissivi quale fia l'officio di questo primario e massimo moderator degli altri, quale vi confesso, persino da quella età che questi mie' capelli eron biondi, persino a questa che ora sono canuti e bianchi, sempre desiderai, sempre quanto in me fu ingegno e attitudine, con ogni studio, fatiche, vigilanza, cercai de essere: non questo tanto per darmivi duttore, quanto per essere in me atto a tanto vostro bene."

118. Ibid., 267. "Tutte le multitudini da natura sono distinte in due ragioni di persone, de' quali alcuni di loro per prudenza, uso e cognizione delle cose, e per autorità sono atti a inducere e reggere gli altri a buono e desiderato fine. Simili omini sempre furono in ogni congregazione rari e pochi, e a costoro si conviene certa opera e officio proprio loro."

119. Orlandi, *De re aedificatoria*, 269. "Hinc igitur prima nobis patebit divisio, ut paucos ex omni multitudine seligamus, quorum alii sapientia consilio ingenioque illustres. . . ." Such a division was an intellectual commonplace going back to Cicero, who writes "Ne vobis multitudine literarum molestior essem." Cited in: *An Abridgment of Ainsworth Dictionary: English and Latin*, ed. T. Morell (Philadelphia: Urich Hunt and Son, 1845), 747.

120. Grayson, *Opere Volgari*, vol. 2, pp. 220–21. "Diventasi virtuoso imitando e assuefacendosi a esser simile a coloro quali sono iusti, liberali, magnifichi, magnanimi, prudenti, constanti e in tutta la vita ben retti dalla discrezione e ragione."

121. Ibid., 278. ". . . ma il procede nostro in esplicare con qual moderazione di vivere colla multitudine simile agli altri privati cittadini, massime fra coniunti e familiari, ciascun di voi diventi primario e pervenga a tanta eccellenza in quello che sia in lui

posto, non in la fortuna, che nulla più vi si possa desiderare, onde sequiti che insieme la famiglia tutta si trovi beata, onorata e felicissima."

122. Ibid., 297, 298.

123. Ibid., vol. 1, p. 297. "Tu con ciascuno di questi ramenterei immitassi Alcibiade, quale in Sparta, terra data alla parsimonia, essercitata in fatiche, cupidissima di gloria, era massero, ruvido, inculto; in Ionia era delicato, vezzoso; in Tracia con quelli s'adattava a bevazzare ed empiersi di diletto; e tanto sapea sé stessi fingere a quello acadea in taglio, che sendo in Persia, altrui patria, pomposa, curiosa d'ostentazioni, vinse el re Tisaferne de elazione d'animo e di magnificenze. Ma per in tempo accommodarsi e accrescere amicizia, fia luogo comprendere ne' gesti, parole, uso e conversazioni altrui, di che ciascuno si diletti, di che s'atristi, qual cosa el muova a cruccio, ad ilarità, a favellare, a tacere."

124. Bonucci, Opere Volgari, 1, c.

125. Grayson, Opere Volgari, vol. 2, p. 279. "Sono gli animi e mente degli omini vari e differenti; alcuni sùbiti al coruccio; alcuni più facilia a misericordia; alcuni acuti, suspiziosi; alcuni creduli, puri; alcuni sdegnosi, provani, acerbi; alcuni umani, trattevoli, ossequiosi; alcuni festerecci, aperti, goditori; alcuni subdoli, solitari, austeri; alcuni amano esser lodati, soffrano esser ripresi; alcuni contumaci, ostinati a ubbidire niuno altro che la legge; duri nel commandare, crudeli nello sdegno effiminati ne' pericoli, e simili: sarebbe prolisso raccontarli. Conviene che 'l nostro prudente iciarco esplori, tenti, ricognosca ora per ora costumi, vita e fatti di ciascuno de' suoi, e a ciascuno adoperi ottima e accomodata ragione di comandare. Adonque userà non sempre, non con tutti quello uno medesimo moderamento, ma adatterà la varietà degli imperi alla varietà degli animi."

126. Ibid., 278. "Quella emulazione per quale tu cerchi meritar fama e gloria sopra gli altri, viene da prestanza d'ingegno e generosità d'animo, e acquistila non con malignità, ma solo con virtù quale sede in te."

127. Etienne Gilson, History of Christian Philosophy in the Middle Ages (New York: Random House, 1955), 216–24. See also Ernest Renan, Averroes et l'averroîsme, (Paris: M. Lévy, 1866).

128. M. Jamil-ur-Rehman, The Philosophy and Theology of Averroes (Baroda: Arya-Sudharak Printing Press, 1921), 51–52.

129. Grayson, Opere Volgari, vol. 2, p. 130. "Così adunque a noi; e in questo così essercitarci faremo come fa el musico che insegna ballare alla gioventù: prima sussequita col suono il moto di chi impara, e così di salto in salto meno errando insegna a quello imperito meno errare."

130. Ibid., vol. 1, p. 255.

131. Charles E. Butterworth, "Philosophy, Ethics and Virtuous Rule: A Study of Averroes' Commentary on Plato's 'Republic,'" Cario Papers in Social Science 9, monograph 1 (Spring 1986): 31. This is part of an early Humanist conflation of rhetoric and ethics. Salutati has no lesser authority than St. Augustine for the traditionally Sophistic argument that there is no point in letting the wrong side take advantage of you. See: Nancy S. Struever, The Language of History in the Renaissance: Rhetorical and Historical Consciousness in Florentine Humanism (Princeton: Princeton University Press, 1970), 55.

132. *Studi e Documenti di Architettura,* no. 1 (December 1972): 139. "Quare istos admonendos puto, prius advertant quid sit, quod efficere instituerimus, subinde spectent, an ex instituto succedant res; postremo de nobis, et de se judicent statuantque uti lubet. Nam quum intelligent, quibus ex fontibus certitudinis hausta haec sint, quidvis poterunt credere quam in his rebus rarissimis, et reconditissimis tractandis me frustra labores comsumpsisse, tantumque aberit, ut poeniteat operae, ut etiam majorem in modum gratulentur, sese istis monitis, et sua diligentia eximiis pictoribus esse effectos pares, quam rem magis experiundo intelligent, quam a me verbis possit explicari." (To avoid such skepticism, I think from the first you should direct the work of your charges, before they realize what ends we are determined to accomplish. Then let them see whether results follow from these lessons. Finally, let them judge and evaluate us and themselves as they wish. For when they understand from what fonts of certainty these precepts are drawn, they may think if they wish that my labors have been wasted in treating the finest points and the most recondite aspects of this art. But I think that far from being dissatisfied with my writing, they shall be exceedingly grateful, for through these precepts and their own careful effort, they will be rendered equal to the task of producing distinguished pictures.)

133. Ibid.

134. Ibid.

135. Grayson, *Opere Volgari,* vol. 2, p. 270. "Altro sarà tenere in mano la squadra, la linea, lo stile: altro adatterlo bene al tuo lavoro."

The Intact City

136. Orlandi, *De re aedificatoria,* 665. "Militarem viam, quae per agrum sit, vehementer ornabit ager ipse, per quem dirigatur, si erit ille quidem cultus consitus refertus villis diversoriis rerumque amoenitate et copia; si modo mare, modo montes, modo lacum fluentum fontesve, modo aridum aut rupem aut planiciem, modo nemus vallemque exhibebit."

137. Ibid., 707. "Sequitur ut intra urbem ingrediamur."

138. Ibid., 759. "Sed sunt quoque publica nonnulla, quae nonnisi primariis civibus et publicum negotium gerentibus pateant, uti est comitium curia senatusque."

139. Ibid., 549.

140. The itinerary does not come from Vitruvius, who organizes his description of the city in a markedly different manner.

141. See: Creighton Gilbert, "The Earliest Guide to Florentine Architecture, 1423," *Mitteilungen des Kunsthistorischen Institutes in Florenz* 14, hft. 1 (June 1969): 33–46; and Hans Baron, *The Crisis of the Early Italian Renaissance,* rev. ed. (Princeton: Princeton University Press, 1966).

142. Ernst H. Kantorowicz, *The King's Two Bodies: A Study in Medieval Political Theology* (Princeton: Princeton University Press, 1957), 71.

143. Grayson, *Opera Volgari,* vol. 2, p. 62. "Genipatro, quel vecchio qua su, quale in queste selve disopra vive filosofando, omo per età ben vivuta, per uso di molte varie cose utillissime al vivere, per cognizion di molte lettere e ottime arti prudentissimo e

sapientissimo. . . . A Genipatro viveno più e più figlioli, e' libri suoi da sé ben composti ed emendatissimi, pieni di dottrina e maravigliosa gentilezza, grati a' buoni e a tutti gli studiosi, e quanto dobbiamo sperarne immortali."

144. Ibid., 85. "Rendone a te grazia e a Genipatro, quale uomo come in tutti suoi altri detti, così in questo a me parse simile all'oraculo di Appolline."

145. Ibid., 62. This has been condensed from the following passage: "A Genipatro né manca, né mancherà iusto padre d'ogni suo instituto e santissima madre d'ogni sua voluntà, l'intelletto sincero e la ragione interissima."

146. Ibid.

147. Ibid., 79. "Benché io ivi sono assiduo ne' templi, ne' teatri, in casa de' primari cittadini, ove e' buoni fra loro di me e de' miei studi spesso e leggono e ragionano."

148. Ibid., 76. "Da me, quale sempre diedi opera che niuna mia cosa altrove sia che solo presso a me, nulla può essere rapito. Mie sono e meco la cognizion delle lettere, e insieme qualche parte delle bone arti, a la cura e amore della virtù, quale cose ottime a bene e beato vivere possono a me né da' casi avversi né da impeto alcuno o fraude essere tolte."

149. Ibid., 119.

150. Orlandi, *De re aedificatoria*, 665. "Apud veteres, praesterim, Graecos, assuevere urbe in media ponere aedificia, quas palestras appellarunt, ubi philosophantes disputando versarentur. Illic quidem inerant spatia fenestrata et apertionum prospectus et sedendi ordines amoeni et honestissimi, aderant et porticus virentem herbis aream et floribus vestitam circuentes."

151. Garin, "Intercenali Inedite," 16. "Quinto loco simulachrum pictum est: mulier gravi et maturo aspectu, que fasciculo coacto et belle edificato pro pulvinari utitur, et florido in prato inter librorum multitudine recumbit, solem superne levatis oculis adornas, et manibus pronis venerans."

152. Grayson, *Opere Volgari*, vol. 1, p. 184. ". . . nelle publiche piazze surge la gloria; in mezzo de' popoli si nutrisce le lode con voce e iudicio di molti onorati. Fugge la fama ogni solitudine e luogo privato, e volentieri siede e dimora sopra e'teatri, presente alle conzioni e celebrità; ivi si collustra e alluma il nome di chi con molto sudore e assiduo studio di buone cose sé stessi tradusse fuori di taciturnità e tenebre, d'ignoranza e vizii."

153. Ibid., 201. "E anche, Giannozzo, nella terra la gioventù impara la civilità, prende buone arti, vede molti essempli da schifare e' vizii, scorge più da presso quanto l'onore sia cosa bellissima, quanto sia la fama leggiadra, e quanto sia divina cosa la gloria, gusta quanto siano dolci le lode, essere nomato, guardato e avuto virtuoso. Destasi la gioventù per queste prestantissime cose, commove e sé stessi incita a virtù, e proferiscesi ad opere faticose e degne di immortalità. . . ."

A Iove Principium Musae

154. Orlandi, *De re aedificatoria*, 171.

The Great Defect

155. Grayson, *Opere Volgari*, vol. 2, p. 47.

Per li pungenti spin, per gli aspri istecchi,
per le turbe marin, per cruda guerra
dove io mi varchi, un pensier mi sotterra
e vuol che innanzi tempo imbianchi e 'nvecchi.

Tanto son fatti e' miei pensier parecchi,
che sì no nel capo mi s'aferra,
quand' un si chiude e l'altro si riserra,
onde di duol mestier sarà ch'io assecchi.

Ma tu, padre sincer, che l'opere e 'l core
cognosci di noi gente maladetta,
che non provedi a tanto nostro errore?

La tu' iustizia che tanto s'aspetta,
ben dice Dante, ond'io prendo vigore:
la spada di lassù non taglia in fretta.

Microtiro

156. Ibid., 94.

157. Ibid., 75. By the thirteenth century *contemptus mundi* was a commonplace intellectual stance. The great classic of the genre was Pope Innocent III's *De miseria humanae conditionis* (1195), which was universally read well into the seventeenth century. These writings argue that worldly life is mutable and transitory, that its pleasures are vain and disappointing, and that man is fallen, his nature corrupt, and his body infirm. They often depict human society as a caldron of vices and hypocrisies, and a good many of them end with apocalyptic passages describing the punishments of hell and the joys of heaven. For a discussion see Donald Howard, "Renaissance World Alienation," *The Darker Vision of the Renaissance*, ed. Robert Kinsman (Los Angeles: University of California, 1974), 47–76.

158. Grayson, *Opere Volgari*, vol. 2, p. 75.

159. Ibid., 78. "Alcibiade, ricco, fortunato, amato, d'ingegno quasi divino, e in ogni lode principe de' suoi cittadini, nobilitata la patria sua con sua virtù e vittorie, morì in essilio perduti e' suoi beni in povertà, tanto sempre alla moltitudine dispiacque chi fosse dissimile a sé in vita e costumi."

160. Ibid., 104.

161. Ibid., 79.

The Final Shriek

162. Ibid., 5.

S'i' sto dogliosi, ignun si maravigli,
poiché sì vuol chi può quel che le piace.

Non so quando aver debba omai più pace
l'alma ismarrita infra tanti perigli.
Misero me! A che convien s'appigli
mia vana speme, debile e fallace?
Né rincrescer mi può chi chiò mi face.
Amor, che fai? Perché non mi consigli?
Ben fora tempo ad avanzar tuo corso,
che la stanca virtù ognor vien meno,
né molto d'amendue già mi confido.
Ma s'ancora a pietà s'allarga il freno,
tengo ch'assai per tempo fia il soccorso.
Se non, tosto, udirai l'ultimo istrido.

The Mortal Gods

1. Eugenio Garin, *Leon Baptista Alberti: Intercoenali inedite* (Florence: G. C. Sansoni, 1965), 31–32.

2. Hieronymo Mancini, *Opera inedita et pauca separatim impressa di Leon Battista Alberti* (Florence: G. C. Sansoni, 1890), 141–42. The passage begins as follows: "Sed jam heus exhibe summes honores illis quos ab omni turba segregatos illuc vides."

3. See: Steven Ozment, *The Age of Reform, 1250–1550* (New Haven: Yale University Press, 1980), 30.

4. I will discuss the question of *De pictura*'s novelty in a forthcoming article in *Renaissance Studies*.

5. Cecil Grayson, *Leon Battista Alberti: On Painting and on Sculpture: The Latin Texts of "De Pictura" and "De Statua"* (New York: Phaidon, 1972), 36 and 106.

6. Giovanni Orlandi, *Leon Battista Alberti: l'Architettura—De re aedificatoria* (Milan: Edizioni il Polifilo, 1966), 441.

7. Ibid., 531. ". . . ita et hominibus praeponendum intelligeret genus aliud animatium, quod multo praestaret sapientia atque virtute." *Intelligere*, for Augustine, indicates man's participation in God. The difference between *intelligentia* and *ratio* is described by Aquinas: "intellect (*intelligere*) is the simple grasp of an intelligible truth, whereas reasoning (*ratiocinari*) is the progression toward an intelligible truth by going from one understood (*intellecto*) point to another. The difference between them is thus the difference between rest and motion or between possession and acquisition." See also: David N. Bell, *The Image and Likeness* (Kalamazoo, Mich.: Cistercian Publications, 1984), 29. John Scotus Eriugena makes a similar distinction in *On the Division of Nature*. See: *Medieval Philosophy: From St. Augustine to Nicholas of Cusa*, ed. John F. Wippel and Allan B. Wolter (New York: Free Press, 1969), 120.

8. Mancini, *Opera inedita*, 127.

9. Giovanni Farris, *Leon Baptista Alberti: De commodis litterarum atque incommodis, Defunctus* (Florence: Olscki Editore, 1976), 148. "Quam quidem virtutem qui animo, voluntate et usu comprehenderit, qui solidam et expressam et virtutem non in plebis iudicio esse, sed in animi elegantia et splendore sitam meminerit, is nullum sibi cum fortuna commercium esse volet, is omnia sua in se bona esse posita putabit, ex quo profecto ornatissimam et beatissimam atque deorum persimilem vitam ducet."

10. C. Grayson, *On Painting*, 60. "Has ergo laudes habet pictura, ut ea instructi cum opera sua admirari videant, tum deo se paene simillimos esse intelligant."

11. This is from the closing of Alberti's treatise on codes and code breaking, *De componendis cifris*. See: Dr. Aloys Meister, *Die Geheimschriften im Dienste der Päpstlichen Kurie von ihren Anfängen bis zum Ende des XVI Jahrhunderts* (Paderborn: Ferdinand Schoning, 1906), 141. "Hoc quod et commodissimum et pulcherrimum est atque ad salutem Reipublicae atque ad maximas res agendas mirifice conferat posteritati sacratum dicasse velim."

The Discourse on the Good and Happy Life

12. Cosimo Bartoli, *Opuscoli Morali di L. B. Alberti* (Venice: Francesco Franceschi, 1568), 129–30.

13. Ibid., 136. "Noi ci reisolviamo che le cose divine debbin lasciare a Dio & alli suoi ministri in maniera che noi deliberiamo che con i premii & con le pene si vadino, contrapesando dal Giudice solamente le cose humane parlando delle leggi pure humane & che egli amministri le cose comprese dalle leggi, come ricordevole di Dio & amicissimo del dovere."

14. Ibid., 138.

15. Garin, *Intercoenali inedite*, 18. "Nam deorum nullus est, qui non se vehementer studeat illi esse in loco patris dee prepotenti, que quidem humana divinaque iura omnia pro arbitrio queat pervertere, queve sanguinis affinitatis cognationis amicitiaumque vicula omnia, etiam diis invitis, valeat dirimere."

16. Grayson, *Opere Volgari*, vol. 2, 262–63. "Dieci leggi non più a numero dopo Moisé, resse tutta la nazione ebrea cento e cento e cento e più volte cento anni con venerazione di Dio e osservazione della onestà, equità e amor della patria. A' Romani bastò per amplificare la sua republica, vendicarsi tanto principato, solo dodeci brevissime tabule. Noi abbiamo sessanta armari pieni di statuti, e ogni dì produchiamo novi ordinamenti."

17. Bartoli, *Opuscoli Morali*, 132–33.

18. Elizabeth McDonough, *Canon Law in Pastoral Perspective: Principles for the Application of Law According to Antoninus of Florence*, Ph.D. diss. The Catholic University of America, Washington, D.C., 1982, 44ff.; Rev. Bede Jarrett, *S. Antonino and Medieval Economics* (London: Manresa Press, 1914).

19. Though Coluccio Salutati was partially responsible for reintroducing the rhetorical style in Florentine politics, there were many humanists who preferred *stilus humilis* on account of its commitment to brevity and restrained elegance. See: Ronald G. Witt, *Coluccio Salutati and His Public Letters* (Geneva: Librairie Droz, 1976), 28.

20. Bonucci, *Opere Volgari*, 1, xcviii.

21. Giuseppe Martini, *Leon Battista Alberti: Momuso Del Principe* (Bologna: Nicola Zanichelli Editore, 1942), 5. "Itaque sic deputo, nam si dabitur quispiam olim, qui cum legentes ad frugem vitae melioris instruat atque instituat dictorum gravitate rerumque dignitate varia et eleganti, idemque una risu illectet, iocis delectet, voluptate detineat, quod apud Latinos qui adhuc fecerint, nondum satis extitere: hunc profecto inter plebeios minime censendum esse."

22. Farris, *De commodis litterarum atque incommodis*, 142. "Nam tantum quidem a me abest ut litteras non maximi faciam, ut pro litterarum cultu prosequendo multas anxietates, multos labores, multa incommoda, damna, detrimenta, multas erumnas, atque calamitates in vita pertulerim, dum omnino me litteris deditum atque admodum invitis plerisque, quorum ope et suffragio vitam ducebam, dedicatum habui. Et enim paupertatem, inimicitias, iniuriasque non modicas neque (ut molti norunt) leves in ipso etiam fere perficiendi flore. . . ."

23. Grayson, *Opere Volgari*, vol. 2, p. 128. ". . . el parlare nostro lo riconosceremo datoci non per detraere, non per eccitar discordie e danno ad altri, ma per commutare nostri affeti, nostri sensi e cognizione a bene e beato viver."

24. Farris, *De commodis litterarum atque incommodis*, 140. "Bone idcirco littere, honestissime artes, sanctissimeque discipline prostant, et questum faciunt. Tune igitur divinarum humanarumque rerum cognitio, bonorum morum et glorie tutrix, optimarum rerum et inventrix et parens extitisti? Que animos hominum ornare, ingenia excolere, laudem, gratiam et dignitatem conferre, rempublicam moderari, ipsumque terrarum orbem, summa lege et ordine, ager consuevisti?"

25. Ibid., 144.

Mother Humanism

26. Garin, *Intercenali inedite*, 15. "Namque loco primo mira imago adest picte mulieris, cui plurimi variique unam in cervicem vultus conveniunt; seniles, iuveniles, tristes, iocosi, graves, faceti et eiusmodi. Complurimas item manus ex iisdem habet humeris fluentes, ex quibus quidem alie calamos, lyram, alie laboratam concinnamque gemmam, alie pictum excultumve insigne, alie mathematicorum varia instrumenta, alie libros tractant. Huic superadscriptum nomen: Humanitas mater." Alberti here is basing himself on a long-standing classical critique of mimesis. See *Republic*, 488a ff., or *Natural History*, 36. The picture is one of twenty described by Alberti in "Picturae" from *Intercenli*. Garin, "Intercenli inediti." Alberti describes an Indian temple in which there are two walls depicting good and evil. On the left wall are Indignation, Hostility, Envy, etc., and on the right wall are Peace, Happiness, Benevolence, and Humanism. The progression works from the central mother figures toward the ends: *Calamitas, Vindicta, Iniuria, Contentio, Ambitio Mater, Invidia Mater, Calumnia, Indignatio, Inimicitia, Miseria–Felicitas, Pax, Benivolentia, Beneficentia, Humanitas Mater, Modestia Mater, Securitas Animi, Cura Virtutis, Laus, Immortalitas.*

27. Partha Mitter, *Much Maligned Monsters: History of European Reactions to Indian Art* (Oxford: Clarendon Press, 1977), 5; See also J. Baltrušaitis, *Le Moyen Âge fantastique; antiquités et exotismes dans l'art gothique* (Paris: A. Colin 1955), 11; Giovanni Boccaccio, *Amorosa Visione*, introd. Vittore Branca (Hanover: University of New England, 1986), 18–20; Mary E. Bernard, *The Myth of Apollo and Daphne from Ovid to Quevedo: Love, Agon, and the Grotesque* (Durham: Duke University Press, 1987), 60; and F. P. Pickering, *Literature and Art in the Middle Ages* (London: Macmillan, and Co.), 1970, 198.

28. The themes associated with Prometheus changed from classical mythology to the Middle Ages and the Renaissance. See Olga Raggio, "The Myth of Prometheus," *Journal of the Warburg and Courtauld Institutes* 21 (1958): 44–55. As Raggio explains, by the fourteenth century the image of Promethius enlivening man with a spark of divine fire seems to have been commonplace. The ring and the gem were iconographic devices of particular importance.

29. Aristotle, *Politics,* III.6.5, 91281b. See also 1460b10ff.

30. Ernst Robert Curtius, *European Literature and the Latin Middle Ages,* trans. W. R. Trask (New York: Pantheon Books, 1963), 70–71, 154–66.

31. James J. Murphy, *Three Medieval Rhetorical Arts* (Berkeley: University of California Press, 1971), 33.

32. Claude Luttrell. "The Figure of Nature in Chretien de Troyes," *Nottingham Medieval Studies* 17 (1973): 6. "Solers Nature studium, que singula sparsim Munera contulerat aliis, concludit in unum."

33. Charles W. Jones, "Bebe as Early Medieval Historian," *Medievalia et Humanistica* 4 (1946): 30.

Baptista and his Texts

34. Grayson, *On Painting,* 65.

35. Ibid., 34.

36. Ibid., 102, 104. "Ea si eiusmodi sunt ut pictoribus commodum atque utilitatem aliquam afferant, hoc potissimum laborum meorum premium exposco ut faciem meam in suis historiis pingant, quo illos memores beneficii et gratos esse ac me artis studiosum fuisse posteris praedicent."

37. Grayson, *Opere Volgari,* vol. 2, p. 132. "Dicea Ennio poeta: non mi piangete, non mi fate essequie, ch'io volo vivo fra le parole degli uomini dotti."

38. For an account of Alberti's will refer to Girolamo Mancini, "Il testamento di L. B. Alberti," *Archivo Storico Italiano* (Rome) 72 (1914): 48; and Franco Borsi, *L. B. Alberti* (New York: Harper and Row, 1975), 17–18. Alberti left a certain amount of money as a stipend for future students from the Alberti family. However, if the male branch was to die out, as it soon did, the money was to be distributed among ten choir boys, whose obligation it was to sing High Mass every Sunday in S. Petronio.

Versipellem

39. Bonucci, *Opere Volgari,* 1, cvi. The term appears also in relation to Ulysses in *Profugiorum ab aerumna.* Grayson, *Opere Volgari,* vol. 2, pp. 151–52.

The "Civic" Functionary

40. Grayson, *Opere Volgari,* vol. 1, p. 17.

41. Martini, *Momus,* 57–58. "In tabellis ista continebantur: principem sic institutum esse opertere ut neque nihil agat, neque omnia, et quae agat, neque solus agat, neque cum omnibus, et curet ne quis unus plurima, neve qui plures nihil habeant rerum aut nihil possint. / Bonis benefaciat etiam invitis, malos non afficiat malis, nisi invitus. Magis notabit quosque per ea quae pauci videant, quam per ea quae in promptu sunt. Rebus novandis abstinebit, nisi multa necessitas ad servandam imperii dignitatem

cogat, aut certissima spes praestetur ad augendam gloriam. / In publicis prae se feret magnificentiam, in privatis parsimoniam sequetur. Contra voluptates pugnabit non minus quam contra hostes. Otium suis, sibi vero gloriam et gratiam artibus pacis potius quam armorum studiis parabit. Dignari se votis patietur et humiliorum indecentias ita feret moderate, uti a minoribus suos fastus volet."

42. Grayson, *Opere Volgari*, vol. 2, 165. "In questa, dove tu non puoi presentarti e averti libero, ubbidisci a chi più può. Ad Euripide poeta parea la inobbidienza della moltitudine più che 'l fuoco valida, e più atta a destruere e consumare le cose. E dicono che la moltitudine sempre fu insuperabile. Omero dicea che 'l male sempre vince; ma quanto e dove e a chi bisogni credere t'insegnerà la necessità." One is also reminded of the opening of Alberti's treatise on codes and code breaking. See: Dr. Aloys Meister, *Die Geheimschriften im Dienste der Päpstlichen Kurie von ihren Anfängen bis zum ende des XVI Jahrhunderts* (Paderborn: Ferdinand Schoning, 1906). The opening paragraph reads: "Hi qui maximis rebus agendis praesunt iudices experiantur quanti sit habere aliquem fidissimum, cui secretiora instituta et consilia ita communicent ut ex ea re sibi nunqum penitendum sit. Id quia non facile ob communem hominum perfidiam datur ut possint, ex sententia inventae sunt scribendi rationes quas cyfras nuncupant, commentum quidem non inutile ni contra essent qui suis artibus et ignenio talia interpretentur atque explicent. Atque hos ego quidem esse non inficior valde utiles principibus quoniam per eos aliorum machinationes et cepta discantur."

43. Mancini, *Opera inedita*, 85. This is spoken by Peniplusius, to be discussed later.

44. Grayson, *Opere Volgari*, vol. 1, 255.

45. Mancini, *Opere inedita*, 175.

Operae Perdae

46. Grayson, *Opere Volgari*, vol. 2, p. 82. Or more precisely: ". . . intesi non avere per rispetto alcuno tanto da dolermi della morte de'miei, che la morte di chi io nulla mi dolea, Omero, Platone, Cicerone, Virgilio, e degli altri quasi infiniti dottissimi stati uomini, non a me molto più che la morte de' miei dovesse essere gravissima e moletissima, da' quali se fussero in vita, senza comparazione potrei ricevere e dottrina a bene e beato vivere e modo a qualunque utile instituto e voluttà in ogni mio pensiero molto e molto più che da qual si fosse nel numero de' miei. . . . (78) Benché io ivi sono assiduo ne' templi, ne' teatri, in casa de' primari cittadini, ove e' buoni fra loro di me e de' miei studi spesso e leggono e ragionano."

47. Farris, *De commodis litterarum atque incommodis*, 132. "Missa facio reliqu obscena litteratis a plebe imposita ignominia. Illud vero pretermittamus quod aiunt: nescire se qua re nostros litteratos debeant magnificare, quos plane videant circa vite usum ea negligere, que bene beatque vivendum admodum necessaria sunt."

48. Mancini, *Opera inedita*, 125.

49. Grayson, *Opere Volgari*, vol. 2, p. 121. "La multitudine perpetuo vive; mutansi di prole in prole; vola loro età; tardi a spaienza, presti a morte, queruli in vita, abitano la terra."

50. Ibid., 144. "Oh lume de' tempi nostri! Ornamento della lingua toscana! Quinci fioriva ogni pregio e gloria de' nostri cittadini."

51. Ibid., 144–45. "Ma dubito non potrete, Battista, recitare vostre opere; tanto può l'invidia in questa nostra età fra e' mortali e perversità. . . . O cittadini miei, seguirete voi sempre essere iniuriosi a chi ben v'ami?"

52. Bonucci, *Opere Volgari*, 1, c. "Cum libros *De Familia* primum, secundum atque tertium suis legendos tradidisset, aegre tulit, eos inter omnes Albertos, alioquin ociosissimos, vix unum repertum fore, qui titulos librorum perlegere dignatus sit, cum libri ipsi ab exteris etiam nationibus peterentur; neque potuit non stomachari, cum ex suis aliquos intueretur, qui totum illud opus palam, et una auctoris ineptissimum institutum irriderent. Eam ob contumeliam decreverat, ni principes aliqui interpellassent, tris eos, quos tum absolverat, libros igni perdere."

53. Farris, *De commodis litterarum atque incommodis*, 138. "Iuris peritia, sacrorum disciplina, cognitioque nature ac forma morum, reliqueve egregie et solis liberis hominibus decrete littere (execrandum facinus!) quasi hasta posita, publice veneunt. Infiniti venalitii licitatores bonarum artium circumvolant, ex agro, silvis, ex ipsaque gleba, et ceno emergunt innumerabiles non homines sed bestie potius ad serviles operas nate, qui spreto rure ad disciplinas venditandas et profanandas irruunt. O pestem litterarum!"

54. Grayson, *On Painting*, 90.

55. Ibid., 106. "Aderunt fortasse qui nostra vitia emendent et in hac praestantissima et dignissima re longe magis quam nos possint esse pictoribus adiumento. Quos ego, si qui futuri sunt, etiam atque etiam precor ut hoc munus alacri animo ac prompto suscipiant, in quo et ipsi ingenium excerceant suum et hanc nobilissimam artem excultissimam reddant."

56. Farris, *De commodis litterarum atque incommodis*, 204. "*Neofrono:* Vide quid sors afferat; nam mihi quidem hac in re tametsi partim temporum nostrorum calamitas deploranda videretur quod etate nostra tanta ad emendandum libellos esset eruditarum aurium penuria, partim mea mihi negligentia improbanda videbatur, quod libellos, quoad in me fuit, non diligentius emendatos reliquerim. . . . (pp. 196–98) Exciditne tibi memoria, qua ipse vigilantia, laboribus atque assiduitate me ab conscribendos annales dederim? / *Polytropo:* Teneo id, teque laude ex re dignissimum puto. . . / *Neo:* Frusta, mi Polytrope, frustra omnia."

57. Diogenes Laertius, *Lives and Opinions of Eminent Philosophers* iv, 24–27.

58. Farris, *De commodis litterarum atque incommodis*, 198, 208. "*Neo.:* Quoniam existimaram meis vigiliis futurum, ut amplissima premia redderentur; lucubrationes meas posteris non ingratas fore opinabar; quin demens etiam conjectabar illis nostris commentariolis meum immortalitati nomen commendasse . . . Dilacerarunt, mi Polytrope, libellos meos mea manu conscriptos, tantis lucubrationibus evigilatos, magna ex parte excultos, meos libellos dilacerarunt ut unguentum exciperent. / *Pol.:* O factum sceleste! / *Neo.:* Ergo per omnem atatem elaboravi ut eruditissimos cuculos ederem: illic igitur mea studia omnia et vigilie et expectationes mee omnes conciderunt." The relationship between book and author so central to Alberti's thought has a long tradition. It was, for example, an important issue to Ovid. We might recall the eloquent closing of *Metamorphoses:* "Jamque opus exegi, quod nec Jovis ira, nec ignes, Nec poterit ferrum, nec edax abolere vetustas. Cum volet illa dies, quae nil nisi corporis hujus Jus habet, incerti spatium mihi finiat aevi: Parte tamen meliore mei super alta perennis Astra ferar: nomenque erit indelebile nostrum. Quâque patet dmitis Romana potentia terris, Ore legar populi: perque omnia saecula famâ (Si quid baent veri vatum praesagia)." / (Now I have done my work. It will endure, I trust, beyond Jove's anger, fire and sword, Beyond Time's hunger. The day will come, I know, So let it come, that day which has no power Save over my doy, to end my span of life Whatever it may be.

Still, part of me, The better part, immortal, will be borne Above the stars: my name will be remembered Wherever Roman power rules conquered lands, I shall be read, and through all centuries, If prophecies of bards are ever truthful, I shall be living always.) Trans. Rolf Humphries (Bloomington: Indiana University Press, 1955), 392. Or we might turn to the prologue of *Tristia:* "Little Book, you go to Rome without me (I don't begrudge you that). But alas, your master cannot go, too! Make your way, but shabbily, as befits the book of an exile, keeping the sad appearance of my situation." Harry B. Evans, *Publica Carmina* (Lincoln, Neb.: University of Nebraska Press, 1983), 33. The separation of text from author is also played out in *Tristia,* where Ovid explains that he attempted to burn all copies of the *Metamorphoses* before he left Rome (II. 15– 22). Ovid in turn is making a deliberate allusion to the publication of the *Aeneid* and to Virgil's instructions to his literary executors, Varius and Tucca, to burn the poem after his death. For a discussion see: Evans, *Publica Carmina,* 43.

The Humanist and the Artist

59. The oft heralded distinction Alberti makes in the introduction of *De re aedificatoria* between architect and craftsman may partially derive from the distinction Lucian makes in his so-called "Dream," where he rejects the life of a stonemason for that of literature, philosophy, and education.

60. Orlandi, *De re aedificatoria,* 13. "Boni viri, quod parietem aut porticum duxeris lautissimam, quod ornamenta postium columnarum tectique imposueris, et tuam et suam vicem comprobant et congratulantur vel ea re maxime, quod intelligunt quidem te fructu hoc divitiarum tibi familiae posteris urbique plurimum decoris ac dignitatis adauxisse."

61. Mancini, *Opera inedita,* 43. This comes from *Anuli,* discussed in the chapter "Philoponius and the Twelve Rings."

62. Orlandi, *De re aedificatoria,* 13. "Demum hoc sit rem, stabilitatem dignitatem decusque rei publicae plurimum debere architetecto...."

63. Mancini, *Opera inedita,* 176. "... qui quidem cum publica summa vigilantia et fide semper tutatus, tum privata mea re imprimis nusquam fuerim non contentus: mea igitur haec meorum sunto."

64. Alberti admits his own philosophical interests in *Commentarium Philodoxeos Fabule, De commodis litterarum atque incommodis, De iure,* and elsewhere.

65. Mancini, *Opera inedita,* 175. "Jam enim eorum, quae vos dicere suspicor, meum quod sit haud satis novi, ac fui quidem in istiusmodi errore diutius ab adolescentia usque versatus, ut quae vulgo esse hominis putent, ea imprudens mea esse dijudicarim. Namque, uti ajunt, mea praedia, mea bona, meas divitias, ex communi reliquorum civium loquendi consuetudine, appellabam."

66. Grayson, *On Painting,* 44. "Missam faciamus illam philosophorum disceptationem qua primi ortus colorum investigantur."

67. Orlandi, *De re aedificatoria,* 887. "Non illa philosophantium hic prosequar, petantne aquae mare quasi quietis locum, radione fiat lunae...."

68. Ibid., 863. "Sed ne Zeusim quidem esse pingendo aut Nichomacum numeris aut Archimedem angulis et lineis tractandis volo. Sat erit, si nostra quae scripsimus picturae

elementa tenuerit: si eam peritiam ex mathematicis adeptus sit, quae angulis una et numeris et lineis mixta ad usum est excogitata: qualia sunt, quae de ponderibus de superficiebus corporibusque traduntur, quae illi podismata embadaque nuncupant. His artibus adiuncto studio et diligentia sibi gratiam architectus opes nominisque posteritatem et gloriam nanciscetur."

69. Grayson, *Opere Volgari*, vol. 2, p. 182. "M. Marcello presso a Siracuse commandò a', suoi armati che in tanto eccidio di sì nobile terra servassero quello Archimede matematico, quale difendendo la patria sua con varie e in prima non vedute macchine e instrumenti bellici, aveva una e una'altra volta perturbato ogni ordine suo e rotto l'impeto di tanta sua ossidione ed espugnazione. Trovoronlo investigare cose geometrice quale e disegnava in sul pavimento in casa sua: e trovoronlo sì occupato coll'animo e tanto astratto da ogni altro senso che lo strepito delle armi, e gemito de'cittadini quali cadeano sotto le ferite, le strida della moltitudine quali periano oppressi dalle fiamme e dalle ruine de'tetti e de' tempi, nulla el commoveano."

70. Ibid., 93–94. The end of the passage reads: "Stavansi e' marmi giacendo in terra; noi li collocammo sulle fronti de' templi e sopra a' nostri capi. E tanto ci dispiace ogni naturale libertaà di qualunque cose procreata, che ancora ardimmo soggiogarci a servitù noi istessi. E a tutte queste inezie nacquero e crebbero artefici innumerabili, segni e argumenti certissimi di nostra stoltizia."

71. Orlandi, *De re aedificatoria*, 9, 11 (Prologo). "Quid demum, quod abscissis rupibus, perfossis montibus, completis convallibus, coercitis lacu marique, expurgata palude, coaedificatis navibus, directis fluminibus expeditis hostis, constitutis pontibus portuque non solum temporariis hominum commodis providit, verum et aditus ad omnes orbis provincias patefecit?" It should be noted that Alberti is asking a rhetorical question, but why he does this only becomes clear if we read it in the context of the passage in *Theogenius* (93–94).

72. Ibid., 667 [VIII,1]. Alberti continues the same argument: "Visuntur passim totis viis militaribus proscissae rupes lapidae, delumbati montes, perfossi colles, aequatae valles, impensa incredibili et operum miraculo. Quae omnia et utilitati et certe ornamento sunt."

73. Grayson, *Opere Volgari*, vol. 2, p. 244. ". . . e in questo consiglio, non ti confidare dello ingegno e discurso tuo più che del iudizio de' tuoi denivoli e coniunti, massime esperti e dotti in quella cosa qual tu tratti, però che con loro raro ti sequirà che tu non ti penta. Non par verisimile che 'l iudizio di più omini periti e buoni sia fallace."

74. Ibid., 182. "E talor, mancandomi simili investigazioni, composi a mente e coedificai qualche compositissimo edificio, e disposivi più ordini e numeri di colonne con vari capitelli e base inusitate, e collega'vi conveniente a nova grazia di cornici e tavolati. E con simili conscrizioni occupai me stessi sino che 'l sonno occupò me."

75. It has long been held that Alberti in his treatises on painting and architecture was elevating these arts so that they could be included among the other humanist liberal arts. See: Caroll William Westfall, *In this Most Perfect Paradise* (University Park: Pennsylvania State University Press, 1974), 29. I hate to refute this, but on the present evidence I hold that such an assertion ignores the important distinction Alberti makes between the writer and the author. In our enthusiasm to endorse Alberti as the proponent of the liberal arts, we fail to be sensitive to the nuances of his argument and his own theoretical strategies.

76. Grayson, *Opere Volgari*, vol. 2, p. 163. "Quando molte cose testé non vedi e non odi quali soleano adolorarti, assai vedi quando tu discerni le buone cose dalle non

buone, le degne dalle non degne, e'assai odi quando tu odi te stessi in quelle cose che faccino a virtù e laude. E bene hassi la notte in sé ancora e' suoi diletti."

77. Grayson, *On Painting*, 44.

78. Orlandi, *De re aedificatoria*, 11. "Quam vero grata et quam penitus insideat animis aedificandi cura et ratio, cum aliunde tum hinc apparet, quod neminem reperias, modo adsint facultates, qui non totus ad quippiam coaedificandum pendeat et, siquid ad rem aedificatoriam excogitarit, volens ac lubens non proferat et quasi iubente natura usui hominum propalet."

79. Ibid., 11. "Et quam saepe evenit, ut etiam rebus aliis occupati nequeamus non facere, quin mente et animo aliquas aedificationes commentemur!"

80. Grayson, *On Painting*, 64. "Neque facile quempiam invenies qui non maiorem in modum optet se in pictura profecisse."

81. Ibid., 104. "Tum minime verendum est ne vituperatorum et invidorum iudicium laudibus pictoris quicquam possit decerpere."

82. Ibid., 102. "Modulosque in charitis conicientes, tum totam historiam, tum signulas eiusdem historiae partes commentabimur, amicosque omnes in ea re consulemus [III, 61]. / Ergo moderata diligentia rebus adhibenda est, amicique consulendi sunt, quin et in ipso opere exequento omnes passim spectatores recipiendi et audiendi sunt. Pictoris enim opus multitudini gratum futurum est. Ergo multitudinis censuram et iudicium tum non aspernetur, cum adhuc satisfacere opinionibus liceat. Apellem aiunt post tabulam solitum latitare, quo et visentes liberius dicerent, et ipse honestius vitia sui operis recitantes audiret [III, 62, p. 104]. / Pictos ego vultus, et doctis et indoctis consentibus, laudabo eos qui veluti exsculpti extare a tabulis videantur . . . [II, 46, p. 88]."

83. Orlandi, *De re aedificatoria*, 95. "Ac mirum quidem, quid ita sit, cur monente natura et docti et indocti omnes, in artibus et rationibus rerum quidnam insit aut recti aut pravi, confestim sentimus."

84. Grayson, *On Painting*, 64. "Tametsi haec una ars et doctis et indoctis aeque admodum grata est."

85. Grayson, *On Painting*, 34.

86. John R. Spencer argues that "although the art Alberti advocates is based on training acquired under a master and apprentice system it gives the artist and his art the means of breaking away from such a system to attain the individualism familiar since the High Renaissance." John R. Spencer, *Leon Baptista Alberti: On Painting* (New Haven: Yale University Press), 11. I can find little evidence in Alberti's thought to substantiate this claim, as reasonable as it may sound. Alberti did not want the artist to function as an individual but as a spokesperson for an ideal patron. Since ideal patrons do not exist, the painter can assume the characteristics of a patron in order to preserve the myth of an intact world.

87. Grayson, *On Painting*, 65; Orlandi, *De re aedificatoria*, 853.

88. Bonucci, *Vita di L. B. Alberti*, cii–civ.

The New—Artless—World

89. Martini, *Momus*, 16. "Est apud superos sacer aeterno ab aevo ductus focus, cui quidem cum caetera, tum illud insit admirabile, ut nulla substituta materia, nulloque liquore subfusco sese confovens, perpetuis lucescat flammis: quin et huiusmodi est, ut quibus adhaeserit rebus, eas quoad una constiterit, immortales incorruptibilesque reddat … Accedit quod solis in villis mapparum, quas dea Virtus contexuit, sacer ipse ignis vigeat. Isthoc sacro ex foco hausta flammula ad summum frontis verticem quibusque deorum illucet, atque ea quidem in diis hanc habet vim, ut ea conspicui, in quas velint rerum formas sese queant ex arbitrio vertere … Hoc ex foco cum Prometheus radium subripuisset, ob perpetratum sacrilegium ad Caucasum montem fixum relegarunt." For a discussion of the manuscripts see: Alessandro Perosa, "Considerazioni su testo e lingua del 'Momus' dell'Alberti," *The Languages of Literature in Renaissance Italy,* ed. Peter Hainsworth, Valerio Lucchesi, Christina Roaf, David Robey, an J. R. Woodhouse (Oxford: Clarendon Press, 1988), 45–62.

90. Martini, *Momus*, 245.

91. Ibid., 13.

92. Ibid., 20–21.

93. Ibid., 68. This has been shortened somewhat from the following passage in which Momus relates to Jove his experiences on earth: "Ridebis atque admiraberis Iovemque Momumque, nam in coena non facile dici potest quam inter epulas praeter omnium opinionem iocosum se Momus exhibuerit, multa referens quae suum per exilium pertulerat, cum ridicula, tum et digna memoratu. Inter quae illud fuit, ut referet omnes quidem se voluisse hominum vivendi rationes et artes experiri, quo reperta commodiore acquiesceret; in singulis quidem elaborasse, ut studio et diligentia coniuncta exercitatione et usu evaderet in egregium artificem; nullam tamen ita didicisse ut sibi satis instructus videretur, tam comperisse omnes artes huiusmodi, ut quo plura quae ad peritiam faciant usu et doctrina sis assequutus, co plura discernas tibi deese ad cognitionem."

94. Ibid., 72. The passage, which is too long to quote in full, begins as follows: "Etenim sic—inquit—dicunt quidem geometrae, quaeque versentur in arte sua, aeque teneri a quovis rudi discipulo, atque ab eruditissimo, modo semel ea percepta sint. Idem ferme ipsum in hac erronum arte evenit: ut uno temporis momento perspecta planeque cognita atque imbuta sit. Sed in hoc differunt, quod geometra instructore qui futurus est geometra indiget, erronum vero ars nullo adhibito magistro perdiscitur. Aliae artes et facultates habent edocendi tempora, ediscendi laborem, exercendi industriam, agendive quendam definitum descriptumque modum; item adminicula, instrumenta et pleraque istiusmodi exigunt atque desiderant, quae hac una in arte minime requiruntur."

95. Ibid., 75.

96. Ibid.

97. Ibid., 128.

98. Ibid., 140.

99. Ibid., 117. "Interea apud superos studia partium tantas in simultates et factiones excreverant, ut omne caelum non minus quam tres esset in partes divisum. Namque

246

hinc Iuno, quae aedificandi libidine insanibat, quam poterat maximam suarum partium vim et manum et bonis et malis artibus cogebat, ad hominumque salutem tuendam instruebat; hinc contra turma illa popularium et eorum quidem quibus non ex sententia cum statu rerum suarum agebatur, sponte congruebant, sed immoderatam rerum novandarum cupiditatem, qua flagrabant, studio gratificandi deorum principi honestabant. Medium quoddam tertium erat genus eorum, qui cum ignobilis levissimique esse vulgi caput grave et periculosum putarent, tum et cuiquam privatorum subesse recusarent, contentionum eventum sibi etiam quiescentibus expectandum indixerant, ea mente, ut in quamcumque visum foret partem tuto attemperateque prosilirent, suisque motibus rem quoquo versus vellent, ex arbitrio traherent."

100. Ibid., 89–90.

101. Ibid., 186. "Huiusmodi erant in tabellis complurima, sed illud omnium fuit commodissimum inventum ad multas imperii molestias tollendas: nam admonebat ut omnem rerum copiam tris in cumulos partirentur, unum bonarum expetendarumque rerum, alterum malarum, tertium vero poneret cumulum earum rerum, quae per se neque bonae sint neque malae. Has ita distribuebat, ut iuberet ex bonorum cumulo Industriam, Vigilantiam, Studium, Diligentiam, Assiduitatem reliquosque eius generis deos desumere plenos sinus, et per trivia, porticus, theatra, templa, fora, denique publica omnia per loca, aperto sinu, altro obviis porrigerent et volentibus grate ac lubens traderent. Mala itidem sinu pleno et aperto Invidia, Ambitio, Voluptas, Desidia, Ignavia caeteraeque his similes deae circumferrent atque sponte erogarent non invitis. Quae autem neque bona neque mala sint, ut ea sunt quae bona bene autentibus et mala male utentibus sunt, quorum in numero putantur divitae, honores et talia ab mortalibus expetita, omnia Fortunae arbitrio relinquerentur, ut ex iis plenas manus desumeret, et quantum cuisque videretur, atque in quos libido traheret, conferret."

The Prophet Unmasked

102. Ibid., 22. "Alii praesidem moderatoremque rerum unum esse aliquem arguebant; alii paria paribus, et immortalium numerum mortalium numero respondere suadebant; alii mentem quandam omni terrae crassitudine, omni corruptibilium mortaliumque rerum contagione et commertio vacuam liberamque, divinarum et humanarum esse rerum alumnam principemque demonstrabant, alii vim quandam infusam rebus, qua universa moveantur, cuiusve quasi radii quidam sint hominum animi, Deum putandum."

103. Ibid., 175–76.

104. Ibid., 143.

105. Ibid., 57–58, 59. "Demum sic statuo oportere his quibus intra multitudinem atque in negocio vivendum sit: ut ex intimis praecordiis nunquam susceptae iniuriae memoriam obliterent, offensae vero livorem nusquam propalent, sed inserviant temporibus, simulando atque dissimulando; in eo tamen opere sibi nequicquam desint, sed quasi in speculis pervigilent, captantes quid quisque sentiat, quibus moveatur studiis, quid cogitet, quid tentet, quid aggrediatur, quid quemque expediat, quid necesse sit, quos quisque diligat, quos oderit, quae cuiusque causa et voluntas, quae cuique in agendis rebus facultas et ratio sit. Alia ex parte sua ipsi studia et cupiditates callida semper confingendi arte integant, vigilantes, solertes, accincti paratique occasionem praestolentur vindicandi sui praestitam ne deserant ... Omnino illud unum iterum atque interum iuvabit meminisse, bene et gnaviter fuscare omnia adumbratis quibusdam signis probitatis et innocentiae; quam quidem rem pulchre assequemur, si verba

vultusque nostros et omnem corporis faciem assuefaciemus ita fingere atque conformare ut illis esse persimiles videamur qui boni ac mites putentur, tametsi ab illis penitus discrepemus. O rem optimam nosse erudito artificio fucatae fallacisque simultationis suos operire atque obnubere sensus!"

106. Ibid., 102–3.

Peniplusius: The True One

107. Ibid., 183–84.

Postscript: Alberti as Architect

1. See Caroll William Westfall's excellent book on this subject: *In this Most Perfect Paradise* (University Park, Pa.: Pennsylvania State University Press, 1974).

2. Howard Burns, "A Drawing by L. B. Alberti," *Architectural Design* 49, nos. 5–6 (June 1979): 45–56.

3. Franco Borsi, *L. B. Alberti* (New York: Harper and Row, 1975), 25.

4. For the complete text of Pius II's less than flattering description of Sigismondo see: Borsi, *L. B. Alberti,* 127.

5. Garin, *Intercoenali inedite,* 11. Alberti, drawing on a famous passage from Cicero, describes three flutes representing three different styles of discourse. He aspires to owning the flute that costs the least, but produces a clear sound.

6. Giovanni Orlandi, *Leon Battista Alberti: l'Architettura—De re aedificatoria* (Milan: Edizioni il Polifilo, 1966), 549 (VII,3).

7. Cecil Grayson, *Leon Baptista Alberti: Opere Volgari* (Bari: Gius, Laterza, and Figli, 1966), vol. 1, pp. 183–84.

8. A stain on the drawing obscures what seems to be the bell tower tucked into the recess behind the entrance portico. The tower was indeed constructed, but on the other side, which may mean that the drawing was made in reverse. There are some notable differences between Labaccom's plan and the executed work.

9. Howard Saalman, "Alberti's San Sebastiano in Mantua," *Renaissance Studies in Honor of Craign Hugh Smyth* (Florence: Giunti Barbèra, 1985), 643–52.

10. Saalman explains this in his article.

11. See the image of Benevolence in "Picturae" from *Intercoenales.*

12. Eugene J. Johnson, *S. Andrea in Mantua: The Building History* (University Park, Pa.: Pennsylvania State University Press, 1975).

13. Ibid., 6.

14. Ibid., 6–7.

Bibliography

Works by Leon Baptista Alberti

Balestrini, Nanni. *Leon Battista Alberti, Momo o del principe.* Genoa: Costa and Noli, 1986.

Bartoli, Cosimo. *Opuscoli Morali di L. B. Alberti.* Venice: Francesco Franceschi, 1568.

Bonucci, Anicio. *Opere Volgari di Leon Baptista Alberti per la piu parte inedite e tratte dagli autografi.* 5 vols. Florence: Tipografia Galileina, 1843.

Carotti, Laura Goggi. *Leon Baptista Alberti: De commodis litterarum atque incommodis.* Florence: Leo S. Olscki Editore, 1976.

Farris, Giovanni. *Leon Baptista Alberti: De commodis litterarum atque incommodis, Defunctus.* Milan: Marzorati Editore, 1971.

Fubini, Riccardo, and Anna Menci Gallorini. "L'autobiografia di L. B. Alberti. Studio e edizione." *Rinascimento* 12 (1972): 21–78.

Gambutti, Alessandro. "Nuove richere sugli Elementa Picturae." *Studi e Documenti di Architettura,* no. 1 (1972): 131–172.

Garin, Eugenio. *Leon Baptista Alberti: Intercenali Inedite.* Florence: G. C. Sansoni, 1965.

Gorni, Guglielmo. *Leon Battista Alberti, Rime a versioni poetiche.* Milan: Riccardo Ricciardi Editore, 1975.

———. "Storia del Certame Coronario." *Rinascimento* 12 (1972): 135–82.

Grayson, Cecil. *Leon Battista Alberti: On Painting and On Sculpture, The Latin Texts of "De Pictura" and "De Statua."* New York: Phaidon Press, 1972.
———. *Leon Battista Alberti. La prima grammatica edlla lingua volgare.* Bologna: Casa Carducci, 1964.

———. *Leon Baptista Alberti: Opere Volgari.* Vols. 1 and 2. Bari: Gius, Laterza and Figli, 1966.

———. "An autographed Letter from Leon Battista Alberti to Matteo de'Pasti, November 18, 1454." New York: Pierpont Morgan Library, 1957.

———. *Opuscoli inediti di L. B. Alberti: "Musca," "Vita S. Potiti."* Florence: Leo S. Olschki, 1954.

———. "Four Love-Letters Attributed to Alberti." *Collected Essays on Italian Language and Literature Presented to Kathleen Speight.* Manchester: Manchester University Press, 1971. 29–44.

Mallè, Luigi. *Leon Battista Alberti, Della Pittura.* Florence: G. C. Sansoni, 1950.

Mancini, Hieronymo. *Opera inedita et pauca separatim impressa di Leon Battista Alberti.* Florence: J. C. Sansoni, 1890.

Massetani, Paola Testi. "Ricerche sugli 'Apologi' di Leon Battista Alberti." *Rinascimento* 12 (1972): 79–134.

Martinelli, Cesarini Lucia. "Philodoxeos Fabula, Edizione critica." *Rinascimaneto* 17 (1977); 144–47.

Martini, Giuseppe. *Leon Battista Alberti: Momus o Del Principe.* Bologna: Nicola Zanichelli Editore, 1942.

Meister, Dr. Aloys. *Die Geheimschriften im Dienste der Päpstlichen Kurie von ihren Anfängen bis zum Ende des XVI Jahrhunderts.* Paderborn: Ferdinand Schöning, 1906.

Orlandi, Giovanni. *Leon Battista Alberti: l'Architettura—De re aedificatoria.* Milan: Edizioni il Polifilo, 1966.

Videtta, Antonio. *Leon Baptista Alberti. De equo animate.* Naples: 1981.

Secondary Works

Aiken, Jane Andrews. "L. B. Alberti's System of Human Proportions." *Journal of the Warburg and Courtauld Institutes* 43 (1980): 68–96.

Alfonso, Procaccini. "Alberti and the Framing of Perspective." *Journal of Aesthetics and Art Criticism* 40, no. 1 (Fall 1981): 29–39.

Badaloni, Nicola, "La interpretazione delle arti nel pensiero di L. B. Alberti." *Rinascimento* 3 (1963): 59–113.

Barelli, Emma. "The Sister Art in Alberti's 'De pictura.'" *The British Journal of Aesthetics* 19, no. 3 (1979): 251–63.

Barnard, Mary E. *The Myth of Apollo and Daphne from Ovid to Quevedo: Love, Agon, and the Grotesque.* Durham: Duke University Press, 1987.

Baron, Hans. *The Crisis of Early Italian Renaissance.* Princeton: Princeton University Press, 1955.

———. "Franciscan Poverty and Civic Wealth." *Speculum* 13, no. 1 (January 1938): 1–37.

Bibliography

Baxandall, Michael. "A Dialogue on Art from the Court of Leonello d'Este." *Journal of the Warburg and Courtauld Institutes* 26 (1963): 304–26.

Begliomini, Lorenzo. "Note sull'opera dell'Alberti: il 'Momus' e il 'De re aedificatoria.'" *Rinascimento* 12 (1972): 267–83.

Behn, Irene. *Leon Battista Alberti als Kunstphilosoph*. Strassbourgh: Heitz und Muendel Verlag, 1911.

Benetti-Brunelli, Valeria. *Leon Battista Alberti e il rinnovamento pedagogico nel quattrocento*. Florence: Vallecchi, 1925.

Bialostocki, Jan. "The Power of Beauty: A Utopian Idea of Leone Battista Alberti." *Studien zur Toskanischen Kunst, Festschrift für L.H. Heydenreich*. Munich: Prestel Verlag, 1964, 13–19.

———. "The Renaissance Concept of Nature and Antiquity." *The Renaissance and Mannerism* Princeton: Princeton University Press, 2 (1963): 19–30.

Bisaccia, Giuseppe. "Past/Present: Leonardo Bruni's History of Florence." *Renaissance and Reformation*, n.s. 9, no. 1 (February 1985): 1–18.

Boccaccio, Giovanni. *Amorosa Visione*. Introduction by Vittore Branca. Hanover: University of New England, 1986.

Borsi, Franco. *L. B. Alberti*. New York: Harper and Row, 1975.

———. "I cinque ordini architettonici e L.B. Alberti." *Studi e Documenti di Architettura*, no. 1 (1972): 57–130.

Bouwsam, William. "The Two Faces of Humanism and Augustinianism in Renaissance Thought." *Inerarium Italicum*. Edited by H. Oberman and T. Brady. Leiden: E. J. Brill, 1975, 3–61.

Bretta, G. "L'ideale etico albertiano nel 'De Iciarchia' e il 'De officiis' di Cicerone." *Miscellanea di studi albertiani*. Genoa: Tilger, 1975, 9–34.

Brunetti, Fabrizio. "Le tipologi architettonische nel tratto albertiano." *Studi e Documenti di Architettura, no. 1 (1972): 261–92.

Buck, August. *Die Methode der Humanisten*. Tubingen, 1952.

———. "Zum Methodenstreit zwischen Humanismus und Naturwissenschaft in der Renaissance." *S. B. der Gesellschaft zur Befoerderung der gesamten Naturwissenschaft zu Marburg* 81 (1959): 3–26.

Burns, Howard. "A Drawing by L.B. Alberti." *Architectural Design* 49, nos. 5–6 (June 1979): 45–56.

Butterworth, Charles E. "Philosophy, Ethics and Virtuous Rule: A Study of Averroes' Commentary on Plato's 'Republic.'" *Cario Papers in Social Science* 9, monograph 1 (Spring 1986).

Campana, Augusto. "The Origin of the Word Humanist." *Journal of the Warburg and Courtauld Institutes* 9 (1946): 60–73.

Ceschi, C. "La Madre di Leon Battista Alberti." *Bullettino d'Arte* (1948): 191–92.

Choay, Françoise. *La règle et le modèle: sur la théorie de l'architecture et de l'urbanisme.* Paris: Sevil 1980.

————. "Alberti and Vitruvius." *Architectural Design* 49, nos. 5–6 (June 1979): 26–35.

Classical and Medieval Literary Criticism. Edited by Alex Preminger, Leon Golden, O. B. Hardison, Jr., and Kevin Kerrane. New York: Frederick Ungar Publishing Co., 1974.

Corsi, Giuseppe. *Rimatori del Trecento.* Turin: Unione Tipografico-Editrice Torinese, 1969.

Gilbert, Creighton. "The Earliest Guide to Florentine Architecture, 1423." *Mitteilungen des Kunsthistorischen Institutes in Florenz* 14, Hft. 1 (June 1969): 33–46.

Curtius, Ernst Robert. *European Literature and the Latin Middle Ages.* New York: Pantheon Books, 1953.

————. "Die Lehre von den Drei Stilen in Altertum und Mittelalter." *Römische Forschungen* 64 (1952): 66–69.

D'Amico, John F. "The Progress of Renaissance Latin Prose." *Renaissance Quarterly* (Autumn 1984): 351–92.

————. *Renaissance Humanism in Papal Rome.* Baltimore: Johns Hopkins University Press, 1983.

d'Ancona, Mirella Levi. *The Garden of the Renaissance: Botanical Symbolism in Italian Painting.* Florence: Leo S. Olschki Editore, 1978, 307–8.

Dardano, M. "Sintassi e stile nei 'Libri della Famiglia' di L.B. Alberti." *Cultura neolatina* 23 (1963): 1–36.

Edgerton, Samuel Y., Jr. "A Little Known Purpose of Art in the Italian Renaissance." *Art History* 2, no. 1 (March 1979): 45–61.

————. "Alberti's Color Theory: A Medieval Bottle Without Renaissance Wine." *Journal of the Warburg and Courtauld Institutes* 32 (1969): 109–34.

————. "The Art of Renaissance Picture Making." *Essays Presented to Myron P. Gilmore.* Vol. 2. Florence: Villa i Tatti, 1977, 134–53.

Farris, Giovanni. "Su 'Religio' e 'Templum' in L. B. Alberti." *Miscellanea di studi albertiani.* Genoa: Tilger, 1975, 97–112.

Ferguson, Wallace K. *The Resaissance in Historical Thought: Five Centuries of Interpretation.* Boston: Houghton Mifflin Co., 1948.

Finzi, Claudio. *Matteo Palmieri dall' 'Vita civile' alla "Città di vita.'* Rome: Giuffreè Editore, 1984.

Flemming, Willi. *Die Begründung der modernen Aesthetik und Kunstwissenschaft durch Leon Battista Alberti.* Leipzig: B. G. Teübner Verlag, 1916.

Foster, Susannah Kerr. *The Ties that Bind: Kinship Associations and Marriage in the Alberti Family 1378–1428.* Ph.D. diss. Cornell University, 1985.

Bibliography

Gadol, Joan. *Leon Battista Alberti: Universal Man of the Early Renaissance*. Chicago: University of Chicago Press, 1969.

Galantic, Ivan. *The Sources of Alberti's Theory of Painting*. Ph.D. diss., Harvard University, 1969.

Gallorini, A. *Studio su le Intercoenales di L. B. Alberti*. Florence: Università degli Studi di Firenze, Facoltà di Magistero, 1968–69.

Garin, Eugenio. *La Disputa della arti nel Quattrocento*. Florence, 1948.

————. *Leon Baptista Alberti: Intercenali Inedite*. Florence: G. C. Sansoni, 1965.

————. "Il pensiero di L. B. Alberti nella cultura del Rinascimento." *Accademia Nazionale dei Linei* 209 (1974): pp. 21–41.

————. "Il pensiero di L. B. Alberti: caratteri e contrasti." *Rinascimento* 12 (1972): 3–20.

————. *Portraits from the Quattrocento*. New York: Harper and Row, 1963.

Gellrich, Jesse M. *The Idea of the Book in the Middle Ages*. Ithaca: Cornell University Press, 1985.

Ghinassi, G. "Leon Battista Alberti fra latinismo e toscanismo: la revisione dei 'Libri della Famiglia.'" *Lingua nostra* 23 (1961): 1–6.

Giehlov, Karl. "Die Hieroglyphenkunde des Humanismus in der Allegorie der Renaissance." *Jahrbuch der Kunsthistorischen Sammlung des Allerhöchsten Kaiserhauses* 32 (1915): 1–232.

Gombrich, Ernst H. "A Classical Topos in the Introduction to Alberti's 'De pictura.'" *Journal of the Warburg and Courtauld Institutes* 20 (1957): 173.

Gorni, Guglielmo. "Storia del Certame Coronario." *Rinascimento* 12 (1972): 135–82.

Grayson, Cecil. "Leon Battista Alberti, Architect." *Architectural Design* 49, nos. 5–6 (June 1979): 7–18.

————. "Studi su Leon Battista Alberti." *Rinascimento* 4, no. 1 (1953): 45–62.

Hall, Vernon. *Renaissance Literary Criticism*. Gloucester, Mass.: Peter Smith, 1959.

Hersey, George L. "Alberti's Cubism." *Essays Presented to Myron P. Gilmore*, vol. 2. Florence: Villa i Tatti, 1977, 245–61.

Howard, Donald R. "Renaissance World-Alienation." In *The Darker Vision of the Renaissance*. Edited by Robert S. Kinsman. Berkeley: University of California Press, 1974, 47–76.

Marita Horster, "Brunelleschi und Alberti in ihrer Stellung zur Römischen Antike," *Mitteilungen des Kunsthistorischen Institutes in Florenz*, Vol. 17, Hft. 1: 1973, 29–64.

Kahn, Victoria. *Rhetoric, Prudence, and Skepticism in the Renaissance*. Ithaca: Cornell University Press, 1985.

Katz, Barry. *Leon Baptista Alberti and the Humanist Theory of the Arts.* Washington, D.C.: University Press of America, 1978.

Kendall, Calvin B. "Bede's 'Historia ecclesiastica': The Rhetoric of Faith." In *Medieval Eloquence.* Edited by James J. Murphy. Berkeley: University of California Press, 1978, 145–72.

Kessler, Eckhardt. *Das Problem des frühen Humanismus, seine Philosophische Bedeutung bei Caluccio Salutati. Munich: Wilhelm Fink Verlag, 1968.*

Kinsman, Robert S. *The Darker Vision of the Renaissance.* Berkeley: University of California Press, 1974.

Kisch, Guido. *Gestalten und Probleme aus Humanismus und Jurisprudenz.* Berlin: De Gruyter, 1969.

Krautheimer, Richard. "Alberti and Vitruvius." *Studies in Western Art* 2 (1963): 43–52.

Kristeller, Paul Oskar. *Renaissance Thought and its Sources.* New York: Columbia University Press, 1979.

Jarrett, Rev. Bede, O. P. *S. Antonino and Medieval Economics.* London: Manresa Press, 1914.

Johnson, Eugene J. *S. Andrea in Mantua: The Building History.* University Park, Pa.: The Pennsylvania State University Press, 1975.

Lang, S. "'De Lineamentis' in L. B. Alberti's Use of a Technical Term." *Journal of the Warburg and Courtauld Institutes* 28 (1965): 331–35.

Lee, Rensselaer W. "Ut pictura poesis: A Humanist Theory of Painting." *Art Bulletin* 30 (1940): 197–269.

MacCulloch, J. A. *Medieval Faith and Fable.* London: George G. Harrap and Co., 1932.

McDonough, Elizabeth. *Canon Law in Pastoral Perspective: Principles for the Application of Law According to Antonius of Florence.* Ph.D. diss., The Catholic University of America, Washington, D.C., 1982.

Mancini, Girolamo. *Vita di Leon Battista Alberti.* Rome: Bardi Editore, 1967.

———. *Vita di Leon Battista Alberti.* 2d ed., rev. Florence: G. Garnesecchi e Figli, 1911.

Maraschio, Nicoletta. "Aspetti del bilinguismo albertiano nel 'De Pictura.'" *Rinascimento* 12 (1972): 183–228.

Paolo Marolda. *Crisi e conflitto in Leon Battista Alberti.* Rome: Bonacci, 1988.

Paolo Marolda. "Leon Battista Alberti e il problema della politica: il 'Fatum et Fortuna' e i 'Libri della famiglia.'" *Rassegna della letteratura italiana,* 90 (1986), 29–40.

Marsh, David. *Leon Battista Alberti Dinner Pieces.* Binghamton: Medieval and Renaissance Texts and Studies, 1987.

———. *The Quattrocento Dialogue.* Cambridge: Harvard University Press, 1980.

————. "Alberti as Satirist." *Rinascimento* 23 (1983): 198–212.

————. "Petrarch and Alberti." *Renaissance Studies in Honor of Craig Hugh Smyth.* Florence: Giunti Barbèra, 1985, 363–75.

————. "Poggio and Alberti," *Rinascimento* 23 (1983): 189–215.

Martelli, Mario. "Una della 'Intercenali' di Leon Battista Alberti fonte sconosciuta del 'Furioso.'" *Bibliofilia* 66, no. 2 (1964): 163–70.

Martines, Lauro. *Power and Imagination: City-States in Renaissance Italy.* New York: Alfred A. Knopf, 1979.

Mazzeo, Joseph Anthony. "The Augustinian Conception of Beauty and Dante's Convivio." *Journal of Aesthetics and Art Criticism* 15 (1957): 435–448.

Michel, Paul Henri. *Un idéal humaine au XV siècle: La pensée de L. B. Alberti.* Paris: Sociéte d'Editions "Les Belles Lettres," 1930.

Misch, George. *A History of Autobiography in Antiquity.* Cambridge: Harvard University Press, 1951.

Mommsen, Theodor E. *Medieval and Renaissance Studies.* Edited by E. F. Rice. Ithaca: Cornell University Press, 1959.

————. "Petrarch's Conception of the 'Dark Ages.'" *Speculum* 17 (1947): 226–42.

Mühlmann, Heiner. *L. B. Alberti: Aesthetische Theorie der Renaissance.* Bonn: Rudolf Habelt Verlag, 1982.

————. "Alberti's S. Andrea Kirche und das Erhabene." *Zeitschrift für Kunstgeschichte* 32, Hft. 2 (1969): 153–57.

————. "Über den Humanistischen Sinn einiger Kerngedanken der Kunsttheorie seit Alberti." *Zeitschrift fuer Kunstgeschichte* 33, Hft. 2 (1970): 127–42.

Oberman, Heiko A. "Fourteenth-Century Religious Thought: A Premature Profile." *Speculum* 53, no. 1 (January 1978): 80–93.

Olson, Glending. *Literature as Recreation in the Later Middle Ages.* Ithaca: Cornell University Press, 1986.

Onians, John. "Abstraction and Imagination in Late Antiquity." *Art History* 3, no. 1 (March 1980): 1–24.

————. "Alberti and Filarete." *Journal of the Warburg and Courtauld Institutes* 34 (1971): 96–114.

Ozment, Steven. *The Age of Reform, 1250–1550.* New Haven: Yale University Press, 1980, 73–134.

Panofsky, Erwin. "Hercules am Scheidewege und andere antike Bildstoffe in der neueren Kunst." *Studien der Bibliotek Warburg* (Leipzig) 18 (1930): 164.

Parronchi, Alessandro. "L'operazione del levare dalla pianta nel trattatelo." *Rinascimento* 16 (1976): 207–12.

————. "The Language of Humanism and the Language of Sculpture." *Journal of the Warburg and Courtauld Institutes* 27 (1964): 108–36.

————. "L. B. Alberti as Painter." *The Burlington Magazine* 54 (July 1962): 280–87.

————. "Otto piccoli documenti per la biografia dell'Alberti." *Rinascimento* 12 (1972): 229–36.

————. "Sul significato degli 'Elementi di Pittura' di Leon Battista Alberti." *Cronache di archeologia e di storia dell' arte* 6 (1967): 107–15.

————. "The Language of Humanism and the Language of Sculpture." *Journal of the Warburg and Cortauld Institutes* 26 (1963): 38–52.

Pasquini, Emilio. "Tradizione e fermenti nuovi poesia del'Alberti." *Accademia Nazionale dei Lincei* 209 (1974): 305–68.

Patch, Howard R. *The Goddess Fortuna in Medieval Literature*. N.Y. Octagon Books, 1953.

Patz, Kristine. "Zum Begriff der 'historia' in L. B. Albertis 'De pictura.'" *Zeitschrift fuer Kunstgeschichte* 49, no. 3 (1986): 269–87.

Pelikan, Jaroslav. *The Growth of Medieval Theology (600–1300)*. Vol. 3 of *Christian Tradition: A History of the Development of Doctrine*. Chicago: University of Chicago Press, 1978.

Perini, Bernardi. "La 'Philogia' del Petrarca, Seneca e Marziano Capella." *Atti e Memorie dell'Accademia Patavina di Scienze, Lettere ed Arte* 83 (1970–71): 147–69.

Perosa, Alessandro. "Considerazioni su testo e lingua del 'Momus' dell'Alberti." *The Languages of Literature in Renaissance Italy*. Edited by Peter Hainsworth, Valerio Lucchesi, Christina Roaf, David Robey, and J. R. Woodhouse. Oxford: Clarendon Press, 1988, 45–62.

Pickering, F. P. *Literature and Art in the Middle Ages*. London: Macmillan and Co., 1970.

Ponte, Giovanni. "La datazione del 'Teogenio' di L. B. Alberti." *Convivium* 23 (1955) 150–59.

————. "Il petrarchism di Leon Battista Alberti," *La Rassegna della letteratura italiana* 62 (1958) 216–21.

————. "Lepidus e Libripeta." *Rinascimento* 12 (1972): 237–66.

————. *Leon Battista Alberti: umanista e scrittore*. Genoa: Casa Editrice Tilgher, 1981.

————. "I salmi di L. B. Alberti." *Miscellanea di studi albertiani*. Geona: Tilger, 1975, 123–32.

Raggio, Olga. "The Myth of Prometheus." *Journal of the Warburg and Courtauld Institutes* 21 (1958): 44–55.

Rathke, Christian. *Pictor Civilis*. "Privately released," 1976.

Riess, Jonathan B. "The Civic View of Sculpture in Alberti's 'De re aedificatoria.'" *Renaissance Quarterly* 32, no. 1 (1979): 1–17.

Rykwert, Joseph, and Robert Tavernor. "The Church of S. Sebastiano in Mantua: A Tentative Restoration." *Architectural Design* 49, nos. 5–6 (June 1979): 86–89.

Saalman, Howard. "Alberti's San Sebastiano in Mantua." *Renaissance Studies in Honor of Craig Hugh Smyth*. Florence: Giunti Barbèra, 1985, 643–52.

Salman, Phillips. "Instruction and Delight in Medieval and Renaissance Criticism." *Renaissance Quarterly* 32, no. 3 (1979): 303–32.

Santinello, Giovanni. *L. B. Alberti. Una visione estetica del mondo e della vita*. Florence: G. C. Sansoni, 1962.

Sasso, G. "Qualche osservazione sul problema della virtù e della fortuna nell'Alberti." *Il Mulino* 2 (1953): 600–18.

Schaedlich, C. "L. B. Albertis Schoenheitsdefinition und ihre Bedeutung fuer die Architekturtheorie." *Wissenschaftliche Zeitschrift Hochschule Weimar*, no. 5 (1957–58): 217–84.

Schalk. F. ""Aspetti della vita contemplativa nel Rinascimento Italiano," *Classical Influences on European Culture A.D. 500–1500* Cambridge: Cambridge University Press, 1971, pp. 225–35.

Schlosser, Julius. "Ein Künstlerproblem der Renaissance L. B. Alberti." *Akademie der Wissenschaften in Wien, Sitzungsberichte 210* 2 (1929).

Seigel, Jerrold E. *Rhetoric and Philosophy in Renaissance Humanism*. Princeton: Princeton University Press, 1968.

Seznec, Jean. *The Survival of the Pagan Gods*. Princeton: Princeton University Press, 1953.

Smalley, Beryl. *English Friars and Antiquity in the Early Fourteenth Century*. New York: Barnes and Noble, 1960.

Spencer, John. "Ut Rhetorica Pictura." *Journal of the Warburg and Courtauld Institutes* 20 (1957): 26–44.

Starn, Randolph. *Contrary Commonwealth: The Theme of Exile in Medieval and Renaissance Italy*. Berkeley: University of California Press, 1982.

———. "Reinventing Heroes in Renaissance Italy." *The Journal of Interdisciplinary History* 17, no. 1 (Summer 1986): 67–84.

Stinger, Charles, L. *The Renaissance in Rome*. Bloomington: Indiana University Press, 1985.

Struever, Nancy S. *The Language of History in the Renaissance: Rhetorical and Historical Consciousness in Florentine Humanism*. Princeton: Princeton University Press, 1970.

Tafuri, Manfredo. "Discordant Harmony: Alberti to Zuccari." *Architectural Design* 49 nos. 5–6 (June 1979): 36–44.

Throndike, Lynn. *University Records and Life in the Middle Ages*. New York: Columbia University Press, 1944.

258

Bibliography

Toker, Franklin. "Alberti's Ideal Architect: Renaissance—or Gothic." *Renaissance Studies in Honor of Craig Hugh Smyth*. Florence: Giunti Barbèra, 1985, 667–76.

Ullman, B. L. "Leonardo Bruni and Humanistic Historiography." *Medievalia et Humanistica* 4 (1946): 45–61.

Watkins, Renée Neu. "The Authorship of the Vita Anonyma of L. B. Alberti." *Studies in the Renaissance 4 (1957): 101–12.*

——. "Il Burchiello 1404–1448: Poverty, Politics and Poetry." *Italian Quarterly* 14, no. 54 (1970): 21–57.

——. "L. B. Alberti's Emblem, the Winged Eye, and His Name Leo." *Mitteilungen des Kunsthistorischen Institutes in Florenz.* 9 (1960): 256–58.

Westfall, Carroll William. *In This Most Perfect Paradise, Alberti, Nicholas V, and the Invention of Conscious Urban Planning in Rome, 1447–55.* University Park: The Pennsylvania University Press, 1974.

Whitfield, J. H. "'Momus' and the Language of Irony." In *The Languages of Literature in Renaissance Italy.* Edited by Peter Hainsworth, Valerio Lucchesi, Christina Roaf, David Robey, and J. R. Woodhouse. Oxford: Clarendon Press, 1988, 32–43.

Wind, Edgar. *Pagan Mysteries of the Renaissance.* New Haven: Yale University Press, 1958.

Witt, Roland. "Coluccio Salutati and the Conception of the 'poetus theologus' in the 14th Century." *Renaissance Quarterly* 30, no. 2 (1977): 538–63.

Wittkower, Rudolf. "Alberti's Approach to Antiquity in Architecture." *Journal of the Warburg and Courtauld Institutes* 4 (1941): 1–18.

Woodward, William Harrison. *Studies in Education during the Age of the Renaissance 1400–1600.* Cambridge: Cambridge University Press, 1924.

Zoubov, V. "Leon Battista Alberti et les Auteurs du Moyen Age." *Medieval and Renaissance Studies* 4 (1958): 245–66.

Index

Index

Index

Index

DATE DUE

TLC 3-19-95			
APR 1 8 1996			